★★★★★

"A HOUSE DIVIDED AGAINST ITSELF CANNOT STAND."
–ABRAHAM LINCOLN

DIVIDED WE STAND

THE GLOBALIST SCHEME FOR A ONE-WORLD GOVERNMENT

LTC ROBERT L. MAGINNIS

AUTHOR OF *KINGS OF THE EAST*

DEFENDER

CRANE, MO

Divided We Stand: The Globalist Scheme for a One-World Government
by LTC Robert L. Maginnis

Defender Publishing
Crane, MO 65633

ISBN: 978-1-948014-70-0

A CIP catalog record of this book is available from the Library of
Congress.

Cover design by Dakota Jackson.
Interior design by Pamela McGrew.

To faithful Christians who apply biblical principles
under the guidance of the Holy Spirit to address our
polarized culture for the glory of God.

Acknowledgments

I gratefully acknowledge…

…my wife, Jan, who is always supportive of these writing efforts to address very tough issues, albeit at some sacrifice, given that throughout this writing I had a "day" job. She's a comfort and a supporter through these challenging times.

…my dear friend Mark Shaffstall, who provided welcomed recommendations, edits, and insights about our divided culture and what our polarized nation means for the prophetic end times.

…finally, like all my previous works, my Lord Jesus Christ, who gave me the thoughts, skills, and breath to complete this effort, and I pray it serves His purpose. All the glory is to Him.

Robert Lee Maginnis
Woodbridge, Virginia

CONTENTS

Section IV
Strategies for Overcoming Division

Section V
Christian Living and Prophetic Implications of Division

Preface

A house divided against itself cannot stand.[1]
—ABRAHAM LINCOLN, sixteenth president of the United States

s America at a breaking point thanks to widespread division, and as a result, can we no longer take our nation for granted?

Today, America is incredibly divided, much more than perhaps at its beginnings and especially at the time just prior to our Civil War (1861–1865). We've somehow forgotten the beauty of the American experiment that every one of us—regardless of our race, ethnicity, sex, religion, or ideological background—has a place in these United States. That was the vision our founders had and why they gave us our Constitution and the Bill of Rights and advocated for political pluralism, which meant we each have an obligation to fight for others, especially the little guy, to enjoy the same rights of conscience and speech.

Consider our founders' wisdom about the threat of division. In 1787, founder James Madison wrote the tenth of *The Federalist Papers*, one of a series of essays first penned by founder Alexander Hamilton that argues for the ratification of the United States Constitution. Madison's essay, titled "Publius," *Federalist* Number 10, is among the most highly regarded of all American political writings. His paper directly addresses the subject of "faction," or political division, and offers a solution.[2]

Madison warns in "Publius" about the challenge of "the violence of faction," or division. He argues that "there are two methods of curing the mischiefs of faction: the one, by removing its causes; the other, by controlling its effects." Those "cures" are polar opposite: either we destroy "liberty which is essential to [our republic's] existence" or we destroy "the other, by giving to every citizen the same opinions, the same passions, and the same interests." Therefore, Madison concludes, division is overcome in a democratic republic by protecting civil liberties with "the increased variety of parties [pluralism] comprised within the Union, [which] increase[s] this security."[3]

Founder George Washington obliquely addressed the problem of division by encouraging early Americans to understand and accept our differences, a view similar to Madison's call for more pluralism. After all, one of Washington's favorite Bible verses was Micah 4:4 (NRSV), which he used frequently in his writings. In particular, the Father of our Nation often quoted: "But they shall all sit under their own vines and under their own fig trees, and no one shall make them afraid."[4]

Certainly, Washington's use of the phrase "vine and fig tree" fits the troubled era of the American Revolution and the founding of the country. In fact, he used the phrase in connection with a call for tolerance of immigration, a reference found in the 1787 issue of the *New-York Journal*, which alluded to the idea of the oppressed citizens of other nations having a place to come for refuge: the newly established United States.[5]

Perhaps Washington's best-known use of the phrase "vine and fig tree" is found in a letter to the Hebrew congregation in Newport, Rhode Island. In that letter, President Washington proclaimed:

May the children of the stock of Abraham who dwell in this land continue to merit and enjoy the good will of the other inhabit-

ants—while everyone shall sit in safety under his own vine and
fig tree and there shall be none to make him afraid.

Here, Washington invokes Micah 4:4 and adds "none to make him
afraid," an effort evidently to reinforce his ecumenical leanings and tolerance for our differences.[6]

The early founders anticipated that future Americans would have to
deal with divisions like those in the eighteenth century that threatened
the nation's survival. However, just perhaps they never expected that
America would face the real prospects of divisive implosion as a nation
as it does today.

That's my motivation for writing this book, *Divided We Stand*. I
believe America is at a tipping point; our survival as a nation is at risk.
Will this country endure the current level of rank division that threatens
our civil liberties at every turn and the very existence of America as a
representative republic? What are the root causes of that division, and is
there hope to pull this nation out of its current death spiral?

Divided in five sections addresses these questions, beginning with
the first, which explores the roots of the phenomenon of division: how
it is applied across America; how the worldview of some powerful elite
spawns division; and Satan's use of the instrument to take mankind
captive. The second section examines the role division plays across history, both internationally and in America, as well as identifies some key
accounts of the use of division as an instrument for both good and evil in
the Bible. In the third section, we consider the elites' contemporary use
of division to garner control of America's critical social structures: family,
politics, religion, education, workplace, culture, and government. There
is hope, which *Divided* addresses in section IV by offering strategies to
address the issue at the individual to national levels before it is too late.
Finally, section V describes the unique role the Christian should play in
our current divided world and what Scripture prescribes to overcome
Satan's challenges, as well as how it will have a leading role in the coming
prophetic end times.

The reader needs to understand two things before launching into this volume, however. First, "division" is a powerful word that, once operationalized, can change the course of the world. Second, our true enemy is the fallen angel, Satan, who is reinforced by a legion of demons and his recruited human proxies. Accepting these facts helps Christians engage in life's battles and discern how and why the spiritual and human instrumenting of division plagues much of our lives and will eventually lead to the prophetic end times.

Operationalizing "Division"

"Division" is defined as "separating" or "marking off," whereby "divisions"—plural—can be disagreements between two or more people or groups, typically producing tensions or hostility. *Operationalizing* division is especially useful when it is applied to politics and sociology, the primary topic of this book. The Latin phrase *divide et impera*, or "divide and conquer," is the operationalized political principle that empowers users to divide and then control others, those who likely would otherwise oppose such domination.

No matter where you look across the history of humanity, division is at the root of virtually every societal problem; no social structure, from family to nation-state, is immune from its effects. It is the instrument of choice for those who understand our fallen nature, and thus many nefarious souls across human history have effectively employed it to influence the malleable. American founding father Benjamin Franklin correctly observed people are divided into three classes, but only the latter two are especially ripe for division's persuasion: "Those that are immovable, those that are movable, and those that move."[7]

Unfortunately, most people fall prey to division's power because they, as Franklin wisely said, "are movable" or "move." That provides Satan and his human proxies the mechanism for gaining control over our lives.

Satan and His Human Proxy "Dividers"

It is in this context—one group or individual seeking to control others—that division became a key tool in Satan's hands. The Devil, a biblical synonym for Satan, uses the principle of division to distance us from God's plan by influencing every aspect of our lives, from interpersonal relations within family members to geopolitical tensions that often lead to wars, leaving nations in ruins.

Satan effectively employs division through his human proxies to defeat and destroy mankind at every turn, and it plays an obvious role across both history and at every level of modern society. For example, division is a mighty device in the hands of the godless Marxist who assigns (divides) us into social classes to control entire nations. Division is the instrument the misguided religious leader uses to splinter communities of faith. It is a dangerous idea in the hand of the community organizer who uses it to destroy unity along racial, ethnic, and class lines. The political leader often uses division as a blunt implement to sabotage the opposition while currying favor with like-minded constituents.

We must also recognize that Satan, his legion of demons, and his human proxies are expert at fostering division to gain control. This reminds me of a statement by the ancient Chinese strategist Sun Tzu: "To know your enemy, you must become your enemy." Essentially, what the author of *The Art of War*, an influential work on military strategy, means by the statement is we must learn the signs and tools of our adversaries. Thus, this volume will demonstrate that Satan and his human proxies use "division" to great effect, which manifests itself when they drive a wedge between us and God and between us and one another. In fact, there are many examples of Satan's use of division in the Bible. In the book of Genesis, chapter 3, Satan (the Serpent) tempts Adam and Eve to abandon (be divided from) God. In the New Testament, Satan tempts Jesus to split (turn away) from God with offers of worldly enrichment in exchange for Satan's control: "All these things I will give You, if You fall down and worship me" (Matthew 4:9, NAS). The Devil's work today is much the same. He tries to turn us away from God and one another to encourage us to decide for ourselves between good and evil and right and wrong, while granting him more control over our lives.[8]

Today, Satan enlists human proxies to do much the same across the world, albeit with the aim of gaining control to serve his evil intentions. After all, the Serpent knows the seed of Adam easily succumbs to their selfish interests, our sinful Achilles' heel. Therefore, in order to control people, the tempter appeals to our selfish interests, which more often than not divides us from others like a hot knife through butter. The Apostle Paul warned as much when he advanced a prophylaxis for man's divisiveness:

> As for a person who stirs up division, after warning him once and then twice, have nothing more to do with him, knowing that such a person is warped and sinful; he is self-condemned. (Titus 3:10–11, EVS)

"Self-condemned" is the state of most humans because they follow the ways of this world and too easily fall prey to the world's evil dividers who tap into our selfish interests in order to gain control. This threat is real and not science fiction. However, British science fiction author H. G. Wells does provide insight into the possible outcome of Satan's earthly plan. Wells wrote in his 1895 novel, *The Time Machine*, that, in the future, all humanity will be divided into two species: the Eloi and the Morlocks. The Eloi live a banal life of ease (a future underclass), while the Morlocks are the superior humanoids who control all aspects of the Elois' lives (the elite).[9]

Contemporary Elois are Ben Franklin's "moveable" or "moved," who, in exchange for getting along, become slaves in a two-tiered system overseen by today's elite Morlocks. Of course, such a system requires a world free of civil liberties similar to present-day communist China, a totalitarian state where every aspect of life is centrally monitored and controlled by the communist elite in Beijing. Citizens who obey Beijing's every command prosper (survive), while those who oppose government's dictates are enslaved or eliminated.

We may not yet be in a world divided into just two human species with one totally controlling the other. However, throughout history, there have been many attempts to realize that outcome.

History Is Replete with "Dividers"

There are numerous accounts of evil people in history who divide others to leverage control for themselves. For example, in the early 1930s, Germany's Adolf Hitler garnered control by dividing himself and his fascist followers from a host of enemies both foreign and domestic, such as the Jews, which Hitler tried to exterminate—albeit he gained total say over the German people through division and almost succeeded in conquering all of Europe. We'll explore other examples of division across world history in the second section of this volume to demonstrate just how common division has been used across humanity's past.

Domestically, the United States experienced many divisions across our nearly 250 years as a nation. America was divided at the start of the Revolutionary War (1776–1789) between those who favored remaining under the tyrannical British boot and others who didn't care and wanted to be left alone, as opposed to following our founding fathers' lead to independence from the European monarchy. Ever since that tough beginning, America has seen plenty of division, often pitting one citizen or group against another and most often ending poorly for both. Some of those efforts polarized previous relationships over money, race, ethnicity, and gender. Others fractured us politically, pitting groups like ideological liberals and progressives against those with libertarian or conservative ideals. Religion is a frequent divider in our history, as there have been cases of violence between American

Catholics and Protestants, and more recently between Muslims and other faith groups.

The perpetrators of much of that division—Satan's human proxies—abound today across every culture and nation. I've written about many of these divisive proxies in a series of recent books.

Divided We Stand: Wraps Up Previous Books Exposing Evil Elites

Five of my recent books are each a puzzle piece that, when put together by this volume, illustrates how the world's Satan-inspired elite seek to control all of our lives.

A few years ago, I called out a host of divisive proxies in my book *The Deeper State*. In that volume, I identified globalists, those who favor global solutions to our challenges as opposed to nationalists, who put America's interests first. That volume also identified a host of exclusive secret societies such as the Bilderbergers, the Council on Foreign Relations, and the Trilateral Commission that seeks to earn for its mostly globalist-elite membership control over the power levers in Washington and other world capitals. That elite cadre also includes not a few members of Washington's present-day deep state who are the bureaucrats manning our executive branch of government and using their administrative powers to "divide and conquer" in order to control our lives through often draconian overreach such as we experienced in Washington's response to the COVID-19 pandemic.

In 2018, I wrote *Progressive Evil: How Radicals Are Redefining America's Rights, Institutions, and Ideals, Making Her Globally Irrelevant for the End Times*. That book exposed a number of evil dividers known as "progressives" who scuttle our civil liberties and impose their godless, big-government agenda on America in order to control every aspect of our lives. Unfortunately, progressives made great strides during the twentieth century as they redefined society by espousing gender fluidity for our children, taking captive much of our media and public education to promote their radical ideas, and elevated big government as the answer to all of our problems, which is similar to George Orwell's "Big Brother" in his dystopian 1949 novel *1984*.

Orwell's "Big Brother" is a fictional character and the leader of Oceania, a totalitarian state wherein the ruling party has total power "for its own sake" over all citizens. They live under constant surveillance and are reminded that "Big Brother is watching you." Today, the term "Big Brother" is a synonym for the abuse of government power—the deep state—especially regarding the respect for our civil liberties.

In 2020, I wrote *Collision Course: The Fight to Reclaim Our Moral Compass before It's Too Late*, which surveyed America's Christian heritage and how our original defining institutions embraced Christian principles and values. However, there arose beginning in the late nineteenth century a cabal of evil proxies who attacked our Christian foundation to threaten our future. These anti-Christian rogues aggressively watered down Christianity's influence across our institutions using division that brought our society to the present moral tipping point.

In 2021, my book *Give Me Liberty, Not Marxism* exposed the elite who embrace the globalists' so-called Great Reset, a Marxist agenda to produce a radically different and divided America—a globalist aim. They fractured us on many fronts to promote a godless society under the boot of a future totalitarian, one-world government that could be ruled by the likes of the tyrants in the Chinese Communist Party (CCP).

In 2022, I wrote *Kings of the East: China's Plan to Eliminate America and Impose a Communist World Order*. That volume explains how China became a global tyrant with America's help. Specifically, *Kings of the East* outlines the CCP's economic, ideological, military, geopolitical, and technological aims that divide the Chinese people and populations across the world in order to gain control for Beijing's totalitarians.

President Biden's Use of Division to Win Total Control

Perhaps one of the best contemporary illustrations of the use of division as a political tool has played out during the first two years of the Joe Biden administration, which operationalized division on many fronts to gain control over the American people and just perhaps could eventually destroy the America many of us love.

Here are a few examples of the Biden administration's use of division as an effective instrument to wrestle control from Americans.

First, Mr. Biden wasted no time in dividing us over energy in order to advance his Green New Deal agenda. Biden came to office promising to reduce our dependence on fossil fuels and began by cutting production just as America emerged from a two-year, pandemic-related lockdown. He canceled the Keystone XL pipeline, declared war on coal and nuclear power, scuttled drilling in the Arctic National Wildlife Refuge oil and gas fields, demonized fracking to tap America's significant natural gas reserves, and cut investment in new energy exploration. Meanwhile, his actions quickly made fossil-fuel power generation far more expensive while they subsidized green energy production.

Second, Mr. Biden divided us by cheapening the dollar and redistributing our wealth through massive giveaway programs and wasteful spending. He and the Democrat-controlled Congress spent trillions of dollars as the lockdowns ended, much of it wasted on saturated COVID-19 subsidies. This "spread-the-wealth" approach caused inflation to spike and hurt the middle class while spreading "free money" to the underclass that destroyed personal initiative.

Third, President Biden divided us over illegal immigration by throwing open our southern border with Mexico. Millions of people poured across our open border clamoring for the American dream, which Biden's policy delivered via government-provided subsidies and at the same time spiked the epidemic of illegal drug use and crime.

Fourth, Mr. Biden and his Democratic Party divided us over elections by marginalizing our trust in our voting system. For many, given the 2020 and 2022 elections, confidence in fair elections is gone, thanks to the normalization of ballot harvesting, the process of third-party agents collecting and turning in voters' completed election ballots, which critics argue is fraught with potential for fraud. Meanwhile, citizens who dared to question the fairness of our elections were labeled "election denialists" and "democracy destroyers." Of course, the evident weaponization of our federal agencies and the Democratic Party's collaboration with social media giants like Facebook and Twitter contributed to our fragmentation and dwindling trust in our election process.

Fifth, Democrats, especially those leading major cities, and with the White House's silence, divided us on the issue of crime. Many of those "leaders" pushed to defund the police in the wake of the 2020 summer of violence marked by a surge in criminal activity. Although the anti-police movement showed signs of waning by late 2022, numerous progressive district attorneys in major cities like New York City, Philadelphia, Chicago, and Los Angeles refused to enforce the law, which gave license to criminals to further divide us.

Sixth, Mr. Biden and many of his fellow Democrats divided us based on our physical appearance; no longer are we united as a county by common ideals. Rather, tribalism is encouraged, defining us by race, ethnicity, and sexual orientation—not the content of our character, as the late Dr. Martin Luther King Jr. (1929–1968) advocated. That divisiveness was accelerated by much of the mainstream media that celebrated so-called social justice by pushing equity, diversity, and inclusion. Sadly, America is no longer blind to our physical differences and united by love of nation.

Seventh, the Democrats, with Mr. Biden's support, divided us by labeling some speech unacceptable, an effort supported by much of mainstream media and the government's education establishment. No longer are we free to express a contrary opinion; dissenting voices are now labeled "hate speech" or are criminalized. Our First Amendment rights are suppressed by social justice warriors who use the power of government to criminalize a dissenting opinion.

Eighth, Mr. Biden divided us by labeling half of our citizenry "semi-fascists" and "potential domestic terrorists." In multiple speeches, the president compared Republican ideology to "semi-fascism." Why? He disagreed with their objections to his radical calls for change, such as packing the Supreme Court with more justices to water down its power, junking the Electoral College, and ending the US Senate's filibuster.[10]

Ninth, Mr. Biden and his fellow Democrats weaponized the COVID-19 pandemic to divide us into two camps: the vaccinated and unvaccinated. While ignoring the origins of the virus, the Biden administration pitted the vaccinated part of our population against the unvaccinated. For months, President Biden said the continued spread of the coronavirus was a "pandemic of the unvaccinated" and repeatedly claimed—contrary to sound scientific evidence—that vaccinated people cannot spread the virus. Meanwhile, the Biden administration ignored our Bill of Rights by mandating vaccinations, mask-wearing, and quarantines.[11]

The Future of Our "Divided" World

Given our recent chaotic and divisive history, there is no reason to believe the use of division as a tool by Satan and his proxies will wane. In fact, from all appearances, the future is a minefield ripe for more polarization, from families to nation-states, in part thanks to giant corporations being in bed with big government, as well as rogue regimes like Communist China growing their influence across the world. Division is creating a bumper crop of elite control across the world.

At this pace, Satan's elite proxies will accomplish what author H. G. Wells long ago predicted as fiction—that is, humans will eventually be divided into two tiers: the elite overseers (Morlocks) and the rest of us underneath (Eloi). The elite who already get away with so much, thanks to double standards of justice, realize their goal can only come about through divisive fascistic acts, and they are just getting started.

We are rapidly approaching that future in which we will be constantly controlled by outside forces. Artificial intelligence harnessed to ever-present surveillance systems will monitor and guide our every action, to include defining what is truth. That frightening point comes about thanks to pervasive technical interfaces such as iPhones that monitor our every click and word; home-based devices that are tethered to the Internet of Things; the all-pervasive social media; our online shopping habits that anticipate future buying decisions; the manipulation of healthcare; government's leverage over most jobs; centralized oversight of our finances; and our public-school ideologically educated children. This control frenzy will continue if not stopped until we become drone-like, compliant without any trace of individuality, faith, and purpose.

This pattern of expanding control over our lives will strip away our civil liberties and, like in present-day China, will make the rest of us beholden to the communist elite. Perhaps this drone-like existence for the underclass will happen in part because of the rapidly advancing transhumanist craze, medicine's mixing of technology with human flesh allegedly to extend life and capability. We're told that in the future most of us will accept microchips in our bodies to identify us when making financial transactions—what some Christians claim is the mark of the Beast (Revelation 16:2). Others of us will have artificially intelligent devices implanted in our bodies to keep us "healthy" or to speed up our thinking, or our genes will be studied to anticipate and then treat future illnesses or disabilities, and possibly to declare some of us unfit to live. These "advances" are here already, and likely they are part of the transformation of mankind. Even more frightening, those with oversight of such technologies—the elite and powerful—will have their fingers on the "switch" of these implants and life-extending technologies.

Where is this leading? No doubt Satan's elite proxies want to transform America and the West into something akin to present-day communist China—a two-class society, with elite (Morlocks) and underclass slaves (Elois). The power-hungry elite seek global government in their hands that dictates every aspect of life: jobs and education; access to money and healthcare; family size; where we live; whether we're free to exercise our faith; and, ultimately, when our lives will end.

Unfortunately, today's elite have their foot on the accelerator, rapidly moving the world in that direction. They intend to subject us to their will by employing power to "divide and conquer," thanks to their control of government, media, education, the economy, technology, and more. If they get their way, every aspect of our lives will fall under their total governance. We will have no freedom, and worse, little discernable identity. Rather, we will be little more than drones, plebes subject to the elites' manipulation.

That's the ultimate destination for today's cabal of elites, Satan's proxies, who are using the tool of division across every aspect of our contemporary lives to gain power. Sadly, given our history, the majority of us will eventually comply with the elites' demands in order to survive, because they already control most of the necessities of life, and those of us who oppose them will suffer or be killed.

Divided We Stand concludes this etymological, social, and political journey by outlining why our ultimate failure to address elite-driven division, a critical spiritual scourge on humankind, will, in spite of both gains and setbacks, eventually result in the rise of the Antichrist and lead to the prophetic end times.

ROOTS OF DIVISION

Democracy is the most realistic way for diverse peoples to
resolve their differences, and share power, and heal social
divisions without violence or repression.[12]
—Condoleezza Rice, sixty-sixth US Secretary of State

There are three key "roots" to explore before diving into the impact division has had across the history of humankind, especially in twenty-first-century America.

In chapter 1 of this section, we explore division as an instrument applied across society by many actors.

Chapter 2 explains how the worldview of powerful people influences their decisions and ultimately whether they serve Satan's purposes.

Chapter 3 provides a glimpse into the person of Satan, his role, his aim, and how he recruits powerful elites as well as others of us into his camp. Further, the chapter provides some rather frightening examples of Satan's current progress in America.

chapter one

Exploring Division

Understanding Its Various Uses

Abuse of words has been the great instrument of sophistry and
chicanery, of party, faction, and division of society.[13]
—JOHN ADAMS, second president of the United States (1797–1801)

Some politicians are guilty of President John Adams' charge of "abuse
of words" that results in "division." President Biden, as illustrated
in the introduction of this book, consistently mastered sophistry with
the intent to deceive us, which has accelerated our national division. He
famously said, contrary to the evidence, that "inflation is transitory";
"this is a pandemic of the unvaccinated";[14] and our withdrawal from
Afghanistan was an "extraordinary success."[15]

The point here is that words are subject to interpretation and outright manipulation to fool the gullible. In the context of this volume, I
want to explore with you my use of the word "division" and then be very
clear as to how it is to be understood throughout.

"Division" has many uses and synonyms—almost two hundred, in fact. It can be used as a noun and often as a verb meaning "to divide." For the purposes of this book, I will use the word as a social construct to separate groups with the intent of one party to control the other. However, first let's explore the depth of the word across some of its more popular uses to prevent confusion.

The word "division," which dates back to the Latin *diviso* and *divisonis*, is used in multiple ways as a noun. As mentioned, it is also used as a verb, which most often means "to split" or "set or force apart."

As a noun, it can mean something that "divides, separates, or marks off." But what it means really depends on the context.

Elementary students are likely to think of division in the context of mathematics. It's the opposite of multiplication. The goal of division, the young students might explain, is separating something into smaller, equal groups, like arranging twelve donuts into three similar groups of four each. Here, division is a process that divides or separates groups.[16]

US Army soldiers would define "division" as a large military formation consisting of between six and twenty-five thousand personnel. Each division is composed of several brigades, and several divisions typically make up a corps. However, ask US Navy sailors, and they would have a completely different meaning for the word. In their Navy context, it refers to an administrative/functional subunit of a department, like the fire-control division on a cruiser. This use is also found in other government agencies, businesses, and educational organizations.

Ask factory workers to define "division," and they might answer that it refers to the segmentation of tasks, with each person focusing on a specific part of the production process. Also, a senior manager at the same plant might call out the three divisions at the facility: finance, operations, and marketing. A vice president would oversee each division and report to the company president.

Sports enthusiasts might think of "division" as it is used by the National Collegiate Athletic Association. The NCAA divides most sports into three divisions to establish the levels of programs in competition. Those designations represent certain standards, and colleges must play in the same division for all sports. In this context, "division" identifies one of the units of a whole, such as a category, type, or group.

Psychologists might understandably think of the fifty-four divisions of interest groups identified by the American Psychological Association. Those groups represent subdisciplines of psychology—e.g., experimental, social, or clinical, and others focus on topical areas such as aging and trauma.[17] This is an example of "division" as an act or process of a whole (all of psychology) being separated into smaller parts.

"Division" is often used as an indication of discord or the lack of agreement or harmony such as strife, friction and war. Geopolitical divisions between nations are the fodder that too often leads to wars.

For the purposes of *Divided*, we will understand "division" in the context of social divisions that stream from the concept that society is separated into the powerful (elite) and the powerless. In fact, we'll explore potentially hundreds of social divisions, such as those due to race, gender, marital status, politics, health, or location that impact our daily lives. These divisions affect the individual's place in the broader society (class), as well as how society views each division.

Conclusion

For the purposes of this book, we will focus on division as a tool to separate people into distinctive groups to satisfy the dividers' purposes. That alignment is more often than not a product of the dividers' worldviews, the aspect of our lives that dictates how we are divided and the topic of the next chapter.

chapter two

Roots of the Powerful Who Use Division

Today, corruption has won and justice has lost. I brought corruption cases in good faith involving powerful people, and the political and legal establishment blatantly covered up and retaliated by targeting my law license.[18]

—ANDREW THOMAS, American politician, author, and former attorney

This chapter defines the term "powerful person"; identifies the beliefs many powerful people share, providing insights into their motivations, and suggests how those beliefs often manifest into divisive action in order to give the powerful control and often redirect the course of society.

What Is a Powerful Person?

Many names (synonyms) are ascribed to people we know as "powerful." We call them a "bigwig," a "heavyweight," the "honcho," a "kingpin," the "biggie," a "real *kahuna*," the "kingfish," and "big shot." We grant them those labels because they have power, prestige, or influence over us and/or our interests. Of course, circumstances dictate whom we identify as powerful, and it's not always a permanent label.

There are temporarily powerful people in our lives. The police officer who stops us for speeding is momentarily a powerful person. However, that view quickly evaporates once we drive away with a warning, a citation, and/or a court summons. Then we transfer that fear to another powerful person: the judge who decides our penalty for speeding.

There are powerful people who are due more consistent attention. For example, our workplace bosses are powerful because they assign us tasks and may even decide whether we are fired or get promoted. Their power is wrapped up in the pay we receive, which sustains our livelihood—a strong incentive to bow to their influence.

There are powerful people who are more incidental, albeit important, to our lives. Elected officials are powerful because we've entrusted them with our taxes to provide our communities with critical services such as public safety, utilities, and schools. We show them deference when they perform those duties, and, in a republic, we replace them with another if they fail.

So, simply, a powerful person is one who exercises influence over others. Obviously, there is quite a difference between the influence of parents over their children and that of the leader over a country. However, it's really a matter of scale, and for our purposes, we will focus at the highest levels of society, where powerful people impact entire institutions and nations.

The Powerful Person's Worldview Matters

We should care about the worldview of powerful people, because it shapes their thinking and decision-making, which either directly or indirectly affect our lives.

The German term *weltanschauung* ("worldview") means "a comprehensive conception or apprehension of the world especially from a specific standpoint." German romanticists explain that cultures create a pattern or common outlook on life expressed in various fora—art, literature, social institutions, religion, and more. In fact, to understand the culture of a country, one must explore the underlying worldview.[19]

I develop this idea in my 2020 book, *Collision Course: The Fight to Reclaim Our Moral Compass Before It's Too Late*. I explain there:

> A Christian worldview addresses important issues as who God is, the world He made, and our relationship with Him. It explains our role in this world in terms of metaphysics, epistemology, and values. It touches every aspect of our life; all areas of this physical domain have a distinctive Christian perspective, which defines our Christian worldview.[20]

Unfortunately, according to Gallup polling, although most (69 percent) Americans identify as Christian, only 29 percent attended a religious service in the past week[21] and just 6 percent say they hold to a biblical worldview.[22] More alarming, only a third (37 percent)[23] of US-based pastors say they have a "biblical worldview."

On a practical basis, our worldview helps us understand the world. It is the basis of our assumptions about things and people we don't fathom, and it helps us navigate everyday life, how we interact with others, the decisions we make, and the values (rights and wrongs) we hold. Everyone has a worldview, but too few can describe it very accurately.

Common Worldview among Powerful People

For average powerful people, their worldview is a fluid set of rights, wrongs, principles, and ideals. It tends to be more secular than Christian, which reflects two common concepts: relativism and humanism.

Relativism is a prevailing philosophy in our culture that states that truth is relative. It declares that all values—even biblical ones—are tied to a respective culture. Relativism claims that no set of values is better than any other. Not surprisingly, for the relativist, all religions are basically the same, and no religion, such as Christianity, should claim exclusivity—i.e., Jesus Christ is the only way to eternal life. Also, for the relativist, morality is a personal preference; good and evil are just labels. Relativists reject Christian views that hold to moral positions on such issues as abortion and homosexuality.[24]

Humanism puts emphasis on the inner man and seeks to improve mankind to the point of perfection. The humanist believes the key to reaching perfection is education—which, if done properly, will cure all social ills. For the humanist, behavior changes with learning, and the stimulus-response theory of man works to help man progress; right learning helps man progress to his ultimate end—perfection. However, that theory shows no accountability to absolutes—there is no infinite god, only one-self. Thus, the humanist, not God, decides on the best course of life and what is ultimately right and wrong (morals).[25]

The modern American secularist—someone who embraces both relativism and humanism—often endorses radical Marxist views, either overtly or covertly. In fact, a 2021 survey by pollster George Barna with the Cultural Research Center found that 10 percent of Americans have internalized Marxist ideology and draw from it in their daily decisions, although few actually admit to such views.[26]

Of course, a Marxist worldview is the polar opposite to Christianity, because it promotes the abolition of all religion; it promotes naturalism (i.e., there is no spiritual component to life); embraces a morality that exclusively advances the "working class"; assumes all human behavior is based exclusively on the material; makes no class distinctions; posits that a communist world government is utopia on earth; and asserts that economics determines the nature of all legal, social, and political institutions.[27]

Granted, it is presumptuous to identify all "powerful" people as either secularists or, worse, Marxists. However, I've already established that many powerful elites identified in my book, *The Deeper State*, are globalists. That view is in itself a humanistic religion that is antithetical to a Christian worldview, and, according to retired US Army Lieutenant General Jerry Boykin, the executive vice president for the Washington, DC-based Family Research Council: "The globalist movement is based on Marxism…their leadership and funding is at the heart, Marxism," and their supporters are "useful idiots thinking they are doing something good for mankind but they are only helping the Marxist movement."[28]

Boykin also explained that every Marxist movement has the wealthy, like the globalists elite, and that every past and present Marxist (communist) regime "always includes a wealthy elite controlling everything—production, distribution, prices." The result is a cabal of globalists elite making a lot of money while most of us are left the crumbs.

That observation begs the question: How many of the truly powerful people in this world actually embrace secular (or worse) worldviews? Frankly, I don't have a conclusive answer to that, but there are available insights about certain powerful people and the groups with which they are associated.

Powerful Technology People: Less Democratic and Religious

A study of some of the most powerful people provides insight into their worldview. Specifically, a 2021 article in *PLOS One*, a peer-reviewed, open-access scientific journal published by the Public Library of Science (PLOS) entitled, "A Class for Itself? On the Worldviews of the New Tech Elite," addresses the research of one hundred of the richest/most powerful people in the high-technology world, according to *Forbes* as cited by *PLOS*, to ascertain three things: whether they "share a common, meritocratic view of the world"; "whether they have a 'mission' for the future"; and "how they view democracy as a political system." The PLOS study found that the "tech elite [which constitute one-fifth of the world's hundred richest people studied] have a more meritocratic view of the world than the general US Twitter-using population [the cohort used by the researchers for a baseline]," and they "promise to 'make the world a better place,'" a view they share with other "extremely wealthy people." However, these tech elite have a dim view of democracy, which is a rather sobering finding.[29]

This unique cohort of world elites are not necessarily entrepreneurs but owe their power/wealth to technologies developed at taxpayers' expense. Further, they are graduates of top-ranked liberal academic institutions such as Stanford and Harvard, and geographically they tend to cluster in places like Silicon Valley, California, and the Washington, DC, metro area. On the revealing issue of democratic checks and balances, they believe rapid technological progress has flushed away many of the ideals of democracy, leaving them with great wealth and the know-how to guide mankind's future development.[30]

It is also a bit reassuring that these tech elite do appear to have strong, "positive sentiments toward the idea of 'making the world a better place.'" However, they are not particularly religious, according to the *PLOS* study.[31]

Powerful People: Ethical Overload Reflects Conflicted Worldviews

What do we know about the ethical decisions made by powerful people? Does their power corrupt them, or does it make the quality of their decisions much stronger?

In 2019, Alexandra Fleishmann, a PhD student at the University of Cologne, Germany, researched how powerful people respond to moral dilemmas. This effort provides some insights about them and their worldviews.[32]

Ms. Fleishmann's thesis was that power corrupts powerful people's reaction to moral dilemmas. So, she investigated what power does to their moral decision-making using four moral thinking styles: "Follow one's emotions, following rules, deliberating about moral dilemmas, and integrating emotions with thinking."[33]

Her research found that "powerful people made the same moral decisions as [do] less powerful people." Why didn't the alleged powerful people's higher moral thinking result in better moral decisions? She concluded that even though powerful people may engage in more moral thinking than less powerful people do, their thinking styles canceled out their more frequent opportunity for moral thinking.[34]

So, the powerful people's position doesn't necessarily mean they make better moral decisions than the rest of us.

Powerful Business People: Swerving Out of Their Lane

Another challenge plagues those in powerful positions, especially those in today's corporate world. The enticement is for the chief executive officers (CEOs) of firms to get out of their corporate lane and fall under the control of outside groups.

Patrick M. Wright, a professor of management at the University of South Carolina, wrote that today's CEOs "face a need to be externally oriented like never before," rather than as CEOs in the past, who primarily focused on "delivering on financial and operating metrics in ways that indicated the company was adequately meeting the needs of shareholders, customers, and employees."[35]

Today's CEOs, wrote Professor Wright, are asked to focus on the environment, social issues, and governance—a woke agenda—which forces them to stake out positions on public-policy ideas such as taking "moral" stands on democracy, human rights, and the environment. However, as Dr. Wright observed, most CEOs today don't have the necessary skills and abilities to deal in "this environment of increasing external pressure to take public stands," and in fact, "many CEOs are ill-equipped to take on this role."[36]

Recent research indicates the public does not want CEOs to "speak out as much as the popular press implies and to do so carries risk." Further, Wright indicated that many CEOs lack the coherent worldview necessary "to allow them to apply philosophical moral values to particular political or social issues." Rather, they may base "decisions on the most visible or highest-pressure groups confronting them, resulting in incoherent decisions across multiple issues and multiple geographies and potentially negatively influence their organizations and society."[37]

In fact, according to Vivek Ramaswamy, a former Biotech CEO who left his position due to his inability to publicly express his conservative beliefs, warned other CEOs:

> Here's what the sincere guys miss: when they create a system in which business leaders decide moral questions, they open the floodgates for all their unscrupulous colleagues to abuse that new-found power. And there are far more CEOs who are eager to grab money and power in the name of justice than there are CEOs who are agnostic to money and power and only care about justice.[38]

Powerful Journalists: Secular, Leftist Worldview

Historically, American journalists were partisans—such as during our Revolutionary War era (1775–1783) with the *Federalist* and *Anti-Federalist* papers or, in the nineteenth century, the Democrat or Republican newspapers. However, only during the mid-twentieth century did Americans develop the now-diminished view that journalists were to be fair and unbiased in reporting.

Today, the problem is that journalism has reverted to the model of previous eras, whereby most seem to report the news with a bias, especially an outright leftist political preference, while still claiming to be fair and unbiased. This becomes a significant challenge when journalists with a cooked-in bias rise to positions where they oversee their media outlets' messaging.

The leftist bias among many mainstream journalists shouldn't surprise us, because they've been conditioned by our leftist public education establishment and culture. Therefore, it's not especially revealing that only 7.1 percent of journalists self-identify with the normally more conservative Republican Party, according to a study cited in *Politico*.[39] Another study from Indiana University found that more than three in four (78.3 percent) American journalists self-identify as either independent or Democrat.[40]

Mr. James Ostrowski wrote an insightful article for the opinion site Lewrockwell.com about journalists, "Why Progressives Make Bad Journalists." In that article, he states that most journalists are ideologically progressive, which he says reflects a fixed worldview about politics; are utopian; favor using democratic government to solve human problems; want government force to produce results; have no theory of costs, thus deny the often-extraordinary costs of their proposed solutions; embrace a form of therapy against existential fears; and have no limiting principle, which makes them prone to totalitarianism.[41]

Based on that definition, Mr. Ostrowski concludes that progressives can't be good journalists, because they fail to set aside their political ideology when reporting facts, nor do they recognize their own political biases. Then he argues that the journalist's progressive worldview is a "self-imposed mental disability that robotically prevents the progressive from noticing certain facts and impels the progressive to exaggerate the importance of other facts."[42]

Powerful Federal Workforce: Deep-State or Apolitical Worldviews?

A number of books address the topic "deep state" within the federal bureaucracy. The theory is that federal government employees draw on their worldviews to secretly manipulate or control the levers of government outside the purview of Congress and the president.

One perspective about the operation of the deep state is espoused by a former congressional aide, Mike Lofgren, in his book, *Anatomy of the*

Deep State. He argues that the deep state is really "a hybrid association of elements of government and parts of top-level finance and industry that is effectively able to govern the United States without reference to consent of the governed as expressed through the formal political process."[43]

Another definition of the "deep state" confines it completely within the US "intelligence community," the so-called military-industrial complex, according to Thomas Knapp, director, and senior news analyst at the William Lloyd Garrison Center for Libertarian Advocacy Journalism. He argues that this view has sinister connotations: "Spies and generals conspiring to put over a coup of some sort, if necessary, maybe even giving inconvenient political figures the JFK treatment."[44]

Mr. Knapp tends to dismiss this view to argue that the deep state is little more than evidence of the nature of our political government, which puts "its own needs first, and its corps of unelected workers (greatly outnumbering the politicians who have to explain themselves to voters) closely identify its needs with their needs and vice versa."[45]

There is some truth to Mr. Knapp's argument. However, what's truly eye-opening about the federal workforce that oversees the levers of government for "our good" is their strong left-leaning political bias. In theory, our federal workforce is apolitical, required to support any administration elected by the American voters.

Although federal workers are expected to be apolitical in their work, they are permitted to establish employee unions that participate in the political process. The vast majority of their unions' political efforts support Democratic Party candidates or Democrat initiatives. However, by exception, the intelligence community is not allowed by law to unionize.

Federal employee political donations expose the workforce's true leanings. In the 2020 political cycle, for example, employees at the Department of Justice gave the vast majority (87.6 percent) of their donations to Democrats. Employees at the Department of Defense gave $5.2 million, of which 65 percent went to Democrats. And perhaps given the well-known bias within the media world, it's not surprising that the employees at the Federal Communications Commission, where many former journalists work, and which oversees our media, gave 99.29 percent of their donations to Democrats.[46]

Although the political giving record of federal employees doesn't necessarily reflect the entire government workforce's ideological inclination, it does suggest a leaning toward Democrats over Republicans—a reflection of a prevailing worldview that perhaps is more representative of lower-ranking minority employees and their bosses. That same bias could well indicate that, by association, a disproportionate number of the government's most senior bureaucrats have a worldview that leads them to favor Democrats over Republicans as well.

What can we conclude about the aforementioned powerful people and their worldviews? Worldview matters because it influences our decisions and actions. In the context of powerful people, a secular worldview tends to be rather fluid, and in the case of the powerful high-tech people, they evidence less respect for democracy and tend to be more secular than the general population. When it comes to ethical decisions, powerful busy people often don't necessarily make better decisions than the rest of us. Our powerful corporate leaders (today's CEOs), no matter their worldview, are vulnerable to being misled by outside influencers when it comes to nonbusiness moral, social, and political issues. Powerful media people tend to have worldviews that are far left of center politically, which influences the messaging from their public platforms. Finally, the federal bureaucrat is expected to be apolitical, but reality indicates that many (perhaps a majority) of the federal workforce demonstrate a worldview that favors the Democratic Party and their policies.

Evidence of Powerful, Divisive People and Our Future

This chapter is incomplete without some mention of the annual World Economic Forum (WEF) meeting in Davos, Switzerland. That conference is a gathering of the world's most powerful elites who have taken it upon themselves to chart our future. They are without exception globalists, mostly narcissists with bankrupt moral compasses and steeped in unfathomable hypocrisy. Consider comments from representative elites who attended the 2023 WEF Summit and what they reveal in their own words about their worldviews.

The WEF is an international nongovernmental and lobbying organization based in Switzerland. Its founder is Klaus Schwab, a German engineer and economist, and the WEF is funded by more than one thousand member companies and some public/government subsidies. Philosophically, the WEF views its mission as "improving the state of the world by engaging business, political, academic, and other leaders to shape global, regional, and industry agendas."[47]

Annually, the WEF hosts a meeting at the end of January in Davos, a Swiss mountain resort. Attending the summit are thousands of hand-picked people, including deep-pocketed investors, business leaders, politicians, economists, and journalists to discuss global affairs. They make the annual pilgrimage to Davos to plan our future. Last year, Mr. Schwab said:

> The future is not just happening. The future is built by us [the elite gathered at the WEF summit], by a powerful community such as you here in this room [at Davos].[48]

The arrogance of these powerful people is palpable. In 2022, the Davos delegates arrived at the summit aboard 1,040 private jets[49] (so much for carbon pollution) believing they are in the business of saving the world in accordance with their vision known as the "Great Reset," which is really an agenda about radically altering the world as we know it to achieve the elites' utopian goals. Most of the participants are either climate religionists or those who prosper from that cult, which may explain their laser focus on that divisive issue.[50]

Consider some of the most shocking, divisive statements erupting from 2023 Davos summit.

John Kerry, the former US senator from Massachusetts, and President Barack Obama's secretary of state, who now serves as President Biden's US Special Envoy for Climate, is quite an alarmist, a climate activist. Mr. Kerry and some of his fellow Davos luminaries evidently think of themselves as gods as well. After all, Mr. Kerry was caught on video at Davos stating: "I mean, it's so almost extraterrestrial to think about saving the planet." Of course, he was serious, believing that he and his fellow elite colleagues are uniquely gifted to save the world. Talk about a divisive statement. But there is more.

In his capacity as Biden's climate czar, Mr. Kerry hysterically called for a "climate revolution" and blamed world businesses for blocking efforts to exchange our future for a few dollars. He left no doubt about the reason for a lack of progress on mitigating what he often calls our global climate crisis. "How do we get there [resolving the climate crisis]?" Kerry asked. "The lesson I have learned in the last years...is money, money, money, money, money, money, money."[51]

Not to be outdone by Mr. Kerry's hysteria, former Vice President Al Gore, also a Democrat, gave an "unhinged" rant about climate change to the Davos delegates. At times he yelled that climate change is "boiling the oceans," causing "rain bombs," and impacting mankind's ability for "self-governance." Of course, like other delegates, Mr. Gore arrived at the Davos summit in his private jet, flown from his Tennessee mansion[52]

Mr. Gore's concern for the climate isn't supported by his energy-wasting real estate holdings, which include a $9 million ocean-view villa in Montecito, California; a twenty-room, eight-bathroom Nashville mansion—which, according to one estimate, uses nineteen times the electricity of the average American household—and two other homes in Virginia and Tennessee.[53]

Evidently, WEF President Schwab has the same weird climate beliefs as do Kerry and Gore, which is why Schwab called for strengthening climate-related "global cooperation." In a similar vein at the Davos summit, Schwab announced the creation of an otherworldly, truly bizarre "Global Collaboration Village," which he said:

> …is the pioneering effort to use the metaverse [a virtual-reality space in which users can interact with a computer-generated environment and other users[54]] for public good, to create global cooperation and strengthen global cooperation in the metaverse or using metaverse technologies. For me, it's a dream coming true because the village allows the Forum to create a more larger [sic] and open platform where everybody can participate.[55]

Climate czar Kerry and Al Gore were joined by many other extremists at Davos, such as Joyeeta Gupta, a professor at the University of Amsterdam, who claimed humankind has but two choices: saving the planet or continuing our current doomed course. The professor said:

> If we do the minimum at this pivotable [sic] moment in our history, then we and our children—even if we are rich—will live in the danger zone. But if we—business people, governments, citizens, cities—take action today, then we and our children will have a future worth looking forward to.[56]

United Nations Secretary-General Antonio Guterres is part of the climate cult and an angry agent of pending global disaster. He called for ending "our addiction to fossil fuels," even if that means massive unemployment and its tragic consequences—especially across the developing world. Mr. Guterres said at Davos:

> So, we need to act together to close the emissions gap, and that means to phase out progressively coal and supercharge the

renewable revolution, to end the addiction to fossil fuels, and to stop our self-defeating war on nature.[57]

Globalists like Spanish Prime Minister Pedro Sanchez blamed Europe's 2023 energy shortage on "mistrust, selfishness [and] xenophobia." He continued:

> Our present struggle is not only against [Russia's] Putin or the energy shortage. It is also against fear, mistrust, selfishness, xenophobia, and environmental disaster. And its outcome will define life in the West and beyond for decades to come.[58]

When the giant egos at Davos weren't threatening climate Armageddon, they pontificated about issues of "political expediencies" that suppress dissent and threaten our civil liberties. Specifically, Věra Jourová, the European Commission's vice president, predicted "illegal hate speech, which you will have soon also in the US," adding, "I think that we have a strong reason why we have this in the criminal law."[59]

WEF's annual Davos summit is a gathering of mostly unelected oligarchs intent on manipulating the world to fit their selfish aim and, evidently, they are a group of egomaniacs who make some rather outlandish statements. Typically, they speak of global interests and governance—as if they run the world. They also trash nationalism and patriotism, which explains why they hate people like former President Donald Trump, a strong American nationalist.

The WEF and especially the annual Davos summit seek to polarize the world to favor the interests of the elite 1 percent, those who have crowned themselves as gods over our planet. They are self-righteous in their aims like John Kerry (Mr. "Extraterrestrial") and look down their collective noses at the rest of the world's population as being mostly expendable. Their narcissism and arrogance are palpable and incredibly divisive.

Conclusion

Many of the world's most powerful people—both within government and the private sector—embrace a worldview that relies on division to maintain control. The outcome of much of that polarization supports Satan's evil agenda, the topic of the next chapter.

chapter three

Satan's Work among the Vulnerable and Powerful

"All this I will give you," he said, "if you will bow down and worship me." Jesus said to him, "Away from me, Satan! For it is written: 'Worship the Lord your God, and serve him only.'"

—MATTHEW 4:9–10, NIV

Satan is very real, and with his army of demons, he uses gullible humans to help wage a spiritual war with the ultimate goal of dethroning God Almighty. In that process, Satan recruits to his cause many powerful people who exercise their considerable influence to divide and conquer this world.

The great deceiver, Satan, even tried to recruit Jesus in Matthew, chapter 4, a familiar account to most Christians. That scene takes place at the start of Christ's earthly ministry. He was just baptized by John at the Jordan River. Then:

...after being baptized, Jesus came up immediately from the water; and behold, the heavens were opened, and he saw the Spirit of God descending as a dove and lighting on him, and behold, a voice out of the heavens said, "This is My beloved Son, in whom I am well pleased." (Matthew 3:16–17, NIV)

Once Jesus was baptized, the Spirit led Him into the "wilderness to be tempted by the devil" (Matthew 4:1, NIV). In the next few verses, we read that the tempter (Satan, the Devil) tried to manipulate Jesus into turning on God. By verse 9 we understand Satan's offer: "All this [the kingdoms of the world] I will give you...if you will bow down and worship me."

This Scripture indicates that Satan tried to entice the Son of God with earthly wealth and power, but Jesus rejected the offer, saying:

Go Satan! For it is written, you shall worship the Lord your God, and serve Him only. (Matthew 4:10, NIV)

That's exactly what Satan does with mankind as well. He tempts us with wealth and promises of power in exchange for our obedience in bowing down and worshipping him. That comes about in many ways, but it's the bottom line when trying to understand how humans are recruited to do the Devil's work on earth.

This chapter answers three key questions: Who is Satan? What does he want? How does he recruit humans to advance his aim—i.e., to become his proxies of evil?

The simplest answer to these questions is: Satan is a fallen angel who wants to control all mankind, and he recruits people to his team with offers not that dissimilar to those he used to tempt Jesus with: earthly riches and power. Unfortunately, humans are weak, sinful, and vulnerable to Satan's temptations, and many surrender to their sinful desires in exchange for obedience: "worship" of Satan.

What Does the Bible Say about Satan?

God created Satan as a holy angel (Isaiah 14:12), perhaps the highest-level angel, the anointed cherub, the most beautiful of God's creations. In fact, he was created with a free moral choice. "Lucifer" (Isaiah 14:12, translated "day star" or "morning star") was Satan's name *before* he chose a path against God that warranted his new label, "Satan," which is a Hebrew word signifying "adversary" and "enemy."

Evidently, according to the Scriptures, Satan was not content with his heavenly stature, so he became arrogant, prideful—narcissistic about his beauty and elevated status. As a result, he desired to sit on a throne above God (Isaiah 14:13–14, 1 Timothy 3:6). In response, God cast Satan out of Heaven (Isaiah 1:15; Ezekiel 28:16–17).

After casting him out of Heaven, God installed Satan as the ruler of this world and the prince of the power of the air (John 12:31; 2 Corinthians 4:4). In fact, Jesus witnessed Satan's fall, as described in Luke 10:18 (NIV): "I saw Satan fall like lightning from heaven."

The timing of Satan's fall is somewhat bracketed by Scripture. We know he fell before the events described in Genesis 3:1–4, wherein he tempted Adam and Eve in the Garden. So, his fall from Heaven happened between when God created the angels and the garden temptation. We also read in the book of Job that Satan evidently continued to have access to Heaven after his fall. Job 1:6–7 (NIV) states:

> One day the angels came to present themselves before the Lord, and Satan also came with them. The Lord said to Satan, "Where have you come from?" Satan answered the Lord, "From roaming through the earth and going back and forth in it."

This suggests Satan was free to move between Heaven and earth and to the throne of God.[60]

The Scripture identifies Satan by his actions. He is described in

God's Word as the angelic enemy of God, a rebel against the Lord, and the leader of other rebellious angels (Ezekiel 28:15; Isaiah 14:12–17). He is also known as an accuser (Genesis 3:1; Revelation 12:9–10), a deceiver (Genesis 3; 2 Corinthians 4:4), and a tempter (Matthew 4:3; 1 Thessalonians 3:5), and he promotes false doctrines to keep unbelievers in spiritual bondage (2 Corinthians 4:4; 11:14). He is also called a "murderer" and the "father of lies" (John 8:44).

In addition to being known by his actions, Satan is known by many titles. He is called "the devil" in the New Testament, which means "false accuser" or "slanderer," a well-deserved title earned by his role in Job 1–2. The Jews refer to him as "Beelzebul," which derives from "Baal-Zebel," a false god of the Philistines in Ekron (2 Kings 12:2–3, 6). Other distinctions associated with him include "tempter" (1 Thessalonians 3:5), "the wicked one" (Matthew 13:19), "accuser of the believer" (Revelation 12:10), "ruler of this world" (John 12:31), and "prince of the power of the air" (Ephesians 2:2).

Scripture is very clear that Satan is a real being, and not like the cartoon depiction of him as an all-red dragon figure with horns. No, he doesn't have flesh and bones like a human, but he's a spiritual being created by God (Ezekiel 28:15) like us in that he has a mind, emotions, and a will (Job 1; Matthew 4:1–12). His key limitation is that he can only do what God allows (Job 1:12) and, like us, he is not omnipresent across all of humanity—even though he does lead his army of demons, and collectively they represent "the powers of this dark world and against the spiritual forces of evil in the heavenly realms" (Ephesians 6:12, NIV).

What Does Satan Seek?

Even though Satan was cast out of Heaven (Ezekiel 28:12–19; Isaiah 14:12–14), he never stopped trying to elevate himself above God. That's why he constantly counterfeits all that God does, aiming to gain our worship and undermine God's kingdom, the motivation identified in Matthew 4:8–9. No wonder Satan is the ultimate inspiration for the world's many cults and false religions that call for the worship of the creature rather than the Creator (Romans 1:24–25). Yes, he will do whatever is in his power to oppose God and believers who follow God's Son, Jesus Christ.

Satan wants to destroy Christians' witness, faith, and joy. We know that from 1 Peter 5:8 (NIV), which calls us to "be alert and of sober mind" so that we can understand Satan's schemes as he "prowls around like a roaring lion looking for someone to devour." This manifests in our lives when he tempts us to doubt God (John 20), to replace our faith with fear (Psalm 34:4), to perceive we are not good enough (Ephesians 2:10), to keep us out of fellowship (1 Corinthians 12), to be led astray by false prophets (Matthew 7:15), and to cause us to fail (2 Corinthians 4:8-10).[61]

Satan is also positioned to exercise dominion over the world and its system (John 12:31; 1 John 5:19), but, as pointed out earlier in this chapter, that's only with God's permission—and his power won't last forever. We know from Revelation 13:2–8 that Satan will deceive mankind and raise up for himself the Antichrist, who will rule for seven years at the coming of the Tribulation.

His mission as the leader of "darkness" is to use his network of demons to nullify the effect of God among people (Matthew 13:3–4, 19) and to blind unbelievers to the Gospel of Christ (2 Corinthians 4:4). Further, he will attempt to destroy Israel (Revelation 12), but at the end of the Tribulation, Jesus returns to destroy the Antichrist and imprisons Satan for one thousand years (Revelation 19:19–20; 20:1–3). At the end of that period, Satan is released to lead one last rebellion (Revelation 20:7–9) before he is once and for all time thrown into the Lake of Fire, where he is forever tormented (Revelation 20:10). (A more comprehensive look at these end-times events is presented in chapter 17 of this book.)

How Does Satan Get What He Wants?

Satan has a kingdom full of helpers, demons who use a variety of methods not dissimilar to how in the wilderness he tried to entice Jesus to abandon God. Although Satan is powerful, he can't do more than God allows.

Satan's earthly successes are irrefutable when it comes to persuading humans to support his aim. Consider a 1965 commentary by famed radio legend Paul Harvey. He captured the attention of his radio audience with a sobering, albeit fictional, story, "If I Were the Devil."

Mr. Harvey's discernment of the Devil's nature, intent, and means is consistent with the Scriptures and clearly demonstrates that Satan knows how to get what he wants.

The legendary commentator said:

If I were the devil… If I were the Prince of Darkness, I'd want to engulf the whole world in darkness. And I'd have a third of its real estate, and four-fifths of its population, but I wouldn't be happy until I had seized the ripest apple on the tree—Thee. So, I'd set about however necessary to take over the United States. I'd subvert the churches first—I'd begin with a campaign of whispers. With the wisdom of a serpent, I would whisper to you as I whispered to Eve: "Do as you please."

To the young, I would whisper that "The Bible is a myth." I would convince them that man created God instead of the other way around. I would confide that what's bad is good, and what's good is "square." And the old, I would teach to pray, after me, "Our Father, which art in Washington…"

And then I'd get organized. I'd educate authors in how to make lurid literature exciting, so that anything else would appear dull and uninteresting. I'd threaten TV with dirtier movies and vice versa. I'd pedal narcotics to whom I could. I'd sell alcohol to ladies and gentlemen of distinction. I'd tranquilize the rest with pills.

If I were the devil, I'd soon have families at war with themselves, churches at war with themselves, and nations at war with
themselves; until each in its turn was consumed. And with promises of higher ratings, I'd have mesmerizing media fanning the
flames. If I were the devil, I would encourage schools to refine
young intellects, but neglect to discipline emotions—just let
those run wild, until before you knew it, you'd have to have drug
sniffing dogs and metal detectors at every schoolhouse door.

Within a decade I'd have prisons overflowing, I'd have
judges promoting pornography—soon I could evict God from
the courthouse, then from the schoolhouse, and then from the
houses of Congress. And in His own churches I would substitute
psychology for religion and deify science. I would lure priests
and pastors into misusing boys and girls, and church money. If
I were the devil, I'd make the symbols of Easter an egg and the
symbol of Christmas a bottle.

If I were the devil, I'd take from those who have, and give to
those who want until I had killed the incentive of the ambitious.

And what do you bet I could get whole states to promote
gambling as the way to get rich? I would caution against extremes
and hard work in patriotism, in moral conduct. I would convince the young that marriage is old-fashioned, that swinging
is more fun, that what you see on the TV is the way to be. And
thus, I could undress you in public, and I could lure you into
bed with diseases for which there is no cure. In other words, if I
were the devil, I'd just keep right on doing what he's doing.

—PAUL HARVEY, good day.[62]

It's pretty obvious that Satan has been quite successful recruiting
mankind to his camp, because virtually everything Mr. Harvey said
decades ago about the Devil and his plans has mostly come true. Unfortunately, that success is the story of humanity through the ages, and it
will continue to be true for the future until the return of Christ.

The fact is that Satan has a host of helpers—spirit beings or demons—which explains his expansive influence. In Revelation 12:3–4, we read that, when he fell from Heaven, Satan brought with him one-third of the angelic host. These demons are his army to help him rule the dark spirit world and directly influence humanity.

The great deceiver deploys his army of fallen angels (Revelation 12) to entice humans to support his aim, and Scripture provides significant examples of that reach. We see in Daniel 10:12 that such spiritual beings have influence and power over governments. Specifically, an angel tells Daniel that his prayers "were heard" and that God would intervene. The angel announced:

> But the prince of the Persian kingdom resisted me twenty-one days. Then Michael, one of the chief princes, came to help me, because I was detained there with the king of Persia. (Daniel 10:13, NIV)

The angel continued:

> So he said, "Do you know why I have come to you? Soon I will return to fight against the prince of Persia, and when I go, the prince of Greece will come." (Daniel 10: 20, NIV)

Numerous New Testament passages indicate that Jesus Christ was very attuned to Satan's demons and what they do, such as in Mark 9:17–29, where He cast out a demon that made a man's son unable to speak. Christ spoke to the demon in the boy:

> "You deaf and mute spirit," he said, "I command you, come out of him and never enter him again." (Mark 9:25, NIV)

The Apostle Paul warned the Gentiles at Ephesus about the war within the spiritual realm. In Ephesians 2:2 (NIV), Paul wrote that they "used to live when you followed the ways of this world and of the ruler of the kingdom of the air [Satan], the spirit who is now at work in those who are disobedient." Later in Ephesians, he further warned:

> For our struggle is not against flesh and blood, but against the rulers, against the authorities, against the powers of this dark world and against the spiritual forces of evil in the heavenly. (Ephesians 6:12, NIV)

These verses make clear that Satan is the "god" of this world, and he greatly influences the actions of human beings. He does this by deploying a number of tools to accomplish his purposes, and the most important is division. In fact, division is just the opposite of what Christ teaches, which is what we would expect from Satan, the adversary, who takes up the mantle of division.

Scripture confirms this view. God's character is represented by four attributes: love (1 John 4:8); peace (Philippians 4:6–9); unity (Ephesians 4:4–6); and truth (Deuteronomy 32.4). In contrast, Satan's character is the polar opposite and is represented by hate (1 John 3:8–15); discord (James 3:13–18); division (1 Corinthians 3:1–4); and lies (John 8:44).

Each of these four divine qualities—love, peace, unity, and truth—is mostly absent from our culture, as outlined in Mr. Harvey's commentary. By contrast, today, Satan polarizes mankind away from these divine qualities by dividing us through fear often associated with our differences: color of skin, sexuality, greed, ego, and much more.

How Does Satan Recruit Humans to Advance His Aim?

Satan recruits human proxies to serve his earthly campaign by tapping into their sinful nature. Our only defense against Satan's campaign is remaining close to Christ, keeping short accounts, and leaning on the Holy Spirit to guard our souls against attack.

Understand that all of human life is Satan's playground, and we are his pawns, nothing more. He recruits us much as he tried to entice Jesus and separate Him from God in the wilderness. His aim is always to get us to worship himself by persuading us to abandon God.

In 2012, Pastor Mark Buchanan of New Life Community Church in Duncan, British Columbia, wrote an article, "Get Behind Me, Satan!" It makes the point that Satan hates humanity and uses us only to satisfy his goal.

Pastor Buchanan said after twenty-two years of pastoral ministry:

> I've come to the conclusion that the devil hates people. Or, more precisely, the devil hates God, and resorts to what any terrorist with a powerful enemy does: goes after his loved ones, wife, and kids. The devil's hatred of people is an act of transference. It's his bitterness toward God aimed at what God loves most. Job's story, in some form or the next, plays out day after day, place after place, world without end.[63]

Pastor Buchanan then explained that the "devil's main act of hatred is not to destroy people (at least not at first), but to get [recruit] them by masquerading as angels of light." This observation is supported by what the Apostle Paul wrote in 2 Timothy 2:26 (NIV), when he said people have fallen into "the trap of the devil, who has taken them captive to do his will."[64]

Many humans are recruited by Satan because they are attracted to power, dominance, and gratification—the essence of Satanism. Satan and his demons extend their power to those who worship him. Sometimes that allegiance takes the form of demon possession or being inhabited. Mark 5:10–13 illustrates the scene wherein Jesus permits the demons to come out of a possessed man and enter pigs (swine), and Luke 11:24–25 cites the parable Jesus told of an unclean spirit entering a person.

Nothing in God's Word indicates that demonic possession or inhabitation ended. Rather, if Satan and his demonic army are still active, then they animate some of the evilest, most powerful people in history—today and, as Scripture promises, even during the prophetic end times.

Revelation 18 tells of that future time in which demons will energize a charismatic political dictator (the Antichrist) who leads a mighty world superpower:

> After these things I saw another angel coming down from heaven, having great authority, and the earth was illuminated with his glory. And he cried mightily with a loud voice, saying, "Babylon the great is fallen, is fallen, and has become a dwelling place of demons, a prison for every foul spirit, and a cage for every unclean and hated bird! For all the nations have drunk of the wine of the wrath of her fornication, the kings of the earth have committed fornication with her, and the merchants of the earth have become rich through the abundance of her luxury." And I heard another voice from heaven saying, "Come out of her, my people, lest you share in her sins, and lest you receive of her plagues." (Revelation 18:1–4, NKJV)

Satan recruits many within our contemporary culture to become proxies of pure evil to advance his goal of gaining power.

The issue of Satan drafting the powerful/influential is important, but it is not the entire picture. He uses others who do his evil work as well. Specifically, I close this chapter with four illustrations of in-your-face satanic action here in the United States.

Abortion as a "religious practice": First, consider an example of the ancient evil practice of human sacrifice that demonstrates the Satan-inspired, contemporary promotion of abortion on demand.

There are many biblical accounts of human sacrifice (Deuteronomy 18:10; Leviticus 18:21; 2 Kings 21:6) associated with so-called religious practices. Unfortunately, in the name of Satan, similar immoral, divisive efforts have come to America thanks to a new "religious" abortion practice in New Mexico.[65]

On February 1, 2023, a New Mexico-based Satanic temple launched a new "religious medical services arm," according to TST Health, the medical services branch of a nontheistic religious organization. Reportedly, members of the "Satanic Temple" believe killing unborn babies is a religious "ritual" they compare to Christian communion and baptism. Also, the name of TST Health's first "telehealth" abortion practice "doubles as a covert death wish to U.S. Supreme Court Justice Samuel Alito, who wrote the decision that overturned Roe v. Wade [410 U.S. 113 (1973) that ruled a woman could choose abortion without excessive government restriction] last year (2022)."[66]

The Satanic Temple's New Mexico "Samuel Alito's Mom's Satanic Abortion Clinic" offers abortion drugs to women who are at least seventeen years old and who are no more than ten weeks pregnant. Fox News indicates the Food & Drug Administration does not recommend abortion drugs after ten weeks.[67]

Malcolm Jarry, the cofounder of the Satanic Temple, in a press statement said about the new abortion services:

In 1950, Samuel Alito's mother did not have options, and look what happened [Samuel was born]. Prior to 1973, doctors who performed abortions could lose their licenses and go to jail. The clinic's name serves to remind people just how important it is to have the right to control one's body and the potential ramifications of losing that right.[68]

That press statement promises that "anyone in New Mexico seeking to perform The Satanic Temple's abortion ritual will be able to receive free online medical services." Although limited to New Mexico at this time, the group claims it intends to expand the new abortion practice to other states.[69]

"The satanic group claims killing unborn babies in abortion is a religious ritual, and restricting it violates its 'fundamental tenets,'" according to an article published by iHeart.[70] Further, the Satanists claim that pro-life laws are rooted in "Christian nationalism."[71]

The Satanic Temple claims it has seven hundred thousand members across the world, and is a recognized religion by the US Internal Revenue Service. The "non-theistic" Salem, Massachusetts-based Satanic organization said in 2019 it received the tax-exempt status because, according to a spokesperson, they sought the recognition in order to "react to and restrict Christianity in public life and claims it does not worship the devil…but advocates for the separation of church and state."[72]

Meanwhile, the British newspaper *The Guardian* published a non-editorial piece on the Satanic Temple's fight against religious conservatives. The article, written by the publication's Adam Gabbatt, featured an interview with Satanic Temple cofounder and spokesperson Lucien Greaves. In the article, Mr. Gabbatt praised the temple's fight for "fundamental issues" that included removing "prayer in classrooms, religious holiday displays and the distribution of Bibles in schools," and evidently now abortion on demand as well. Surprisingly, the Satanic Temple organization's spokespersons claim they don't worship Satan as defined in the Bible.[73]

Satan worship by cultural icons: Satan's influence across the culture is not a laughing matter. Consider another example of in-your-face, evil Satanic influence vis-à-vis a performance at the 2023 Grammy Awards. Evidently, such evil has the endorsement of a leading television network, and one of the event's sponsors was Pfizer, the giant American multinational pharmaceutical corporation that grew quite wealthy thanks to the production of the COVID-19 "vaccination."[74]

Television network CBS caused quite the stir online leading up to the 2023 Grammy Awards. In a response to a tweet from Grammy-performing singer Sam Smith, which featured a photograph of him wearing devil horns, CBS tweeted: "…you can say that again. We are ready to worship."[75]

At the Grammy Awards, Smith and transgender singer Kim Petras delivered a raunchy performance with Smith dressed as the Devil surrounded by dancers acting like demons seemingly bowing down in worship. Robby Starbuck, a music video producer and director, called the CBS tweet an admission that the network was "compromised by evil." He continued, "They [CBS] aren't even trying to hide how compromised by evil they are anymore. It's all out in the open now."[76]

The Media Research Center, a conservative nonprofit media watchdog, asked whether CBS was confirming they worshipped Satan. "Did CBS just admit it worships Satan?" the account asked.[77]

Fashion icon pushes Satanic messages: Another example of Satanic influence in the broader culture is perhaps worse than the Grammy Awards' evil display. In late 2022, Balenciaga SA, a luxury fashion house founded in 1919 by the Spanish designer Cristobal Balenciaga, produced a controversial advertisement campaign that some claim demonstrates a Satanic influence, as evidenced by various symbols seen in the commercials. And perhaps not coincidentally, the word *Balenciaga* in Latin translates to "do what you want" or "do as thou wilt," which was allegedly a "decree of the [nineteenth century] satanist Aleister Crowley," an English occultist, ceremonial magician, and founder of the religion of Thelema, who was known as the "wickedest man in the world."[78]

The top fashion label's advertising campaign featured young children modeling what appeared "to be teddy bears wearing bondage gear." The allegation, according to the *New York Post*, was that the ads normalized "sexual fetishization and abuse of children." Also appearing in the ad, though very briefly, was the cover page from the Supreme Court case *United States v. Williams, 553 U.S. 285 (2008)*, a decision supporting a federal statute prohibiting the "pandering" of child pornography.[79]

Others allege, according to the *Post* article, that the ads pictured demonic paraphernalia in a photograph of a young boy. Specifically, the claim was that Satanic totems included a "child's drawing of the devil" and a black hood of the type allegedly worn by "Satanic cult" members.[80]

As expected, the luxury couturier issued a disclaimer once the ad campaign gained unwelcomed attention: "We strongly condemn child abuse; it was never our intent to include it in the narrative."[81] Further, the fashion house apologized to the public and then filed a $25 million lawsuit against the ad campaign producers.[82]

Face-saving lawsuit aside, the ad campaign also featured a "roll of yellow Balenciaga tape with the label's name misspelled with two As, forming [the word] 'Baal.'" That's the name of an ancient fertility god worshipped in ancient Middle Eastern cultures such as Canaan, and spoken of in the Bible, such as when Jezebel, Ahab's wife, promoted Baal in Israel (1 Kings 18:19) and also in 1 Kings 18:28 when Elijah confronted the people about blood drawing in the rituals to Baal.

It's hard to believe that such blatant, divisive Satanic messaging wasn't done on purpose. After all, Olga Liriano, a fashion industry director and top magazine editor, said: "It is ridiculous to think Demna [Gvasalia, Balenciaga's creative director] and the top echelon at Balenciaga didn't know what the campaigns were going to look like once they were photographed."[83]

Sex reassignment surgery part of a Satanic agenda: Sex-change operations are pushed by an evil part of our culture; unfortunately, that includes the Biden administration. These surgeries are the epitome of Satan's influence especially on vulnerable young people and they represent an incredibly divisive war on families and young people alike.

Human sexuality is clearly outlined in the Bible:

> So, God created mankind in his own image, in the image of
> God he created them; male and female he created them. God
> blessed them and said to them, "Be fruitful and increase in num-
> ber; fill the earth and subdue it." (Genesis 1:27–28a, NIV)

Further, God labels His creation as "very good" (Genesis 1:31, NIV). Therefore, the issue of gender matters to God; there is no confusion from His perspective.[84]

Fortunately, God doesn't stop describing what He calls "very good" in the book of Genesis. His opinions about marriage and sex are recorded throughout the rest of the Bible as well. For example, He outlines appropriate sex-related behavior by addressing monogamous marriage relationships between one man and one woman (1 Corinthians 7:2) and condemns homosexual behavior (Genesis 19:1–13; Romans 1:26–27). God also defines the roles in life based on our gender, such as the man is given the headship of the home and church (Ephesians 5:21–33). Finally, although the Bible affirms the value of both males and females, nowhere does it indicate our sex is negotiable.[85]

As described earlier in this chapter, Satan's divisive agenda includes attacking God's plan for men and women. He seeks to confuse us about who we are, and in particular he creates gender confusion, especially among young people thanks to our corrupted culture. Then he offers a "solution" to his evil-inspired idea of gender dysphoria—sex-reassignment surgery.

Unfortunately, the Biden administration bought into that evil agenda and is advancing Satan's push that is contrary to God's plan for men and women. Specifically, the administration released a series of official documents that encourage gender-reassignment surgery and hormone treatments for minors: "Gender Affirming Care and Young People" and "Gender-Affirming Care Is Trauma-Informed Care."[86]

These Department of Health and Human Services (HHS) documents state that "appropriate treatments" for "transgender adolescents" include: "'Top surgery'—to create male-typical chest shape or enhance breasts" and "'Bottom' surgery—surgery on genitals or reproductive organs, facial feminization or other procedures."[87]

The Biden administration then makes a scientifically unsupported claim about such procedures:

Medical and psychosocial gender affirming healthcare practices have been demonstrated to yield lower rates of adverse mental health outcomes, build self-esteem, and improve overall quality of life for transgender and gender diverse youth.[88]

To further confuse the public, in 2022, the White House released a video to coincide with the new HHS documents featuring President Biden speaking on the issue of transgender children. In that video, Mr. Biden tells parents of transgender children that "affirming your child's identity is one of the most powerful things you can do to keep them safe." Evidently, by inference, Mr. Biden supports HHS' view about sex-reassignment surgery.[89]

Sex-reassignment surgery is not only evil but also dangerous. Ryan T. Anderson with the Washington, DC-based Heritage Foundation is the author of a book on the transgender issue, *When Harry Became Sally: Responding to the Transgender Moment*. He states, based on extensive research:

> "The medical evidence suggests that sex reassignment does not adequately address the psychosocial difficulties faced by people who identify as transgender. Even when the procedures are successful technically and cosmetically, and even in cultures that are relatively "trans-friendly," transitioners still face poor outcomes.[90]

Briefly, the evidence of such invasive, life-altering surgery is pretty tragic. Dr. Paul McHugh, a distinguished service professor of psychiatry at the Johns Hopkins University of Medicine, wrote:

> Transgendered men do not become women, nor do transgendered women become men. All (including Bruce Jenner) become feminized men or masculinized women, counterfeits or impersonators of the sex with which they "identify." In that lies their problematic future.[91]

The consequences of sex-change surgery are often quite tragic. The Obama administration's Centers for Medicare and Medicaid Services reviewed a 2016 Swedish study that resulted in the denial of government funds for reassignment surgery, which resulted in a "19-times greater likelihood for death by suicide, and a host of other poor outcomes."[92]

Conclusion

Satan is real and uses gullible humans as pawns in his effort to wage spiritual war against God Almighty. Ultimately, Satan seeks our worship, and although his demise is settled, according to the book of Revelation, he wants to replace God. In that process, he recruits people to help him accomplish that end, and he is especially keen to enlist powerful people who have the most influence in our culture to use them to advance his divisive ways to leverage control over mankind.

This concludes section I of *Divided*, which provides the "Roots of Division." Section II reviews "Division Across History," which includes the many instances it plays a critical role in international, domestic, and biblical history.

Section II

DIVISION ACROSS HISTORY

The world is polarized. The middle class becomes smaller. The polarization makes the difference between rich and the poor big. This is true.

—POPE FRANCIS, head of the Roman Catholic Church since 2013

This section of *Divided* surveys "polarization," a synonym for division, a process with deep roots across international, American, and biblical history. Here we apply the roots of division discussed in the previous section to real-world settings.

Polarization causes otherwise neutral parties to align as opposing sides in conflict that often leads to increasingly extreme positions. Each party to the conflict defines themselves "in terms of their opposition to a common enemy," according to a 2003 essay, "Polarization," posted on the website Beyond Intractability, which is hosted by the University of Colorado's Conflict Information Consortium.[93]

The consequences of polarization at any level includes declining trust and respect, and "distorted perceptions and simplified stereotypes emerge," according to the "Polarization" essay. As a result, the parties in a polarized situation embrace rigidly opposite positions.[94]

Although polarization is a common problem for all societies at all levels, it is especially associated with the structure of the international system; in particular, it considers "the impact of military alliances on war and peace, and the balance of power." Thus, the study of security relationships necessarily involves an analysis of the polarizing factors that brought the parties into conflict.[95]

The authors of the essay also admit the causes of conflict are complex, in that they are related to "psychological, sociological, and political processes." And, evidently, as polarization fuels conflict, communication and interaction are cut by the parties, "trust diminishes," and the crisis grows. Specifically, as group isolation grows, polarization fuels "the tendency of partisans to try to win bystanders to their side…[and eventually the] conflict intensifies."[96]

This view of the polarization process is a common story of conflict across human history. In this section of *Divided*, we illustrate how the polarization process results in conflict internationally (chapter 4), domestically (chapter 5) and in the Bible (chapter 6).

I expect you will come to appreciate that polarization is an ancient problem fueled by the father of lies, Satan, and his army of demons who recruit powerful people across both time and geography to serve as the locus of division that alters much of human history.

chapter four

Polarization across the World

Yesterday and Today

The founders of the United Nations expected that member nations would behave and vote as individuals after they had weighed the merits of an issue—rather like a great, global town meeting. The emergence of blocks and the *polarization* of the United Nations undermine all that this organization initially valued.[97]

—RONALD REAGAN, fortieth president of the United States

Polarization has been a common problem around the world from ancient times to the present. This chapter will profile examples of polarization across major historic world events—wars and religious movements—that have served Satan's purposes. Then we will consider some of today's most polarizing foreign figures and how they are powerful instruments doing Satan's work.

Reflect as you read these vignettes on the often-dark motivation behind the veil of reality. Specifically, the previous section of this volume explained the phenomenon of worldview, the powerful leader's vulnerability to manipulation by Satan and his demons who exchange earthly wealth and power for collaboration that advances the tempter's aim.

History of War Replete with Polarization

"Polarisation [British spelling] manifesting at the level of nations and empires leads to war," writes David Murrin, a British global forecaster, in an article, "Polarisation: The Road to War." He explains that, "in the process, killing other human beings becomes justifiable because they (the opposition) embrace values that are anathema: they are 'the enemy' and no longer viewed as human."[98]

"Genghis Khan [an Asian twelfth–thirteenth-century warrior and conqueror] had a masterly understanding of this mechanism [polarisation] as he understood the power of unity," wrote Murrin. He continued:

Prior to his rise, the Mongols had been controlled by the Jin Dynasty [AD 1115–1234], which exploited their tribal enmities to play one tribe off against another. The young Genghis, an outcast from his tribe upon the death of his father, bound the stragglers from his tribe into a new combat-ready force, ready to fight their traditional enemies, the Tartars. He then continued to amass his army until it was able to challenge the tribes that dominated the region and, finally, using the threat of the Jin [Dynasty] to unite all of the tribes and create the Mongol nation, a nation that rode out of the steppes and conquered the known world. Today, Mongolians view Genghis Khan as their George Washington. In contrast, students in China are taught that he was a Chinese general. Historical perspective always has two sides![99]

Extreme polarization, what Murrin labels "war fever," approaches madness, but it is a powerful potion. He illustrated how, in wartime, polarization creates some rather irrational decisions. For example, during World War I, the British royal family tried to disguise their German heritage, so King George V changed the family name from the German "Saxe-Coburg and Gotha" to the English name "Windsor." Meanwhile, on the streets of Great Britain at the time, German breeds of dogs were killed or renamed something more acceptable to the British ear.[100]

America was marked by similar wartime polarization. Governor William Harding of Iowa banned all public use of foreign languages during World War II. Even most other American schools stopped teaching German, and the American public renamed "sauerkraut" to "liberty cabbage" and "German measles" to "liberty measles"; it also renamed streets that reminded them of Germany.[101]

Indeed, polarization has played a key role as nations prepared for and eventually went to war. Consider how polarization contributed to the causes for both of our world wars.

Polarization Contributed to the Causes of World War I

World War I, known as the "war to end all wars," occurred between July 1914 and November 1918 and claimed over seventeen million lives. The catalyst that triggered it was the assassination of Archduke Franz Ferdinand on June 28, 1914. He was killed by Gavrilo Princip, a nineteen-year-old Bosnian Serb nationalist, a member of the "Unification or Death" Serbian secret military society. Evidently, Princip's motivation for that attack was the polarization of the Austro-Hungarian from the Balkan states to form a united Yugoslavia.

The archduke's assassination was only the last straw that pushed much of Europe into war, however. Specifically, Austria-Hungary blamed Serbia for the attack and quickly declared war, then turned to its ally, Germany, for help. Meanwhile, Serbia lacked the means to defend itself, so it turned to its ally, Russia, for aid, which prompted Germany to declare war on Russia.

Arguably, these and other nations at the time anticipated the war, which was fed by at least four underlying causes, and each involved some form of polarization: alliances, imperialism, militarism, and nationalism. [102,103]

Alliances are, at the macro level, about the polarization of a group of countries from others. This relationship happens when nations embrace mutual defense agreements (treaties) with their neighbors; if one member of the treaty is attacked, the others rush to that one's defense. Like the North Atlantic Treaty Organization today, prior to World War I, there were a number of alliances, such as the Triple Entente (Russia, Great Britain, and France) and the Triple Alliance (Austria-Hungary, Italy, and Germany).

Those alliances and other less-formal groupings of nations quickly joined the war after the first spark of conflict, which is when Austria-Hungary declared war on Serbia. Soon, Russia, Serbia, and Germany were joined by France, and when the Germans attacked France, the British came to Paris' rescue. Later, the Ottoman Empire joined Germany and Austria-Hungry.

Imperialism is another form of polarization among nations that contributed to World War I. It is the state of being when a country increases its power by controlling more territories, like the colonies both the British and French seized in the nineteenth century. Germany came to imperialism later, which had a polarizing effect among competing colony-seeking nations thirsting for resources, and that competition increased tensions and eventually led to world war.

Militarism is fed by polarization as well. It's about security deterrence and building up the military might to exert a country's will on other nations. Prior to World War I, Germany seeded a European arms race at the start of the twentieth century; by 1914, the German Imperial Navy had nearly one hundred warships and the nation's army had two million soldiers, evidently trying to outdo its neighbors in anticipation of war.

Nationalism is a political ideology whereby individuals identify with a particular national identity, which has a polarizing effect among neighboring countries. Specifically, prior to World War I, various national groups identified themselves to prove their dominance over the others, as indicated by the rivalry between the Slavs and Germans, which was exacerbated when the Slavic people in Bosnia and Herzegovina became part of Austria-Hungary rather than Serbia.

Therefore, World War I, to a large degree, was a product of the instruments of polarization: alliances, imperialism, militarism, and nationalism. We saw much the same leading up to the Second World War (1939–1945).

Polarization Contributed to the Causes of World War II

Polarization was key to the start of World War II, but its arrangement was somewhat different from what had occurred decades earlier with the First World War. Specifically, the cause often attributed to World War II was Germany's invasion of Poland (1939), which pulled other European powers and eventually Russia and the United States into the war. However, it was the polarization inside Germany that brought about the rise of Adolf Hitler and his actions that really triggered the war in Europe.

Consider how Germany came to the point that it started another world war. Specifically, toward the end of the First World War, the Allies met to draft the Treaty of Versailles, the primary document produced by the Paris Peace Conference to end the war. Those leaders, which included US President Woodrow Wilson, were polarized over significant issues, such as whether to seek revenge, a French and British aim, as well as making certain Germany could never start another war.

Eventually, the Allies compromised around Wilson's Fourteen Points plan, despite some deep divisions. The treaty mandated that Germany accept responsibility for starting the war; pay reparations; and disarm and limit the size of any future military. Further, the treaty insisted that Germany forfeit some territory, such as the Alsace and Lorraine, to France. Not surprisingly, those harsh provisions left the German people in a desperate way, especially as their economy collapsed in the late 1920s, largely as a result of paying the required reparations.

By 1930, the German people were ripe for Nazi polarization. A decade earlier, Adolf Hitler, the leader of the Nazi Party, officially the National Socialist German Workers' Party, had begun making a name for himself and his populist ideals by hosting small-scale rallies across Germany. Hitler's campaign was interrupted by jail time because he attempted to seize power by force during the 1923 Beer Hall Putsch. Meanwhile, he used his time during incarceration to write his infamous book, *Mein Kampf* ("My Struggle"), an autobiographical manifesto that outlines his views about the Jewish race, nationalism, World War I, and other topics of interest to a growing segment of the polarized German population.[104]

On January 30, 1933, thanks in part to the crumbling Weimer Republic, widespread economic misery, and the Germans' still-festering anger from the terms of the Treaty of Versailles, President Paul von Hindenburg appointed Hitler to be Germany's chancellor to keep the Nazi party "in check." To win that position, Hitler had tapped the discontent of the polarized electorate to win over half of the seats of the Reichstag, Germany's parliament.[105]

Over the next six years, Chancellor Hitler mostly ignored the provisions of the Treaty of Versailles by expanding German territories, rebuilding the military, and cementing a number of geopolitical military agreements. Specifically, in 1936, Hitler established two alliances that polarized Germany from the rest of Europe. He formed the Rome-Berlin Axis Pact, which allied Germany with fascist Benito Mussolini's Italy, and the Anti-Comintern Pact, an alliance with the imperial Japanese who, at the time, were preparing to occupy China (1936).

Leading up to World War II, Hitler managed to further polarize the German people to his ideological views by identifying scapegoats for Germany's many challenges, the so-called stab-in-the-back myth (German: *Dolchstoßlegende*). Specifically, he used the threat of Russian communism—a polarizing fear across much of Europe at the time; his divisive eugenics policy intended to eliminate undesirable people; and his anti-Semitic views. All were meant to distract attention from his Nazi Party's plans that led to World War II.

History of the Polarization of Religious Groups

World history is replete with examples of the polarization of religious groups, which often resulted in wars or permanent divisions. Consider three of the most notable examples of religious-based polarization: the split within the Muslim world; the theological division between the Roman Catholic and Greek Orthodox churches; and the Reformation, which polarized Roman Catholicism and led to Protestantism.

Islam Polarized into Sunni-Shia Camps

The seventh-century Muslim Empire known as the Rashidun Caliphate (Islamic political-religious state) encompassed much of the modern Middle East. It collapsed into a civil war over the polarization issue of succession. One party argued that only the founder Prophet Muhammad's descendants could rule, a polarization that developed into the modern Muslim world's Sunni-Shiite split.[106]

In AD 630, the Prophet Muhammad founded Islam in the city of Mecca in modern-day Saudi Arabia, which became the first Muslim Empire. Upon Muhammad's death, he was replaced by Abu Bakr, his father-in-law, who initiated a period known as the Rashidun Caliphate ("Rightly-Guided"). Under Abu Bakr and his successors, the Muslim Empire rapidly expanded.

In AD 656, the fourth caliph's leader, Uthman ibn Affan, the second cousin, son-in-law, and companion of Muhammad, was assassinated, and a faction of Muslims installed Ali, Muhammad's cousin, as the new caliph. Uthman's kinsman, Muawiyah, the governor of the empire's Syrian province, rebelled against Ali, leading to civil war in which Ali was killed. Muawiyah went on to establish the Umayyad Caliphate, which grew to be quite powerful.

Muslims who accepted Muawiyah as the legitimate caliph became Sunnis, while those who sided with Ali became Shiites. That division has resulted in many wars among the Muslims ever since.

Christians Polarized by the Nicene Creed

The medieval Christian Church suffered the "Great Schism" of 1054 between the Roman Catholic and Eastern Orthodox churches over the polarization of a single point of contention with the Nicene Creed: the Holy Trinity.

In AD 325, Constantine, the first Christian leader of the Roman Empire, directed 318 bishops to gather at the town of Nicaea, in modern-day Türkiye, to resolve the question of Jesus' divinity. The bishops proffered that Jesus and God were of the same "substance," a view they codified in the Nicene Creed, which formed the fundamental basis for Christianity. The text of the creed identifies the bishops' belief in one God, Jesus Christ, and the Holy Spirit. (Note: The Creed as read today was expanded upon at the Second Ecumenical Council in Constantinople in AD 381.)

Centuries later, there arose a dispute over the addition of the phrase "and the Son," which came to be included in the Nicene Creed's statement on the Holy Spirit: "I believe in the Holy Spirit, the Lord, the giver of life, who proceeds from the Father and the Son." The addition of "and the Son," translated *filioque*, became popular among Western liturgies but speaks of a fundamental theological difference in the understanding of the Holy Trinity. The Eastern Church came to believe it was from the Father that both the Son and the Holy Spirit flow. However, the Western Church (Rome) embraced the view that all three are unified by divine essence, which for the Easterners diminished the Father's role.

The different theological interpretations in the Nicene Creed polarized Eastern and Western Christendom, as did their geographic separation and linguistic differences.[107]

Another Theological Disagreement Polarized Roman Catholics

The sixteenth century's Protestant Reformation was the product of polarization within the Roman Catholic Church over key theological issues. It began with Martin Luther (1483–1546), a teacher and monk who famously nailed his *Ninety-five Theses* (1517), the "Disputation on the Power of Indulgences," on the door of the church in Wittenberg, Germany. Luther expected his action to spark a debate over controversial ideas about Christianity that contradicted Roman Catholic teachings.

One of Luther's disputes was over the Catholic Church's role as the intermediary between people and God, and especially the Church's indulgence system, which allowed Catholics to purchase pardons for their sins. The controversy that ensued over indulgences soon led to other challenges to Church doctrine from John Calvin in France, Huldrych Zwingli in Switzerland, and the Anabaptists, who objected to infant baptism.

Although these public challenges to Catholic doctrine were important, the real issue for many of the Catholic "protestants" was the belief that Christians should be independent in their relationship with God rather than dependent on the Church, the pope, and priests for spiritual guidance and salvation.

Thus Catholic-Protestant polarization took center stage across much of Europe and was the cause of the Thirty Years' War (1618–1648), one of the longest and most brutal wars ever, with an estimated eight million casualties. It started among Catholic and Protestant states that formed the Holy Roman Empire. Emperor Ferdinand II, head of the Holy

Roman Empire, fomented the religious war by forcing citizens to adhere to Roman Catholicism, even though religious freedom was promised by the 1555 signing of the Peace of Augsburg, which allowed the head of state to adopt either Catholicism or Lutheranism/Calvinism.[108]

A major outcome of the Thirty Years' War was polarization across the European continent based on the fault lines of ethnicities and religious faiths—an outcome that arguably continues today.[109]

The Catholic-Protestant tension ultimately had an impact on the American colonies thanks to sixteenth-century England's King Henry VIII, who abandoned Catholicism because the pope refused to grant him a marriage annulment to Catherine of Aragon. King Henry rejected the pope's authority and installed himself as the authority over the Church of England, which embraced a combination of Catholic and Protestant ideas. For decades, religious turbulence followed the king's decision to separate from Rome. Specifically, Mary I, daughter of Catherine and Henry VIII, tried to return England to Catholicism by killing Protestant heretics and marrying Philip of Spain, a Catholic. However, Queen Elizabeth I, daughter of Anne Boleyn and Henry VIII, succeeded Mary and changed the state religion back to Protestantism. Meanwhile, many English Protestants known as Puritans were skeptical about the queen's true intentions about the switch.

By the early seventeenth century, many of these Puritan separatists left England for the Netherlands to start new lives. However, their failure to assimilate in the Netherlands prompted some to return to England to continue their separatist protests; others (known today as Pilgrims) set sail for New England in 1620 aboard the British ship Mayflower, landing near the tip of Cape Cod, Massachusetts.

Ultimately, the legacy of the Protestant Reformation created a diversity of religious thinking that was brought to New England and eventually came to influence America's founders, who wrote in the US Constitution's Bill of Rights a provision that explicitly forbids "establishment of religion or prohibiting the free exercise thereof." Today, Americans have the polarization of mostly fifteenth-century former Catholic clergy over key theological issues to thank for severing our government from any particular religion.[110]

Contemporary Polarizing International Figures

Polarization continues today among powerful heads of nations, religious groups, and even independent people with the resources to push their views across the world.

Today, polarization continues tearing apart many countries around the world, including Brazil, India, Poland, and Türkiye. A Carnegie Endowment for International Peace study by Thomas Carothers and Andrew O'Donohue, "How to Understand the Global Spread of Political Polarization," found that a variety of contemporary powerful leaders are putting democracy in the crosshairs, and polarization is their tool of choice.[111]

Their study methodology was to assemble a group of scholars with deep expertise in the focus countries, then produce case studies on each country. From these studies, Carothers and O'Donohue extracted cross-cutting findings that document polarization as a decisive tool for powerful national leaders.

They found significant similarity across powerful leaders like Narendra Modi in India and Recep Tayyip Erdogan in Türkiye, who relentlessly inflamed basic divisions throughout their countries. These powerful leaders demonized their opponents and shuttered democratic processes, as well as harnessed technology to fuel disruption of their media.[112]

In Türkiye, for example, the "head of the main opposition party stoked tensions by calling on the military to oppose Erdogan's potential bid for the presidency in 2007," according to the study. The India case study found that a growing economy could contribute to polarization support for Hindu nationalist narratives, a surprising outcome.[113]

Patronage and corruption can temporarily reduce polarization by aiding politicians to grow their voter support. However, the rise of divisive populist figures like the late Hugo Chavez in Venezuela tend to disgust most voters, not an uncommon problem across the world's authoritarian leaders.[114]

Other consequences of polarization tend to undermine the independence of the judiciary, reduce legislative bodies to gridlock, or worse. It can also lead to the abuse of executive powers and lead voters to conclude the chief executive represents only his supporters, not the whole country.[115]

Contemporary Foreign Leaders with Divisive Worldviews

Many contemporary foreign government leaders are incredibly polarizing. A short list of those leaders includes China's Xi Jinping, Russia's Vladimir Putin, and Saudi Arabia's Crown Prince Mohammed bin Salman al Saud. They are not that dissimilar from other rogues ruling the world's 195 countries, such as in North Korea, Syria, Iran, Chad, and the Central African Republic.[116]

Each of these rulers is a classic authoritarian who maintains control over his population by using force and polarization. They are clearly in Satan's camp, as evidenced by their actions and policies that advance evil outcomes.

Consider insights into their worldviews and associated divisive actions.

China's Xi Jinping

Xi Jinping is the uncontested leader of the world's most populated country (1.4 billion) and serves as the general secretary of the Chinese Communist Party (CCP), chairman of the Military Commission (the entire armed forces), and president of the People's Republic of China (PRC). He has absolute authority over the ninety-five million CCP members who are scattered across that country embedded in literally every company and involved in every community. Mr. Xi rules with an iron fist through his party members by using a governing template established by Vladimir Lenin, a hardened Soviet-era revolutionary who took his intellectual doctrine from Karl Marx and translated it into a formula for a totalitarian police state.

Chairman Xi is an incredibly divisive ruler, which is evidenced by his human-rights agenda. Even though that nation's constitution includes a promise that ensures human rights of its citizens, Mr. Xi pursues an agenda that suppresses freedoms of press, expression, speech, assembly, association, religion, and movement. The Beijing dictator tightly controls all sophisticated technologies to limit access and usage of the Internet as well.

Mr. Xi's abuse of the Uighurs, a Turkic-speaking Muslim people in Xinjiang Uighur Autonomous Region, is legendary. A 2018 report by the Global Slavery Index indicates that "on any given day in 2016 there were over 3.8 million people living in conditions of modern slavery in China."[117]

Despite the PRC's efforts to suppress the truth, the regime's human organs for money activities are thoroughly documented as well. A 2019 report from a London-based "people's tribunal" found that Beijing "had engaged in forced organ harvesting for years 'on a significant scale,' and continues to do so." The main victims of such a brutal practice are practitioners of Falun Gong, a spiritual discipline based on the principles of truthfulness, compassion, and forbearance.[118]

President Xi's worldview is a product of his Marxist-Leninist ideological background. He will do whatever is necessary to promote a radical socialist agenda, including suppressing all dissent through division, which is necessary for him to maintain control.

Russia's Vladimir Putin

Vladimir Putin of the Russian Federation ranks near the top of the list of the world's most powerful people. Four times he served as Russia's president, and, despite claims that his country is a democracy, Mr. Putin rules that country with an iron fist as a true authoritarian.

Stephen Crowley, a professor of politics at Oberlin College, Ohio, said:

> Most political scientists that I'm aware of would say that Russia is in between a democracy and an outright dictatorship, what some would call a "hybrid regime" or "electoral authoritarianism," though Putin has certainly been drifting more toward [the] authoritarian side.

However, Crowley cautioned that Putin is not nearly as perverse as North Korea's Kim Jong-un, an unmitigated tyrant. After all, Russia does have "contested elections, opposition parties, and at least some degree of freedom of speech," cautioned Crowley.[119]

In 2022, Mr. Putin launched a "special military operation" (war) against the former Soviet Union member state Ukraine, ostensibly to protect ethnic Russians from genocide at the hands of "a Nazi regime." That campaign used virtually every means at the Kremlin's disposal to destroy not just Ukraine's military, but to cause great suffering among innocent Ukrainians.[120]

German Prime Minister Olaf Scholz explained Putin's polarizing war aim. Mr. Scholz wrote for *Foreign Affairs* that Putin "seeks to redraw borders by force and to divide the world, once again, into blocs and spheres of influence." According to the German leader:

> Under Putin's leadership, Russia has defied even the most basic principles of international law as enshrined in the UN Charter: the renunciation of the use of force as a means of international policy and pledge to respect the independence, sovereignty, and territorial integrity of all countries.[121]

Mr. Putin's authoritarian, arguably Marxist, worldview is reflected in his actions against Ukraine and other former Soviet republics like Georgia with the intention of recapturing Russia's former greatness, both during the days of the nineteenth-century Russian Empire (1721–1917) and of the former Soviet Union (1917–1991). As a result, Putin uses the powers of the state to vanquish those who oppose his hegemonic polarizing ambitions both at home and abroad. Further, he frequently rattles his nuclear saber against the West that has come to Ukraine's aid, threatening a much larger conflict.

Saudi Arabia's Mohammed bin Salman al Saud

Mohammed bin Salman al Saud (aka MBS) is the crown prince who consolidated power and controls for Saudi Arabia and formally leads that country as its head of government, the prime minister. He has a reputation as a harsh and cruel dictator, evidence of his Islamic and totalitarian worldview. The prince's hate crimes include the heinous murder of journalist Jamal Khashoggi, the torture of women who demand broader rights, and the ongoing military campaign in Yemen marked by numerous war crimes.

The crown prince is widely known for his brutality. In late 2021, *60 Minutes* reported on MBS' plots to murder his uncle, then-King Abdullah bin Abdulaziz Al Saud, and Saudi exile Saadi al-Jabri, a former Saudi intelligence official who exposed the prince as a violent and sick man "who has and continues to commit egregious and lawless acts."[122]

Agnes Callamard, the United Nation's Special Rapporteur on extrajudicial or arbitrary executions, echoed a similar view. She wrote:

> Like [Iraq's] Saddam Hussein before him, Mohammed bin Salman concluded that he was righteous. As he ordered women to be tortured in prison, his planes continued to bomb Yemen, and he took the first steps to acquire nuclear weapons, because Western governments do not stop him, until there is too much price to pay.[123]

On other fronts, the crown prince reminds me of the idiom "birds of a feather flock together," because he keeps company with similar rogues. In December 2022, MBS welcomed Chinese dictator Xi to Riyadh, Saudi Arabia, with a gregarious handshake and a lavish ceremony.[124]

Chinese state media reported that MBS' warm welcome and subsequent meeting with Mr. Xi consummated deals worth $30 billion. However, there was no mention in that meeting about China's genocide against multiple Muslim ethnic groups. One would expect MBS to call out Xi's abuses, given that Saudi Arabia is the world's leading Muslim country and home to the two holiest Islamic sites, the cities of Mecca and Medina.[125]

MBS is a true totalitarian tethered to his Islamic faith, and he maintains absolute control for himself and his family. He is known to use all means necessary to keep control, which includes division at home against his political and religious opponents.

Non-government Powers with Polarizing Worldviews

Someone doesn't have to be a powerful government leader to use division to advance an agenda. There are powerful people in the high-tech, business, media, and government worlds, as illustrated in chapter 2, who demonstrate corrupted worldviews that are polarizing.

Some of these powerful people use their wealth to advance evil ends.

For example, Mr. George Soros uses his wealth to seed division across the world and promote his one-world government agenda—a globalist aspiration.

I profiled Mr. Soros' radical agenda in my book *The Deeper State*. I explained there that he arguably impacts world politics and culture more profoundly than any other nongovernment person—and besides, perhaps not surprisingly, he admits to fantasies about being a god.

"I admit that I have always harbored an exaggerated view of self-importance—to put it bluntly, I fancied myself as some kind of god," Soros wrote in his 1987 book, *The Alchemy of Finance*. That self-image hasn't changed much over the past decades; in fact, he has grown more megalomaniacal. Then, of course, he admits: "Next to my fantasies about being god, I also have very strong fantasies of being mad," which evidently might be a genetic issue. He told a British audience: "In fact, my grandfather was actually paranoid. I have a lot of madness in my family. So far, I have escaped it."[126]

Soros was born in Budapest, Hungary, to Jewish parents who survived the 1944 Nazi invasion by hiding and running from the Germans and their collaborators. This period of his life significantly contributed to the formulation of his worldview. Soros said:

> [My] view of the world, I would say, was formed very much in the traumatic experience in the Second World War when Hungary was occupied by Nazi Germany, and they were deporting Jews to Auschwitz. I was lucky enough to have a father who understood that this is not normalcy. This is far from equilibrium. And if you go by the rules that you normally go by, you're going to die. I learned from a grand master in the Second World War, and I basically applied this view of the world to the financial markets and also to my political vision.[127]

Soros has a radical progressive worldview that includes virtually every left wing issue: drug legalization, abortion on demand, normalizing homosexuality, climate change, wiping out national borders for unfettered migration, one-world government, and much more. He doesn't hesitate to throw millions of his own dollars at these issues.

He is blamed for Europe's 2015–2016 migration crisis, which brought more than a million illegal migrants to Western Europe.

Soros uses his nonprofit Open Society Foundations, which are active in 120 countries including the United States, to funnel funds to most left-wing efforts. In 2021, he poured an estimated $100 million into promoting Biden administration initiatives.[128]

Soros money is also given to political action campaigns controlled by attorney and criminal justice reform activist Whitney Tymas. She oversaw funds going to Chicago's Kim Foxx, the city's district attorney, as well as to George Gascon in Los Angeles and Larry Krasner in Philadelphia; all three of these district attorneys are known for their pro-criminal, so-called justice-reform actions.[129]

One of the worst of the batch of Soros-backed criminal justice reform activists is Alvin Bragg, the Manhattan, New York, district attorney who became well-known for his indictment of former President Trump. Bragg was elected in 2021, largely due to Soros' $1.1 million donation. He quickly made a name for himself when he released a memo stating his office would not seek sentences for armed robbery, drug dealing, and burglary.[130]

On March 30, 2023, Bragg announced the indictment of Mr. Trump allegedly for misreporting a hush-money payment to adult film star Stormy Daniels. Former Vice President Mike Pence said: "I think the unprecedented indictment of a former president of the United States on a campaign finance issue is an outrage." He continued: "It appears to millions of Americans to be nothing more than a political prosecution that is driven by a prosecutor who literally ran for office on a pledge to indict the former president."[131]

Harvard Law School Emeritus Professor Alan Dershowitz predicted a judge would likely dismiss the case on statute of limitations grounds. It's also noteworthy that the indictment came despite the Justice Department's decision not to prosecute Mr. Trump, and the Federal Election Commission declined to pursue the case as well.[132]

The broader issue at play in the Trump indictment is the weaponization of the law to attack a political opponent. That is a very serious, divisive precedent, and until recent years such behaviors were confined to foreign tyrants—no doubt Mr. Soros' intent.

Tom Anderson, director of the Government Integrity Project at the National Legal and Policy Center in Virginia, said:

> George Soros has quietly orchestrated the dark money political equivalent of "shock and awe," on local attorney races through the country, shattering records, flipping races and essentially making a mockery of our entire campaign finance system.[133]

On so many fronts, Mr. Soros is a powerful, divisive figure who promotes what many of us label as pure evil, doing the work of Satan.

Contemporary Powerful Religious Leader with Divisive Worldview

The religious community has powerful dividers as well. Pope Francis is a polarizing leader who in 2013 said: "If someone is gay and he searches for the Lord and has good will, who am I to judge?" For that statement, the LGBTQ (lesbian, gay, bisexual, transgender, queer, or questioning] magazine, *The Advocate*, named Francis its 2013 person of the year.[134]

The pope further shocked his conservative Catholic constituents when, at the 2014 Synod, he included a line about "welcoming homosexual persons." Later, Francis commented, "Who am I to judge?" Then, in 2016, in a footnote of his encyclical *Amoris Laetitia*, he suggested the Catholic Church should grant communion to divorced and remarried couples, despite that the Church believes in the indissolubility of marriage.[135]

Evidently, Pope Francis' worldview allows him to be divisive and act counter to the Bible's teachings in order to maintain control over the Catholic Church…or perhaps the pontiff is advancing another, more sinister agenda.

Conclusion

Polarization is a powerful process across the history of mankind. This chapter briefly outlined its impact on great events—world wars and religious movements. It also concluded with profiles of some of the most polarizing and powerful figures in the world today.

Chapter 5 looks at polarization in America through our nearly 250-year history and identifies some of our most divisive citizens.

chapter five

America's Polarized History

There is nothing I dread so much as the division of the republic into two great parties, each arranged under its leader, and concerting measures in opposition to each other. This, in my humble apprehension, is to be dreaded as the greatest political evil under our constitution.[136]

—JOHN ADAMS, second president of the United States

America has a rich history of polarization, beginning with its founders, and not until the twentieth century did the phenomenon momentarily wane. For example, George Washington's vice president, John Adams, won the presidency in 1797, but avenged himself by jailing his most vocal critics. Then, when Adams ran for reelection, fellow founder Alexander Hamilton, a member of Adam's own party, published a pamphlet arguing that the sitting president was "emotionally unstable, given to impulsive and irrational decisions, unable to coexist with his closest advisers and generally unfit."[137]

One of the best examples of political polarization was the rivalry between founding fathers Aaron Burr, the sitting vice president at the time, and Alexander Hamilton. Increasing tensions between the men finally led to the dueling ground at Weehawken, New Jersey, on July 11, 1804, where the confident, cocky Hamilton was forever silenced by Burr, who shot and killed Hamilton. .[138]

Polarization was especially widespread for the balance of the nineteenth century. Historian Mark Wahlgren Summers with the University of Kentucky writes in *Party Games* (2004) that America's polarization in the 1850s was like "Armageddon with brass bands," a situation that brought politics to the battlefield with the Civil War (1861–1865). An example of such unhinged polarization took place in 1856, when ardent abolitionist, US Senator Charles Sumner (MA), delivered a speech, entitled "The Crime Against Kansas," in which he described the excesses that occurred in that territory and across much of the South. Mr. Sumner termed his address as the "most thorough philippic [bitter attack] ever uttered in a legislative body." Further, he accused fellow US Senator Andrew P. Butler of South Carolina "as having a mistress, slavery, which was polluted in the sight of the world," and he said US Senator Stephen Douglas of Illinois was the "squire of slavery, its very Sancho Panza [a fictional character in the novel Don Quixote], ready to do its humiliating offices."[139]

Days later, on May 22, 1856, Senator Butler's nephew, US Congressman Preston Brooks, a South Carolina Democrat and strong advocate of slavery, beat Senator Sumner into unconsciousness with a cane while the senator sat in the Senate chamber, rendering him unable to resume his duties for three years. Meanwhile, the deep polarization over slavery and Brooks' attack on Sumner made the congressman an instant hero in the South. The cane beating landed him the role of an honored guest at testimonial dinners and earned him a large collection of canes from admirers.[140]

Eventually, Congressman Brooks faced a resolution of censure in the House of Representatives, but in July 1856, he resigned his seat to permit his constituents the opportunity to express their view of his conduct. They approved; in fact, they reelected him that August to fill the vacancy his resignation had created. Meanwhile, Senator Sumner was widely lauded as a martyr across the North, and although reelected, he was unable to return to his seat in the Senate due to his injuries.[141]

The Civil War didn't put a stop to the political polarization, especially, for example, when one considers that, in 1888, Republican presidential candidate Benjamin Harrison fought off Democrat campaign slurs that Chinese immigrants, aka "Mongolian Republicans," were allegedly bankrolling his campaign.[142]

The 1896 presidential election of William McKinley over William Jennings Bryan not only gave the Republicans a victory, but also, for at least the first half of the new century, political hostilities diminished. However, polarization continued to be an issue on a number of cultural fronts.[143]

This chapter now reviews the polarization that marked America's involvement in two wars, the Civil War and the Vietnam War. Further, the country experienced considerable cultural polarization thanks to a number of issues, two of which are considered here: the emergence of the racially divisive Ku Klux Klan after the Civil War, which continues even today; and the emergence of the women's suffrage movement. Finally, we consider a number of other notable polarizing American groups across our history that continue to this day.

Polarization Marked Two American Wars

Carl von Clausewitz, a nineteenth-century Prussian general and military theorist, wrote in his book *On War (Vom Kriege)* that "war is not merely a political act, but also a real political instrument, a continuation of political commerce, a carrying out of the same by other means." That's precisely what happened to the United States as it entered the combustible Civil War period (1861–1865).[144]

Polarization Led to the American Civil War

America's Civil War resolved two issues: 1) whether the US was a dis-
solvable confederation of sovereign states or an indivisible sovereign
national government; and 2) whether all people were created with an
equal right to liberty, or whether the nation would continue as a slave-
holding country. Of course, the North's victory preserved the US as one
nation and ended the institution of slavery. But the costs were stagger-
ing, at 625,000 lives, roughly 2 percent of the total population, and the
total "casualty" count—personnel lost through death, wounds, injury,
sickness, internment, capture, or missing in action—was approximately
1.5 million.[145]

Prior to the Civil War, polarization of the young nation became pronounced during the antebellum period (1812–1861), the time Southern plantations were quite profitable, especially thanks to inventions
like Eli Whitney's cotton gin and the sustained high demand for cotton
at mills in the US and overseas. However, the plantations required a
large workforce of slave labor to cultivate and harvest not just cotton,
but other products like tobacco, rice, and indigo—all major cash crops.
Therefore, for the plantation owners, slaves ensured a cheap and reliable
labor source, the heart of the prosperous region.

The financial benefits of slave labor for plantation owners hit a snag
in 1807, however. As the demand for cotton increased, the US government imposed a ban on importing more slaves from Africa, striking at
the purse strings of the South's agricultural enterprise. Also, about the
same time, the quality of Southern states' land decreased, thanks to over-
cultivation, which prompted many of the owners of large numbers of
slaves to begin looking for new land to expand their way of life.[146]

Resistance to the institution of slavery became a significant national
issue in the early nineteenth century, as the slave ban implies, especially in the North. That effort got a significant boost with the Slave
Rebellion of 1831 in Southampton County, Virginia. Nat Turner, an
enslaved man, organized the effort that resulted in the killing of sixty

whites before the unrest was put down. In response to the rebellion, white militias formed, and some were violent, taking the lives of hundreds of innocent slaves.[147]

Soon, state governments across the South responded to rebellious slaves with new codes and laws that limited their movements. Then, in October 1859, abolitionist John Brown led his militia in a raid to capture the US arsenal at Harpers Ferry, West Virginia, hoping to use stolen weapons to arm a widespread slave uprising. However, the raid failed, and Brown and many of his supporters were executed. Word of the event further fueled Southern plantation owners' fears that the North wanted to exterminate Southern whites and destroy their livelihood.[148]

Slave rebellions and actions like Brown's were part of a larger social landscape of the growing abolition movement at the time. To a certain extent, abolitionism was also aided by the coincidence of the Second Great Awakening (1790–1840), a time of evangelical fervor. Specifically, a growing number of Christian citizens saw slavery as a sin, such as the Pennsylvania Quakers, who considered all people equal in God's eyes. They spoke consistently about the issue and formed the first abolitionist group in the 1790s.[149]

By 1840, the American Anti-Slavery Society grew to include nearly two thousand local auxiliaries with membership approaching two hundred thousand, which included freed Blacks like Frederick Douglass, who had escaped slavery in Maryland and later became a national leader of the abolitionist movement. Those groups passed resolutions against slavery and published numerous abolitionist newspapers that condemned slave owners as sinners and called on all people to refuse to return runaway slaves to their owners. Meanwhile, abolitionists set up the Underground Railroad, a network to help lead slaves to freedom. There was also the Compromise of 1850, a package of five US Congressional bills that were intended to defuse slavery-based polarization, but that ultimately contributed to more division.[150]

The abolitionist movement also created a broad social reform effort that gained widespread traction by the 1850s, aided by author Harriet

Beecher Stowe's book, *Uncle Tom's Cabin*. That bestselling novel increased the ranks of the abolitionists and played a role in national politics.[151]

Division over slavery came to a head in 1860 among Democratic Party members who at the time began preparations for the presidential election. The issue that conflicted the Democrats was whether slavery would be permitted in new American territories, especially with the admission of Kansas and Nebraska.

At the time, the Nebraska Territory was considered too far north for slavery to be profitable. However, whether Kansas would be a free or slave state became a contentious issue. By 1854, the Kansas-Nebraska Act gave those residents the option of forming a slave state, an issue that enraged northern Free Soil Party members (the Free Soil Party was a precursor to the Republican Party), who believed the expansion of slavery in that territory would advance the issue throughout the nation.[152]

By 1860, there were an estimated four million slaves in the US who fueled the Southern agricultural-based economy. Meanwhile, the Kansas-Nebraska Act politically split the Whig Party over slavery, which led to the founding of the Republican Party (July 6, 1854), and soon two Republican candidates announced for the presidency: Abraham Lincoln and William H. Seward, who both expressed strong antislavery positions. However, Democratic Party candidate John Breckinridge, the sitting US vice president at the time, favored a law protecting slave owners' rights in the new territories, reasoning that territorial governments could decide the issue for themselves.[153]

The 1860 Democratic Party's presidential convention was held in Charleston, South Carolina, where slavery was the top issue. The outgoing US president, James Buchanan, a Democrat, endorsed Breckinridge, who was from Kentucky, and wanted the party platform to protect slaves as property, while Senator Stephen Douglas of Illinois, also a candidate for the party's nomination, believed the federal government had no power over slavery. Both failed to earn the nomination, and the convention adjourned without naming a candidate.[154]

Six weeks later, the Democratic Party regathered in Baltimore, Maryland, and the slavery issue continued to fester. The delegations from the ten Southern states quickly left the convention in protest and immediately held their own convention, the Constitutional Democrats, who nominated Breckinridge for president. Those delegates left behind in Baltimore nominated Senator Douglas as their candidate for the presidency. Other Democrats broke with the party to form the Constitutional Union Party and nominated John Bell, a Tennessee moderate who favored federal protection for slave ownership as well.[155]

Not surprisingly, the 1860 election was the first presidential election in which a candidate was elected with less than 50 percent of the vote. After all, because of the polarization over slavery, Lincoln's name didn't appear on the ballot in the Southern states, and Douglas, who ran as a Democrat, was equally hated in the South because of his position on slavery. Thus, Lincoln and Douglas were the only candidates considered in the Northern states, and Breckinridge and Bell competed in the South. Once Lincoln declared victory, South Carolina immediately voted to secede from the Union. By the time Lincoln was inaugurated on March 4, 1861, six other states—Mississippi, Florida, Alabama, Georgia, Louisiana, and Texas—had also seceded.[156]

The trigger for Civil War hostilities came at Fort Sumter in Charleston Bay on April 12, 1861. The Confederate army opened fire on the federal garrison and forced the lowering of the American flag. At that point, President Lincoln mobilized the militia to suppress the "insurrection." Meanwhile, four more slave states seceded, and the war soon stretched across the young nation from Virginia to Missouri.[157]

The Confederate armies surrendered in the spring of 1865, accompanied by the capture of Confederate President Jefferson Davis in Georgia on May 10, 1865. Meanwhile, months before the end of the shooting war, Congress passed the Thirteenth Amendment to the Constitution that abolished slavery.[158]

Polarization in the 1960s

National polarization over slavery led to the Civil War. By contrast, the US' participation in the Vietnam War came to polarize the US population and accelerated the end of our role in that Southeast Asian war.

The Vietnam War pitted the communist North Vietnam government and its allies like Russia and the Viet Cong, a South Vietnamese insurgent group, against the people of South Vietnam and their principal ally, the United States. The conflict spread across the region, and in part became a Cold War-proxy conflict between America and the former Soviet Union.

The conflict was initially about North Vietnam's desire to unify the entire country under a single communist regime similar to the Soviet Union or the communist People's Republic of China. However, the South Vietnamese government fought to preserve its Western alignment, which precipitated the arrival of US military advisers who kept a small presence in that country throughout the 1950s. Those numbers grew to include active combat units by 1969, with more than five hundred thousand US military personnel.

As the US built up its presence in Vietnam, the Soviet Union and China poured weapons and other supplies into North Vietnam. Then, as the war intensified, casualties mounted until Washington abandoned the fight in 1975, which led to the downfall of South Vietnam. Ultimately, the human toll from the war included 2 million civilians on both sides, 1.1 million North Vietnamese and Viet Cong fighters, and an estimated quarter of a million South Vietnamese soldiers. America lost 58,281 who were killed, and 153,372 were wounded requiring hospitalization, with another 150,332 wounded but not requiring hospital care. Also, 1,584 Americans were missing in action, with up to 778 having been taken captive.[159]

The war ended after President Richard Nixon signed the Paris Peace Accord on January 27, 1973, and ordered our withdrawal. Had we abided by the obligations under that accord, and had Congress not pulled the authority to continue the war, the end state may have been quite different. However, once the North Vietnamese realized the US had no intention of abiding by the accord, they quickly seized all of South Vietnam in 1975; as a result, the country was unified as the Socialist Republic of Vietnam.

How did we get to that disastrous outcome, and why had America become so polarized by the conflict?

The war accelerated to a new level shortly after South Vietnamese general officers assassinated Ngo Dinh Diem, the country's president, and at nearly the same time (November 1962), President John F. Kennedy was assassinated in Dallas, Texas. Shortly thereafter, the new US president, Lyndon B. Johnson, agreed to further increase our support to Saigon under the guise of stabilizing South Vietnam.

President Johnson's decision to increase forces got a further justification for action in the summer of 1962, when North Vietnamese torpedo boats allegedly attacked two US destroyers in the Gulf of Tonkin. President Johnson quickly ordered a retaliatory strike on North Vietnam, and shortly thereafter, the US Congress passed the Gulf of Tonkin Resolution, which gave the president broad war-making powers, to include regular bombing raids that came to be known as "Operation Rolling Thunder."[160]

American bombing operations quickly expanded to include attacks on infiltration corridors in neighboring countries that led into South Vietnam, such as Laos, along the famed Ho Chi Minh Trail. Then, by March 1965, Johnson once again increased our forces to 175,000, albeit with the alleged intent to shore up the South Vietnamese army.

America continued to grow its troop presence until late 1967, when it topped out at 500,000 troops in Vietnam. Meanwhile, US casualties reached 15,058 killed and 109,527 wounded, figures that were updated every week on our television screens. The longer the war stretched, the more our soldiers bled, the more politicians in Washington claimed we were winning—and the more the American public began to view the war effort with a jaundiced eye.[161]

Polarization among the American people became especially bad because, at the time, our armed forces depended on conscription to fill the military's ranks. Further, media images about the war seeded a growing lack of desire by many draft-age young men to serve in Vietnam War, as did their distrust for our national and military leaders. Meanwhile, a robust anti-war movement grew among draftees both inside the military and especially with the young adults waiting anxiously at home for a go-to-war call from their local draft boards. Of course, a very polarizing aspect of conscription at the time was the unfair aspect of draft deferments that kept many of the well-connected and/or wealthy from serving while the balance of the less fortunate young men were involuntarily enlisted and shipped to war.

The problems that erupted among draftees became especially daunting and quite public. Our active military forces came to be known for drug use, post-traumatic stress disorder, desertion, and attacks against their uniformed military leaders. In fact, between 1966 and 1973, half a million military personnel deserted; meanwhile, the anti-war movement spawned violent protests fueled by the media, which blasted horrific combat images in every evening newscast. Soon, mass demonstrations were staged across the country, even outside the Pentagon.

The polarization within the ranks and across the nation reached a tipping point in 1970 just as the US-South Vietnamese forces invaded next-door Cambodia and Laos both on the ground and from the air to destroy enemy supply bases. Word of these invasions sparked new protests across American campuses, and the unrest came to a head on May 4, 1970, at Kent State University in Ohio, when federalized National Guardsmen shot and killed four student protesters. A week later, two more student protesters were killed by police at Jackson State University in Mississippi.[162]

Both the news of an escalating war in Vietnam and the killing of anti-war protesters at the hands of National Guardsmen became an accelerant for more domestic tensions over the war. Further, in 1971, the *New York Times* released a leaked top-secret Pentagon study on the Vietnam War that indicated President Nixon ramped it up, arguably for political purposes.[163]

In 1975, America abandoned South Vietnam to its own demise and began the healing process from years of stark polarization.[164]

Polarization over Significant Social Issues

Americans were polarized by significant issues other than those that led to or kept us in wars. Two of the most polarizing social groups in our short history were the race-related emergence of the Ku Klux Klan (KKK) and the women's suffrage movement.

Post-Civil War KKK Fueled Race-based Polarization

The Ku Klux Klan emerged in postbellum America when white segregationists sought to maintain "their economic, cultural, and political power on local, state, and national levels to suppress African Americans' civil liberties." As a result, according to historian Henry Louis Gates at Harvard University:

> The American South [with the encouragement of the KKK] developed and implemented Jim Crow segregation laws, which spread throughout the country, to maintain African Americans' second-class status and ensure white supremacy.[165]

The KKK, a secretive group, persists even today to advance its bigotry against African Americans, Jews, Catholics, and other groups. The white supremacist organization surged three times in this country over the past 160 years, each time promoting its radical polarizing ideas.

The group initially formed after the Civil War, thanks to resentful

Southerners who desired to put African Americans back into a permanent plebeian class by denying them civil liberties, social mobility, and economic opportunity.

At the time, the Klan formed in the summer of 1866 in Pulaski, Tennessee, allegedly at the law office of Judge Thomas M. Jones. The KKK's name comes from the Greek word *kyklos*, translated "circle" or "band," with "clan" spelled with a "K." The group borrowed from the Greeks some of their leadership titles, such as "Grand Magi."[166]

Very soon after forming, the Klan became a vigilante "society" perpetrating crime, especially against African American freedmen. The KKK donned distinctive white robes that often concealed their faces with masks as they invaded Black homes and lynched some ex-slaves— all allegedly to "protect" the public.[167]

"The Klan became in effect a terrorist arm of the Democratic Party, whether the party leaders as a whole liked it or not," wrote Allen W. Trelease in *White Terror: The Ku Klux Klan Conspiracy and Southern Reconstruction*. The group's popularity drew membership across the Southern states, and soon stories emerged about its use of violence and destruction of property.[168]

The KKK's second surge came in the wake of D. W. Griffith's 1915 silent epic drama film that romanticized the Klan's origins, *The Birth of a Nation*, aka *The Clansman*. During that period, which lasted at least a decade, the KKK expanded to the west, both to rural and urban areas, which was a response to political and economic changes associated with the post-World War I era's uncertainties. Further, the group's bigotry reached beyond just African Americans to include anti-Semitism and anti-Catholicism. Similar to their initial manifestation, the group's actions involved cross burnings and an assortment of other violent acts, as well as mass parades and promoting like-minded people for public office.[169]

The third KKK surge in polarizing popularity took place during the civil rights movements of the 1950s and 1960s. It was triggered especially by notable actions such as the 1954 Supreme Court's *Brown v. Board of*

Education of Topeka, 347 U.S. 483 (1954) decision, which declared separate public schools for students of different races unconstitutional. Also, the 1964 Civil Rights Act and the growing profile of prominent African American citizens like Dr. Martin Luther King Jr. energized the Klan's popularity among a segment of the population.

There was no doubt about the KKK's polarizing, racist agenda. A 1964 leaflet produced by the KKK in Mississippi began: "Here are twenty reasons why you should, if qualified, join, aid and support the white knights of the Ku Klux Klan of Mississippi." A few of those reasons include:

Because it is a Christian, fraternal and benevolent organization.

Because it is a democratic organization, governed by its members.

Because it is a legal organization and no one can be prosecuted for being a member.

Because it is a Pro-American organization that opposes any thing, person or organization that is Un-American.

Because it is an organization that is sworn to uphold the lawful Constitution of the USA.

Because it is composed of native-born, white, gentile and protestant American citizens who are sound of mind and of good moral character.

Because the goals of the KKK are the total segregation of the races and the total destruction of communism in all its forms.

Because a Christian-like brotherhood among men must be revived in America.

Because the KKK needs you today to help fight America's battles.[170]

Unfortunately, the KKK still exists in some form across America today. It will continue to adjust to our social landscape, but hopefully it will have a weaker polarizing effect in the future.

Women's Suffrage Movement Overcomes
Patriarchal Polarization

The age-old struggle for women to gain equality within a patriarchal society evidences a first-order form of human polarization, a fight American women launched under the guise of the "suffrage" movement, a word taken from the Latin *suffragium*, which simply refers to the right to vote. Of course, voting was just the tip of the proverbial iceberg for women. Over the nineteenth and early twentieth centuries, and due to the tenacity of some very determined women, the Nineteenth Amendment to the US Constitution gave women not only the right to vote but removed many of the draconian, anti-female obstacles long rooted in our male-dominated social structure.

The nineteenth-century American woman enjoyed few of the rights accorded to male citizens. They lived in a culture that endorsed the view that women were subordinate to men by nature, evidently created as less intelligent, and biologically unfit for the rigors of business, much less politics. That view was sewn into the common law, which stuck women in an eternal second-class status.

Those laws robbed women of a civic identity as well. Specifically, once a woman married, her "separate civil existence ceased, and she was assumed to function 'under the cover of, or as a part of her husband,'" according to Virginia Sapiro, writing for the Boston University *Law Review*. That meant she could not own property, even if she had an income, nor could she seek employment without her husband's permission. Even a married woman's children "belonged" to her husband by law. Further, if she left her husband, even due to his abuse of her, all family property stayed with the man. Even within the relationship, once the woman consented to marriage, her husband had unlimited sexual control over her body, which meant the man could never be charged with raping his wife while he lived with her.[171]

Thus, the nineteenth-century woman, at best, was a second-class citizen with few meaningful rights. Even our all-male founders failed to provide a constitutional basis for recognizing more women's rights. Therefore, for much of our early history, half of our population was polarized as being "unfit" to be full citizens, which gave women a significant challenge to overcome.

In 1995, the history of American women's efforts to win full rights was outlined in a speech by Sandra Day O'Connor, an associate justice to the US Supreme Court. She spoke to commemorate the seventy-fifth anniversary of the ratification of the Nineteenth Amendment, which guaranteed women the right to vote.[172]

Justice O'Connor began her speech about the Nineteenth Amendment and the suffrage movement with an interesting anecdote. In 1776, Ms. O'Connor explained, the wife of future President John Adams "implored her husband to 'remember the ladies' in drafting our new nation's charter, [but] her plea fell on deaf ears." After all, the American Constitution, written exclusively by fifty-five men, failed to acknowledge women in the text, permitting each state to continue their practice of prohibiting women from voting.[173]

Even our Bill of Rights gave no quarter to the plight of female citizens. Evidently, its framers saw no role for women in the new American government, much less in commerce, which meant women were forever relegated to domestic chores. Even by the turn of the twentieth century, women still couldn't serve on a jury or even as a notary public. They couldn't hold an elected office, make a contract, convey property, bring legal action, or acquire a passport without male oversight.[174]

The nineteenth-century American female citizen's place in American society was aptly described at the time by Alfred Lord Tennyson (1809–1892), the British poet who wrote that a "wife stood in relation to her husband as something just 'better than his dog, a little dearer than his horse.'"[175]

Many insightful women saw their opportunity to gain basic citizens' rights (voting) by attaching their future to the growing abolitionist movement of the mid-nineteenth century. In fact, women came to constitute the majority of Northern antislavery societies and were the backbone behind most abolitionist petition drives.

Some of those female abolitionist leaders won the opportunity to participate in the 1840 World Anti-Slavery Convention in London, England. Although women were welcomed at the convention, the men who oversaw the event refused to allow them to speak. That exclusion from speaking became a light-bulb moment for two female convention participants, Lucretia Mott and Elizabeth Cady Stanton, who recognized the need to take concerted action to advance women's rights.[176]

Many years later, Mrs. Stanton, the wife of Henry Stanton, an abolitionist leader from New York, reflected on her participation in the World Anti-Slavery Convention and the silent treatment given all women at the time. She wrote about her growing conviction to take action: "All I had read of the legal status of women, and the oppression I saw everywhere, together swept across my soul, intensified now by many personal experiences."[177]

Nearly eight years after Mott and Stanton attended the London convention, they met with other women in Seneca Falls, New York, and decided to call their own congress, a "woman's rights convention," in July 1848. It's noteworthy that Henry Stanton threw cold water on his wife's suffrage ambitions. After reading Elizabeth's draft resolution demanding that women be given the right to vote, Henry said if she presented her demand, "he would have nothing to do with it and would go so far as to leave town to avoid embarrassment." However, Frederick Douglass, the black abolitionist leader at the time, approved of Elizabeth's resolution and promised to support it at the convention.[178]

The convention took place with many speeches and much discussion for days. Elizabeth Stanton's reading of the ninth resolution was the key point of the gathering: "Resolved, that it is the duty of the women of this country to secure to themselves their sacred right to the elective franchise." That convention was the first of other congresses for the next ten years, and gradually women across young America came to agree on their dissatisfaction with the state of affairs.[179]

These women saw the rank discrimination against women, but realized the only way to really change the paternalistic culture was to gain the right to vote. Then came the Civil War and subsequently the emancipation of the former slaves, which brought the plight of female citizens to the forefront. After all, if freed former slaves got all the civil liberties of citizenship, including suffrage, then there was no justification to exclude women from having the right to vote.

Evidently, many men at the time were of a different opinion. In 1866, Congress drafted the Fourteenth Amendment, which declared the right to vote should not be "denied to any of the male inhabitants" of a state. At the time, Mrs. Stanton realized that such an amendment would be a setback for the women's suffrage movement. However, the amendment, which included the word "male" three times, was ratified in 1868, stating that no citizen could be denied the right to vote because of their "race, color or previous condition of servitude," but there was no mention of gender in the language.[180]

After failing to get gender included in the Fourteenth Amendment, the frustrated women took new steps to gain attention. In 1871, Victoria Woodhull, another suffragette, presented a petition to the US House of Representatives Judiciary Committee, arguing that the "constitutional amendments had secured the vote for women as well as blacks." The committee rejected her petition, and the Supreme Court later dismissed their request for a hearing because "women had no right to vote under the United States Constitution."[181]

Susan B. Anthony, a suffragette, tried a new tactic. She illegally voted in the presidential election of 1872 with other women. They were quickly arrested. At trial, Anthony intended to argue the Fourteenth Amendment as her defense. However, she never got the opportunity to speak, because the judge concluded that, as "a person of the female sex," her vote made her guilty, and therefore there was "no issue to be presented to the jury."[182]

As the fight continued in the eastern US, the American territories saw the issue differently. For example, in the Wyoming Territory, a bill passed to enfranchise women in 1869, and soon they voted and assumed with enthusiasm all the rights of full-fledged citizenship.[183]

By 1900, the leading suffrage groups, the National Woman Suffrage Association and American Woman's Suffrage Association, com-
bined into a single entity and changed their strategy. These American
women took a lesson from British suffragettes who were equally fed up
with all the male foot-dragging on the issue and launched a more direct
approach. Specifically: "One English suffragette went so far as to throw
herself in front of the King's horse as it was winning the derby, sacrificing
her life to garner attention for the suffrage movement," explained Justice
O'Connor. Soon, American suffragists under the leadership of Elizabeth Stanton's daughter, Harriot Stanton Blatch, organized the Women's
Political Union, which hosted open-air meetings, posted messages at
public settings, and held parades. Those actions ratcheted up pressure
on the non-suffrage states. Meanwhile, a fight with suffrage opposition
used a host of tools, such as bribes to threaten vulnerable state legislators
to defeat women's voting bills.[184]

Just prior to World War I, and in the wake of eight states granting full suffrage to women, a group of young, well-educated women
decided to directly lobby then-President Woodrow Wilson by picketing,
parades, pilgrimages, and petitions. In fact, they successfully pulled off
a stunt inside the halls of the US Congress just as President Wilson rose
to address that body. Specifically, five women sat in the House gallery
and, as the president spoke, they dropped over the balcony a banner that
demanded: "Mr. President, what will you do for woman suffrage?" Wilson faltered momentarily, surprised by their protest, but the message got
through, and soon other suffragists took more direct action, including
picketing the White House.[185]

The more direct-action strategy had its intended effect. The suffrage
movement earned the endorsement of both parties' 1916 presidential
campaigns. Two years later, a national amendment to extend the vote
to women came to the Congress, which passed the House by two votes
more than the required two-thirds majority. The issue once again passed
the House in 1919 and then earned a two-thirds majority vote in the
Senate, making the outcome a foregone conclusion. At that point, the

suffrage movement worked to get three-fourths of the states to support amending the Constitution. And, on August 26, 1920, Secretary of State Bainbridge Colby signed the Nineteenth Amendment into law. It states:

> The right of citizens of the United States to vote shall not be denied or abridged by the United States or by any state on account of sex. Congress shall have power to enforce this article by appropriate legislation.

The suffrage movement fought the polarizing effect of deeply rooted patriarchy—not that different from the injustice perpetrated on the black slaves.

Contemporary Polarizing Powerful Americans

Consider two categories of powerful Americans who polarized our nation under the guise of leadership and profit: some of those who lead our government and the otherwise influential in political parties and the media who collaborate. These groups have historically polarized the population to gain and sustain control, because they are at the pinnacle of power, where they have access to the levers of society, which grants them that control.

US Government Leaders with Divisive Worldviews

A 2018 survey of two hundred political science scholars of the American Political Science Association ranked American presidents whom they believed to be the most polarizing/divisive. The majority (57 percent) of the respondents identified as Democrats and just 13 percent were Republicans. Perhaps it's not surprising that Presidents Donald Trump and Barack Obama were ranked among the most polarizing/divisive presidents in US history.[186]

In 2019, Gallup's Jeffrey Jones attributed polarization to the "extreme partisan views of presidents," which, he said, "are the new norm in politics." Mr. Jones went on to explain that "the past 15 presidential years account for 14 of the top 15 most polarized years since Gallup began regularly measuring both job approval and party identification in the 1950s."[187]

The label "polarizing" is identified, according to Jones, when the average presidential approval rating from an opposing party is low. In Barack Obama's case, his approval rating slipped from his post-inauguration high because he pursued policies that displeased his opposition.

President Trump is known by many as a polarizing leader. From the start of his administration, he pursued what his opponents considered fractious policies, such as dismantling Obamacare, withdrawing from a global climate pact, and agreeing to move the US Embassy in Israel to Jerusalem—all campaign promises.[188]

Further, polarizing presidents more often than not appoint staff members who will advance their contentious agendas. That's why those appointees become the tip of the president's ideological spear—wielding influence over vast national resources, like the Secretary of Defense, who literally oversees millions of military and civilian personnel, and in fiscal year 2023, a budget of $813 billion. These appointees use their power to get the job done in accordance with guidance from the White House, which can become part of a divisive, polarizing campaign to remake the government in their ideological image.

President Biden is very polarizing, as are his underlings. In 2023, his national polling hovered around 40 percent approval, which suggests that most Americans disagree with his policy agenda on a host of issues: immigration, inflation, environment, and more.

What's clear among presidential administrations is that the policies—and, by direct correlation, the worldview—of the president himself translates by his actions into division, which angers the majority of the country, not just his political opposition. Not surprisingly, too often the federal workforce—which is already biased to the Democratic Party, according to a variety of polls—is frequently pleased to do the bidding of a Democrat administration and may even drag their feet on controversial issues when a Republican is in the White House.

Social Media Giants and Democrats Who Share a Divisive Worldview

The otherwise powerful polarizing Americans include many corporate and wealthy people who support especially the Democratic Party and too often employ divisive tactics. Don't believe me? Then consider what columnist Adriana Cohen wrote in the website RealClearPolitics.

In August 2022, Ms. Cohen confirmed that big tech has long been in cahoots with the Biden administration to help the Democrats maintain power and win elections. In her article, "Big Tech Continues to Collude with Democrats," she wrote: "Take long-time Facebook COO and Meta board member Sheryl Sandberg's high-profile wedding last weekend [August 2022] at the Four Seasons hotel in Jackson Hole, Wyoming."[189]

US Secret Service personnel were crawling over the Jackson Hole hotel because "top Biden administration officials—including U.S. Secretary of State Antony Blinken—jetted in [at taxpayers' expense] for the weekend long celebration." Why was the secretary at the wedding? He was there, according to Cohen, to "schmooze with big tech brass like Facebook CEO Mark Zuckerberg." After all, as Cohen wrote:

Facebook and Twitter [before Elon Musk took over the company] are run by an army of left-wing political activists who gleefully censor and ban conservatives with impunity.

She continued:

What's actually happening is these unchecked and far too powerful social media oligarchs are designating virtually any content that damages Democratic candidates and/or their associates as "misinformation" and swiftly burying it from voters' view to help tip elections to their preferred candidates.[190]

The next section of *Divided* will expose in great detail the many other divisive and powerful Americans who use their influence on the country's most important institutions.

Conclusion

America has a history rich in significant polarizing events. Arguably, polarization motivated the start of the Civil War and, conversely, it quickened the end of America's involvement in the Vietnam War. On issues like the role of the KKK, that group galvanized Americans mostly against rank bigotry, leading to a Supreme Court decision against racist policies and legislation that gave justice to oppressed African Americans. The suffrage movement exposed the evil of patriarchy and gave all women a more equal opportunity.

The next chapter demonstrates that the Bible's sixty-six books are chock-full of examples of division/polarization—as a necessity by God's design and, in other cases, as real evil fostered by Satan and his demonic army.

<u>chapter six</u>

Division across Biblical History

These are the people who divide you, who follow
mere natural instincts and do not have the Spirit.
—JUDE 1:19, NIV

No study of the phenomenon of division would be complete without an examination of its various uses in the Bible. Across the
Bible's sixty-six books, we find division employed to fulfill God's will
for man as well as the means Satan uses to separate us from God's plan.

This chapter surveys some of those uses, providing insights that
inform our understanding of the phenomenon in preparation for the
next section of the book, which exposes division's extensive role in contemporary American culture. Further, this chapter is quite different from
chapter 3, which focused on a review of Scripture regarding how Satan
employs division to enlist powerful people.

Division from the Beginning: Genesis

Genesis chapters 1–11 outline God's relationship with our cosmos and declare theological truths that apply to this day. The term "division" plays a prominent role in those early chapters, outlining a template for its use for both good and evil throughout the balance of human history.

In Genesis chapter 1, we see God's power evidenced when He divides the light from the darkness (1:4) and the sea from the dry ground (1:9). We also understand that God is holy, but humans are not, and—thanks to the account in Genesis chapter 3—the Serpent (Satan) introduces sin to humanity, thus dividing us from God's perfect plan for His creation.

Template of "Enmity": From Feud to Restoration

Satan comes to the Garden of Eden in Genesis chapter 3 to tempt Eve, who then brings Adam into the Fall, and both disobey God. Thus, God banishes (separates, divides) Adam and Eve from Paradise for their disobedience. The impact of that division is stark: Eve and all future women are to suffer in painful childbirth and must submit to their husbands' authority. Adam and all future men are cursed to toil and work the ground for food, unlike during their previous idyllic life in Eden's Paradise. But there is much more to this division, what the Bible calls "enmity." God divides (puts "enmity" between) the Serpent's seed and the woman's seed, which means the feud between Satan and mankind will involve all her offspring.

"Enmity" is a twofold promise. It refers to the spiritual battle started with Adam and Eve's banishment from the Garden of Eden that continues today between Satan, his demonic army, all the ungodly children of Satan (John 8:38–44), and the godly seed of the woman. It is also the very first prophecy of the death and resurrection of Jesus Christ, because God's curse on the Serpent (Satan) was part of His plan to restore what had been lost by humanity's betrayal in Eden and rebellion against their Creator.

God gave Satan dominion over the earth at the time (Luke 4). However, God's rich mercy would, for a time, allow the Serpent to strike the heel of the offspring of the woman. In doing so, Satan would have his head crushed (Colossians 2:15). Specifically, God will restore mankind after the failure of the first Adam and with the success of the Last Adam (Christ). Thus, those who put their faith in Christ will taste restoration in this life and eternity in Heaven in the full renewal of the next life.

Template of Sin

Division continues to show aspects of its template in Genesis 6, whereby God expresses His disappointment once again with His creation, sinful humans. The descendants of Adam and Eve passed their sinful nature forward, and, as we read in chapter 6, God saw that the "wickedness of man was great" then declared that He "was sorry that He had made man on the earth" (6:5, NAS). Therefore, the righteous God said, "I will blot out man whom I have created from the face of the land" (6:7, NAS). However, "Noah found favor in the eyes of the Lord" (6:8, NAS). So, God separated (divided out) Noah and his family from the balance of wicked humanity, then utterly destroyed all people by the Flood, but He spared Noah and his immediate family (6:13).

Parenthetically, it's interesting to note Professor Peter Gentry's interpretation of the expression "sons of God" in Genesis 6:2 and 4, which addresses efforts by some to put the blame of human sin on fallen angelic beings. The Southern Baptist Theological Seminary professor notes there are three common interpretations of "sons of God," including the view that the expression refers to the progeny of the union between angels and human women. Thus, divisively, some pursue this interpretation to then blame sin (division from God) on the offspring of fallen angels. However, Professor Gentry dismisses this view by restating that Genesis 3 is clear: God made a covenant with the first humans (Adam and Eve), and they "cheated on God." Thus, sin became the human condition, and not the fault of fallen angels procreating with women. Further, the professor cites the book of Jude, which affirms that sin marks mankind because of human disobedience, not because of the activity of angelic beings.[191]

Now, picking up with Noah: After the Flood, his family reestablished humanity. However, people quickly returned to the sinful ways of Adam and Eve. In Genesis 11, we read that "now the whole earth used the same language and the same words" (11:1, NAS). They said:

> Come, let us build ourselves a city, and a tower whose top will reach into heaven, and let us make for ourselves a name, otherwise we will be scattered abroad over the face of the whole earth. (11:4, NAS)

Evidently, they disagreed with God, and under the corrupt leadership of Nimrod (likely Satan's envoy, 10:8), the people built a tower to worship a false god and replace the true God's authority.

The text states that God was displeased with the idolatry and said:

> Behold, they are one people, and they all have the same language. And this is what they began to do, and now nothing which they purpose to do will be impossible for them. Come, let Us go down and there confuse their language, that they may not understand one another's speech. (11:6–7, NAS)

Thus, God scattered (divided) the people across the whole earth, to confuse them and defeat their wicked, idolatrous' plan.

The message from Genesis 1–11 is that God's created people sinned at every opportunity. Therefore, to address that sin, God either divided them or allowed Satan to divide them. The byproduct of that division was in each instance a fresh start for the human race that inevitably returned to the same old ways—sin. This pattern repeated until Jesus came to pay the penalty for all sin once and for all, which will lead to one last division at the end time, when the saved go to Heaven and the lost are doomed to eternity in Hell.

Division across the Old Testament

The division seen in Genesis 1–11 plays out across the balance of Genesis and the other thirty-eight books of the Old Testament. A few familiar accounts of division illustrate the prominence of the phenomenon.

Israelites Divided from the Balance of the World's Humanity

In Genesis 12, God called Abram to leave his home in Ur of the Chaldees, a pagan civilization. Although Abram did not know the true God or His plans for him and his descendants, he obeyed the call to be divided from his people and follow the unknown God's instructions. We read that commission in Genesis 12:1–2 (NIV):

> The Lord had said to Abram, "Go from your country, your people and your father's household to the land I will show you. I will make you into a great nation, and I will bless you; I will make your name great, and you will be a blessing."

After reading a few chapters later in Genesis, we understand why God chose—divided from His people—Abram. Specifically, he was chosen to become the father of the Israelites, God's chosen people, who were divided out from all nations, which God intended to use to bless all the earth through the coming of the Messiah (Galatians 3:16). Later, we see the Israelites' special status with God once again in Exodus 19:5–6 (NIV), where we read that God said:

> Now if you obey me fully and keep my covenant, then out of all nations you will be my treasured possession. Although the

whole earth is mine, you will be for me a kingdom of priests and
a holy nation.

God further divided Israel by calling on Aaron and his descendants
to serve as priests (Exodus 28:1, 44). Israelite priests had special quali-
fications (divisions), such as they must be male; descendants of Aaron;
of a certain age (Numbers 4:3); unblemished (Leviticus 21:16–23);
properly married (Leviticus 21:9, 14); and not unclean (Leviticus
22:3–9).[192]

Job Refuses to Be Divided from God Despite Great Suffering

The story of Job is another early account of division. The book deals
with the age-old question of humanity being divided from God. It poses
and then answers a key question: Why do the righteous suffer if God is
loving and merciful?

The storyline portrays Job as prosperous, blessed by God. But Satan
comes to test (divide) him, and God allows that challenge. The text
states Satan approaches the throne of God, and the Lord asks him:

> Have you considered my servant Job? For there is no one like
> him on the earth, a blameless and upright man, fearing God and
> turning away from evil. (Job 1:8, NAS)

Satan responds to the Lord's inquiry: "Does Job fear God for nothing?" (1:9, NAS). He accuses God of placing a protective shield around
Job. "But put forth your hand now and touch all that he has," says Satan,
and "he (Job) will surely curse you to your face" (1:11, NAS).

The Lord agrees to allow Satan to test Job: "Behold, all that he has is
in your power, only do not put forth your hand on him" (1:12, NAS). So,
Satan departs from the presence of the Lord and immediately the Devil
removes all of Job's possessions—his flocks and children—to which Job

responds, "Naked I came from my mother's womb, and naked I shall return there" (1:21, NAS). The text continues, "Through all this (suffering Job) did not sin nor did he blame God" (1:22, NAS).

Satan returns to God's throne to insist that "touch his (Job's) bone and his flesh; he will curse you to your face" (2:5, NAS). God responds: "Behold, he is in your power, only spare his life" (2:6, NAS). Soon Satan inflicts Job with sore boils from the sole of his foot to the crown of his head (2:7, NAS).

Job's wife sees his suffering and then asks, "Do you still hold fast your integrity?" She then urges him to "Curse God and die" (2:9, NAS)! Her call for Job to turn away (divide himself) from God is soon echoed by Job's three friends who hear of his adversity. They sit with Job seven days and seven nights, with no one speaking a word to him, for they see his pain is very great. Finally, his friends conclude that Job suffers from loss and sickness because of his sin.

Satan's infliction of pain on Job and the human (wife's and friends') calls for him to abandon—be divided from—God fail, however. Job refuses their advice to conclude in Job 19:25 (NAS): "As for me, I know that my redeemer lives. And at the last he will take his stand on the earth."

Yes, Job comes to question God. However, in his conversation with God, Job recognizes his insignificance before his all-knowing Creator. Then Job declares after a conversation with God: "Behold, I am insignificant; what can I reply to you? I lay my hand on my mouth" (40:4, NAS).

The conclusion is that God is sovereign over the affairs of mankind. Yes, we suffer, which God allows. However, God's plans that may include painful division are for His purposes, and after life's tests, Job rejoiced in his renewed relationship with God and the return of His rich blessings.

Joseph's Division from His Family Saved Israel

Joseph was divided from his father Jacob because of the jealousy of his brothers, who sold him into slavery (Genesis 37:27). However, as we read in Genesis 37, God used what Joseph's brothers intended for harm to save the nation of Israel.

Jacob favored his youngest son, Joseph, over the others, which resulted in jealousy that compelled his brothers to sell him as a slave to a caravan of Ishmaelites. Then the brothers lied to their father that Joseph had been killed by a wild beast (Genesis 37:32).

Joseph was further divided from his family when his captors sold him to Potiphar, the captain of the Egyptian Pharaoh's bodyguard. That second division got worse for Joseph when Potiphar's wife "looked with desire at Joseph" (39:7, NAS). However, the young man fled Potiphar's unfaithful wife only to be falsely accused of a sexual advance that landed the Israelite in jail.

In time, the incarcerated Joseph interpreted the dreams of the cup-bearer and the baker, his fellow jail mates. Eventually, after two years behind bars, Joseph had the opportunity to interpret Pharaoh's dream, earning the Israelite elevation to a position "over all the land of Egypt," second only to Pharaoh (41:41, NAS).

The account of Joseph is marked by multiple significant instances of division but ends well for him and all of Israel. After all, the division from his family, what Joseph's brothers meant for evil, God used for Israel's ultimate good. It saved the nation from a devastating drought at home and allowed the number of Israelites to grow to multiple millions while in Egypt, then to eventually return to the promised land.

Predictably, there are many other examples of division within Old Testament families. One of the best-known examples of Satan's efforts to divide the family is found in 2 Samuel 15:13, where we read that Absalom turns on his father, King David. Scripture tells us Absalom was angry with David, and in retaliation the king's son turned (divided) the entire nation against the king. It's noteworthy that Absalom's name, which means "peace of my father," resulted in no peace for his family, much less for the nation.

God Ordered Israelites to Divide (Separate) from Other Nations

God told the Israelites that when they entered the promised land after wandering in the Sinai Desert forty years, they must totally destroy everything—including the foreigners and their flocks (Deuteronomy 2:34; 3:6). Why? To prevent the foreigners from teaching the Israelites to follow all their detestable practices related to worshipping foreign gods, which might cause the Israelites to sin against the Lord (Deuteronomy 20:16–18). Of course, the Israelites failed in that mission as well, and the result was precisely what God had said would occur (Judges 2:1–3; 1 Kings 11:5; 14:24; 2 Kings 16:3–4): They abandoned God and turned to pagan deities.

God commanded His people to exterminate the foreigners to prevent greater evil from occurring in the future. Specifically, the First Commandment (Exodus 20:3, NAS: "You shall have no other gods before me") was appropriate for the people of Israel. After all, they had a long history of abandoning God to worship idols.

We saw the Israelites quickly turn from God while Moses was on Mount Sinai receiving the Ten Commandants. At that time, Moses' brother Aaron saw the desperation in the eyes of his people, who said to him: "Come, make us a god who will go before us; as for this Moses, the man who brought us up from the land of Egypt, we do not know what has become of him." Then Aaron melted the people's gold rings into the form of a calf, and said: "This is your god, O Israel, who brought you up from the land of Egypt" (Exodus 32:4, NAS).

Turning to idols was quite common throughout the history of Israel. In Hosea 10:1–2, for example, we read that God exposes the problem of idolatry once again. Israel abused its prosperity for the purposes of idolatry, which divided their hearts from God. Most major prophets like Isaiah and Jeremiah and other prophets like Amos called out God's judgment on the nation for turning their hearts to idols.

Today, too many of us get taken captive by created idols such as financial security or politics, which divert our attention away from the True God.

Exiled Jews Refused to Be Divided from God

The book of Daniel provides multiple examples of division that serves God's purposes. Perhaps the best-known temptation came when, as we read in Daniel 3, King Nebuchadnezzar had an idol made and commanded all people to "fall down and worship the golden image" (3:5, NAS). The consequence for failing to worship the idol was being cast "into the midst of a furnace of blazing fire" (3:6, NAS).

Three Jewish exiles—Shadrach, Meshach, and Abednego—refused to bow down to the idol—in other words, they refused to be divided from the True God. When threatened with certain fiery death, the three said:

> If it be so, our God whom we serve is able to deliver us from the furnace of blazing fire; and he will deliver us out of your hand, O King. (3:17, NAS)

King Nebuchadnezzar tied up the disobedient Jews and threw them into the fiery furnace. However, the three were not consumed by the fire and, accordingly, the king looked into the inferno and saw four, not three, men walking about the fire. The fourth man, the king said, "is like a son of the gods" (3:25, NAS).

The king ordered the men to come out of the furnace and noted "the fire had no effect on the bodies of these men nor was the hair of their head singed" (3:27, NAS). Nebuchadnezzar responded:

> Blessed be the God of Shadrach, Meshach, and Abednego, who has sent His angel and delivered His servants who put their trust in Him.... Therefore, I make a decree that any people, nation or tongue that speaks anything offensive against the God of Shadrach, Meshach, and Abednego shall be torn limb from limb and their houses reduced to a rubbish

heap, inasmuch as there is no other god who is able to deliver in this way. (3:29, NAS)

God used division in this case to bring glory to His name.

Positive Principle of Being Undivided

The Old Testament also includes teachings about the importance of being united, rather than divided. For example, the book of Ecclesiastes has many wise instructions from the author identified by the Hebrew word *qoheleth*, which means "preacher." There is good reason to believe the author of the book was King Solomon, the "son of David, king in Jerusalem," the one who had increased in "wisdom more than all who were over Jerusalem before me," and the one who collected many proverbs (Ecclesiastes 1:1, 16; 12:9, NAS).

Solomon writes in Ecclesiasts 4:12 (ESV):

And though a man might prevail against one who is alone, two will withstand him—a threefold cord is not quickly broken.

This verse expresses the antithesis of division, the importance of not being alone (divided from others). Earlier in the book, Solomon says life is vanity for someone who is alone and toils for nothing. However, Solomon extols the virtues of having partners—thus being united, not divided.

So, the Old Testament has numerous accounts of God dividing or allowing His people to be divided in order to serve His purposes. Teachings in books like Ecclesiastes and some of the Psalms—like 22:18 (NAS), which are prophetic of those who crucified the Christ ("divide my garments among them")—illustrate the concept. Yet other biblical passages wisely point out the virtues and potential harm associated with division.

Division in the New Testament

There is division in the New Testament for both good and bad purposes: the division that honors God and that which is overseen by Satan to divide people from God's best intentions. These uses have general application in our contemporary world, which we'll see played out in section III of *Divided*.

There are four Greek words in the New Testament translated "division," according to *Strong's Concordance*. *Diamerismos* (διαμερισμός) means "breaking up," "discord," or "hostility." It is found in Galatians 5:19–21 to describe one of the works of the flesh and in Romans 16:17 to urge believers to avoid those who cause divisions.

The word *dischostasia* (διχοστασία) means "division," "dissension," or "standing apart." It is used in Luke 12:51 (NAS), where we read that Jesus asks: "Do you suppose that I came to grant peace on earth? I tell you, no, but rather division." In this context, Jesus indicates His followers may be rejected (divided) from close friends and family because of Him. Therefore, people who place others ahead of their service for Christ are divided and are called "not worthy" in the Scripture.

The third word for "division" in the New Testament is *schisma* (σχίσμα), which means "to rent, as in a garment," or "dissension." It is used eight times, such as in Matthew 9:16 (NAS): "But no one puts a patch of unshrunk cloth on an old garment; for the patch pulls away from the garment, and a worse tear [schisma] results."

The fourth word, *apodiorizo* (ἀποδιορίζω), is found in Jude 19 (NAS): "These are the ones who cause divisions, worldly-minded, devoid of the spirit." Sensual people are divided, split from God when they join themselves to Satan, the world, and the flesh by their ungodly and sinful practices.

Consider examples of division within the context of several New Testament passages.

Christ Called for His Disciples to Be United, not Divided

Christ, just prior to the Crucifixion, calls for His disciples to be united (John 17:20–23) as opposed to being divided. This appeal for unity applies more universally as well—for all believers to be united with Christ and with one another. Thus, the lesson here is to avoid division. After all, in Romans 16:17 (NAS), the Apostle Paul warns:

Now I urge you, brethren, keep your eye on those who cause dissensions and hindrances contrary to the teaching which you learned, and turn away from them.

This teaching continues in Paul's first letter to the Corinthians. He states:

Now I exhort you, brethren, by the name of our Lord Jesus Christ, that you all agree and that there be no divisions among you, but that you be made complete in the same mind and in the same judgement. (1 Corinthians 1:10, NAS)

The conclusion is that division is a result of the flesh (sin) and is contrary to the true fruit of the spirit.

Yes, Paul identifies division among our many sinful, fleshly tendencies in his letter to the Galatians:

Now the works of the flesh are evident: sexual immorality, impurity...dissensions, *divisions*, envy...and things like these. I warn you, as I warned you before, that those who do such things will not inherit the kingdom of God. (Galatians 5:19–21, ESV; emphasis added)

How are we to respond to such division when it shows its ugly head in the Body of Christ? We are instructed to discipline believers who cause division. In Titus 3:10–11 (NAS), we read:

Reject a factious [divisive] man after a first and second warning, knowing that such a man is perverted and is sinning, being self-condemned.

Clearly, the Bible teaches there can be no unity without truth, and the toleration of teaching that divides is unacceptable. We are called to remove that sin or the false teaching.

Division is also often the result of selfishness, and as Philippians 2:1–4 (ESV) states:

So if there is any encouragement in Christ, any comfort from love…do nothing from selfish ambition or conceit…let each of you look not only to his own interests, but also to the interests of others.

The application here is to oppose division and embrace unity within the Body.

Jesus Warns Christians: Expect Division from the World

Jesus Christ is clear that Christians are divided, or separated, from this world because we belong to Him. He explains in John 15:18–19 (NAS) that we are to expect division/polarization because we are His:

If the world hates you, you know that it has hated me before it hated you. If you were of the world, the world would love its own; but because you are not of the world, but I chose you out of the world, because of this the world hates you.

Therefore, by belonging to Christ, we are automatically ostracized (divided) from this world.

Being hated is disturbing but understandable, because we know that followers of Jesus Christ should expect to be rejected by nonbelievers and even by some church leaders. Specifically, we read Christ's words in John 16:2 (NAS):

They [some church leaders] will make you outcasts [divide you] from the synagogue [church], but an hour is coming for everyone who kills you to think that he is offering service to God.

That rejection makes sense when we read Christ's follow-up explanation regarding why some church leaders reject true believers:

These things they will do because they have not known the Father or Me. (John 16:2–3 NAS)

We are further divided because the Lord is very clear about certain human behavior and His teaching.

Jesus Opposes Division in and Distortion of Marriage

When Jesus was questioned about divorce, the division of a marriage of one man and one woman (Mark 10.6–8, NAS), He quoted from Genesis 1:27 and 2:24, saying the purpose of marriage is for one man and one woman to "become one flesh." Unfortunately, Satan's efforts to divide marriages and redefine the institution of marriage sparked the sexual revolution that has divided married couples throughout history—especially during the last half century.

Satan also seeks to divide entire families, if not just married couples. Jesus warned about family division in Luke 12:51–53 (NAS):

Do you suppose that I came to grant peace on earth? I tell you, no, but rather division; for from now on five members in one household will be divided, three against two and two against three. They will be divided, father against son and son against father, mother against daughter and daughter against mother, mother-in-law against daughter-in-law and daughter-in-law against mother-in-law.

Another aspect of Satan's efforts to cause division in marriage is the abuse of sexuality, something God created for good. Satan distorts human sexuality to draw people away from God's purpose for marriage (procreation), such as with the abomination of homosexuality (Leviticus 18:22). God's Word is clear about His intent regarding homosexuality:

If a man lies with a male as with a woman, both of them have committed an abomination; they shall surely be put to death; their blood is upon them. (Leviticus 20:13, NAS)

The New Testament is equally clear about God's view of divisive homosexuality as a lifestyle. The Apostle Paul writes in 1 Corinthians 6:9 (NAS):

Do you not know that wrongdoers will not inherit the kingdom of God? Do not be deceived: neither the sexually immoral nor idolaters nor adulterers nor men who have sex with men.

Christ's Answer to Eternal Division

Perhaps the most pronounced division in the New Testament is between believers and nonbelievers (those who are spiritually lost). Satan uses his powers to steer nonbelievers from God's truth. We see that, upon Christ's Second Coming (Matthew 25:31–46, NAS), He "will divide man into two groups, his sheep [followers] on his right, but the goats [nonbelievers] on the left." Until that time, believers are called to "test the spirits" to see whether they are from God so they won't be "deceived" (divided). We read in 1 John 3:24–46 that we are not to believe every spirit unless it confesses that Jesus Christ has come from God in the flesh. We must recognize that the spirit of the divisive Antichrist is in the world, seeking to draw us away from God's purposes.

Believers Should Avoid Dividers

Titus 3:10 (ESV) states:

> As for a person who stirs up division, after warning him once and then twice, have nothing to do with him.

Also, Romans 16:17 (ESV) calls on believers to "avoid" those who cause division. Why? Because "such persons do not serve our lord Christ, but their own appetites, and by smooth talk and flattery they deceive the hearts of the naïve" (Romans 16:18, ESV).

What should we then conclude about divisive people who teach something other than the "sound words…of our Lord Jesus Christ"? We read in 1 Timothy 6:3–5 (ESV) that such divisive people are "puffed up with conceit and understand" nothing. They have, the passage continues:

> …an unhealthy craving for controversy and for quarrels about words, which produce envy, dissension (division), slander, evil suspicions, and constant friction among people who are depraved in mind and deprived of the truth, imagining that godliness is a means of gain.

These divisive people cause others to stumble, and they don't follow New Testament teaching. Rather, as we read in Romans 14, dividers follow a "different gospel" and their acts are outlined in Galatians 5:19–21: sexual immorality, impurity, idolatry, dissensions (divisions), and more.

Jesus Warns Followers of Division

It is true that Jesus teaches about division, the outcome when believers apply God's Word in their lives. According to Luke 6:22–23, when we stand for Jesus, others will hate us and seek to divide us, set us apart from society for persecution. However, we must understand from Luke 12:51–53 that Jesus did not come to bring peace, but division. His Word will divide families and set us at variance with nonbelievers. We see the same situation in Acts 14:1–4, whereby the people at Iconium were divided by the preaching of the Gospel: Some believed, and others were disobedient.

Conclusion

Division plays a critical role throughout the Word of God. It is often used to set apart first the Jews from the idol-worshipping world and then, with the New Covenant, to distinguish the Christ-followers from those who are lost in their sin.

Division is also a tool Satan and his demonic army use to manipulate vulnerable people to disobey God's direction and, as a result, sin seeks to destroy every good thing created by God. However, we know Satan and his minions are ultimately doomed, and that our path between now and when Satan is "thrown into the lake of fire and brimstone" (Revelation 20:10, NAS) will continue to be marked by frequent division.

Section III of *Divided* considers the contemporary roles division plays across twenty-first-century American life in seven chapters addressing critical institutions: family, politics, education, religion, the workplace, culture (media), and government.

Section III

DEEPLY DIVIDED TWENTY-FIRST CENTURY AMERICA

The root cause of all the problems we have in the world today
is ignorance of course. But most, polarization.[193]
—MAYA ANGELOU (1928–2014), American memoirist,
poet, and civil rights activist

A 2022 survey of Americans found we are sharply divided not just on economic issues, but on our nation's political system, our global leadership, and whether most people will ever achieve the American dream.[194]

Overwhelmingly, Americans (83 percent) describe the current state of our economy as poor or, at best, not good. One-third (35 percent) are dissatisfied with their financial situation, with only a quarter (27 percent) believing they have any chance to improve their standard of living.[195]

Dissatisfaction isn't just about pocketbook issues. In fact, most (86 percent) of the 2022 respondents to a *Wall Street Journal* poll said they are deeply divided across most issues, and more than half of those people expect things to worsen in the future.[196]

One of those surveyed was Robert Benda, a sixty-nine-year-old retiree from Colorado, who told the *Journal* he "considers freedom the most important value in America and thinks Democrats who control Washington are trying to take that away from people." Mr. Benda continued: "Our government is doing what's right for their special-interest groups, and everybody else be damned." In fact, according to the *Journal*, the poll found that only a third of respondents were optimistic that people of different races or religions would ever come together to solve the country's problems.[197]

Perhaps not since the American Civil War have Americans been so radically polarized regarding so many issues. It is true that polarization can help democracies by keeping voters engaged in the political process, but it hurts governance when large swaths of the electorate refuse to consider alternative views, much less compromise their hardened beliefs.[198]

Currently, I don't believe we are at the point of no return. However, the path to civil disputes that result in violence can't be ruled out going forward. After all, America's current polarization is marked by growing subsets of the population that embrace radically dissimilar attitudes not just about political parties, but about ideologies, government policies, education, religion, sexuality, workplace policies, and other cultural norms that too often violate traditional rights and values. Further, of significant concern, there is an increase in domestic terrorism, which is a key act of insurgent groups and often precedes attacks on law enforcement.

A recent behavioral science study supports that view. The study, hosted by the National Center for Biotechnology Information, National Library of Medicine, found that "80% of Americans today feel unfavorable towards their partisan [ideological] foes, and the portion feeling very unfavorable has nearly tripled since 1994." In fact, some behavioral science scholars believe a cross section of our population demonstrates "hate for [their] opponents [that] exceeds their affinity for co-partisans."[199]

This level of polarization and hatred should concern all Americans, because it can contribute to the unraveling of the democratic process. For example, sometimes, highly polarized citizens refuse to engage with their opponents or dismiss alternative views outright. Under such a situation, constructive debate is impossible, and mutually acceptable policies are never reached. Thus, impasse is inevitable across all institutions.[200]

Today, America is at such a crossroads. We are experiencing unprecedented division across the country, the likes of which have been unseen since the period preceding the Civil War, with some of the most polarizing citizens intent on remaking this country into something our founders sought to avoid.

This section of *Divided* considers the impact division has for seven American institutions: family, politics, religion, education, the workplace, culture (media), and government. Admittedly, polarization affects some institutions more than others. However, the byproduct of this cultural cancer is a deeply alienated population, and if we are to survive as a democratic nation, then America must find a space that allows our basic freedoms to flourish once again freely.

chapter seven

Divided Family

The foundation of national morality must be laid in private families.... In vain are schools, academies, and universities instituted, if loose principles and licentious habits are impressed upon children in their earliest years.[201]

—JOHN ADAMS, second president of the United States (1797–1801)

The family is the crucible of civilization. Destroy it and society collapses, which is the aim of Satan and his human proxies. Unfortunately, those evil entities have the American family under siege. In the past, this country has been known for having large families, higher fertility rates, and intact families. All of that changed in a major way beginning in the 1960s and it accelerated during this century.

This chapter outlines the critical role the family plays in building healthy adults for society. Unfortunately, our contemporary crucible is threadbare with severe consequences for our future. Finally, we consider some of the agents of evil working overtime to divide and destroy the American family.

Family's Place in Society

Founding father James Wilson (1742–1798), a legal scholar and associate justice of the US Supreme Court, wrote:

> That important and respectable, though small and sometimes neglected establishment, which is denominated a family…[is] the principle of the community; it is that seminary, on which the commonwealth…must ultimately depend…. It is the duty of parents to maintain their children decently, and according to their circumstances; to protect them according to the dictates of prudence; and to educate them according to the suggestions of a judicious and zealous regard for their usefulness, their respectability and happiness.[202]

Healthy families are critical to society, as Justice Wilson wrote. They are God's creation to bring life to the world through newborn babies, equipping the innocent, helpless infants over time to become productive members of humanity. Strong, ideal families do this by providing for children's basic needs to grow physically, emotionally, and intellectually.

The particulars of the child-development process involve years of parental supervision and significant resources that lead to growth and learning. If at all possible, this socialization metamorphosis takes place in a secure environment, whereby children are protected from life's many dangers. That security umbrella—again, in an ideal setting—remains in place even after children are adults, because the family is always a safe haven with unconditional love and support.

Another role the family plays in the child's development is education. Long before entering a formal educational setting, young people learn manners and pick up other behaviors and skills from parents and siblings. Further, in that learning environment, children can cultivate a sense of belonging, especially when a family offers a secure emotional support system, which helps maturing kids develop a positive attitude about life and foster healthy self-esteem.

Unfortunately, the "ideal" American family environment described above isn't always the case today. In fact, the traditional American family is in decline, and society is beginning to pay a high price, thanks to a large extent to divisions imposed by outside forces.

Declining American Families

The American family experienced dramatic changes in the twentieth century, and that transformation accelerated in the early twenty-first century. Specifically, for decades we've seen the decline in the number of traditional nuclear families due to divorce (division of the marriage relationship), delayed remarriage, shifting economic roles, women having fewer children, and a sizable part of the general population deciding against marriage while some still have children.

In the post-World War II era, the nuclear family consisted of a working husband, a wife who did not work outside of the home, and their children. A variety of new family structures have replaced that structure today. However, no longer can we say there is a "typical" American family structure, because contemporary family composition is very diverse.

Today, half (50 percent) of all adult Americans are unmarried; that's the lowest that statistic has ever been.[203] Further, the trend is for marriages to occur later in life, if at all, with more frequent instances of people living alone and having fewer children.[204]

That structural shift took place over many decades. In 1970, only 7 percent of children lived with a mother who had never been married. The US Census Bureau reports that by 2017, that figure—never-married mothers with children—reached a whopping 49 percent. Further, in 2017, 83.9 percent of children living with just one parent lived with their mothers, a rate that remained steady over the previous decade.[205]

The fact is the disintegration of families is driven by the disintegration of marriages. Many young adults eschew marriage for alternative relationships such as nonmarital cohabitation or singleness. To a certain extent, "hooking up"—living together—has displaced marriage among many young adults. After all, according to the Pew Research Center, the rate of marriage among those ages eighteen to thirty-two fell from 65 percent married in 1960 to only 44 percent of Millennials married in 2022 (in marriages they tended to delay). The median age of first marriages for Millennial males is 30.4 years and 28.6 years for women.[206]

Multiple factors contribute to the drop in the numbers of marriages, such as the value attributed to the institution and the absence of religious beliefs. In 2014, a Pew Research survey found that fewer than half of all Americans agreed that society is "better off if marriages and children are given priority, while 50 percent of those surveyed responded that society is 'just as well off if people have other priorities.'"[207]

Those other priorities that make marriage less appealing today include what US Senator Elizabeth Warren (MA) calls the "two-income trap." She explains that marriage "simply no longer offers the financial security it once did." It's simple math. As expenses rose, wages tended to stagnate, which made it very difficult for many families to live on one breadwinner's income. This stark reality often forces moms of children at home to join the workforce, even though many prefer to stay at home with their kids.[208]

Another troubling factor is the growing absence of religion in the American family life, especially when couples are divided over faith. For example, of couples married before 1972, 81 percent shared the same faith as their partner. By contrast, today, just over half (52 percent) of couples married in the past decade are of the same faith, and 16 percent are in secular (religion-free) marriages.

Recent research strongly suggests certain faith pairings result in higher divorce rates. Among self-identified evangelicals, a third of those marriages end in divorce. That figure rises to nearly 50 percent when evangelicals marry non-evangelicals. Further, the divorce rate is especially high (61 percent) for evangelicals who marry someone with no religious affiliation.[209]

Naomi Schaefer Riley, author of *Til Faith Do Us Part: How Interfaith Marriage is Transforming America*, wrote for the *New York Times*:

> Evangelicals and black Protestants in interfaith marriages reported the least satisfaction. Mormons, remarkably, reported high levels of satisfaction…. Catholics in interfaith marriages were no more likely to divorce than those married to other Catholics.[210]

Divorce is not the only alternative relationship that contributes to the disintegration of marriage. The evidence of this crisis also comes at the hands of so-called same-sex marriage. That came about with the 2015 US Supreme Court case of *Obergefell v. Hodges*, 576 U.S. 644 (2015) ruling that all states must legalize same-sex marriage. The court settled the constitutional question, but few inquiries about social and political acceptance, much less legitimacy. However, the result of that decision was to further marginalize the ages-old, one-man and one-woman institution of marriage.

So, as the rate of marriage has declined for a variety of reasons, the incidence of cohabitation and singleness has grown across American society. This trend has some troubling implications for our future.

The National Marriage Project at Rutgers University produced a comprehensive review about cohabitation and the impact it has for our future generations. The authors of the study reported:

> A careful review of the available social science evidence suggests that living together is not a good way to prepare for marriage or to avoid divorce. What's more, it shows that the rise in cohabitation is not a positive family trend. Cohabiting unions tend to weaken the institution of marriage and pose clear and present dangers for women and children.[211]

The researchers also found the following:

- Living together before marriage increases the risk of breaking up after marriage.
- Living together outside of marriage increases the risk of domestic violence for women, and the risk of physical and sexual abuse for children.
- Unmarried couples have lower levels of happiness and well-being than married couples.

Yes, the American family is in serious trouble. A significant aspect of that crisis is the incidence of fatherlessness for children.

America's epidemic of fatherless homes produces an enormous void in society, and the children pay the price. For example, in 2018, there were approximately four million Black, single-mother-headed families compared to .6 million Asian families headed by a single mom and 3.25 million Hispanic families with only a mom present. By comparison, in 2019, there were 6.69 million white families with a single mother living in the United States.[212]

That devastating lack of fathers in the home translates to 15.76 million children in 2019, who, as a result, suffer higher occurrences of the social ills facing America: crime, poor academic performance, out-of-wedlock births, poverty, suicide, and much more.[213]

Those ill effects are directly traceable to the breakdown of the American family, especially the absence of fathers, according to Mary Eberstadt of the Faith and Reason Institute. She writes:

Some people, mainly on the left, think there's nothing to see here. They're wrong. The vast majority of incarcerated juveniles have grown up in fatherless homes. Teen and other mass murderers almost invariably have filial rupture in their biographies. Absent fathers predict higher rates of truancy, psychiatric problems, criminality, promiscuity, drug use, rape, domestic violence, and other less-than-optimal outcomes. Here's another pertinent, albeit socially radioactive fact: Fatherlessness leads to a search for father substitutes. And some of these daddy placeholders turn out to be toxic.[214]

Dark Enemies of the Family

The American family has numerous enemies tearing it apart, and too often even the Christian community is oblivious to what's happening. Consider three dark enemies that divide the family: progressive politicians, an amoral popular culture, and the father of lies (Satan and his demonic army working through powerful human proxies).

Progressive Politicians

The political class of many stripes has a long history of attacking the family. We know from history that families are often the target of rising totalitarian regimes. Looking back hundreds of years, we see that totalitarian regimes always targeted the family for destruction: the French Revolution (1789–1799), the Russian Revolution (1917–1923) and even Germany's Nazi regime (1933–1945). After all, a nation's families are the socioeconomic bulwark of a country; they pay more taxes, evidence more religious ties, tend to be law-abiding, and are typically self-sufficient. Each of these factors is a threat to evil totalitarians who seek control.

For all these reasons, totalitarians target families because they typically push back against tyrants who object to families that support the rule of law, strong economies, good schools, and local decentralized governance. We've seen similar assaults on the family in America.[215]

America's far-left, mostly progressive politicians attack the traditional family, what they perceive as an obstacle to their control. For example, progressive Democrats are especially guilty of promoting policies that take power away from families and grant the leverage to big government, which progressives then run.

President Lyndon B. Johnson's War on Poverty, an expansive list of social welfare legislation, is a case study in attacking families by giving big government more control. That 1964 federal program, the Great Society, virtually destroyed Black families through welfare dependency and fueled the epidemic of fatherlessness. This view is shared by columnist Thomas Sowell, an African American author, economist, and senior fellow at the Hoover Institution, who attributes the devastating situation among Black families to political manipulation. He wrote:

> Many successful political careers have been built on giving Blacks "favors" that look good on the surface but do lasting damage in the long run. One of these "favors" was the welfare state. A vastly expanded welfare state in the 1960s destroyed the Black family, which had survived centuries of slavery and generations of racial oppression.[216]

Amoral Culture

Another enemy of the family is America's amoral culture. Our culture remains in the moral gutter because of the unending onslaught of media presentations that mock traditional families, celebrate single- and same-sex parent households, encourage a decadent lifestyle, and reward sexualized narcissism.

Decades ago, televised situation comedies—sitcoms—entertained us and promoted wholesome family settings with respect for marriage, such as in the programs *Leave it to Beaver* and *Father Knows Best*. Today, some of the most debased and anti-marriage programming depicts a radically new normal, such as an episode of *Friends* that portrays "pregnant lesbians and three-parent households as not only normal, but admirable," an observation made by Ben Shapiro, an American lawyer and conservative political commentator.[217]

Our so-called woke culture has infiltrated many institutions of higher education as well. Consider the case of Annabella Rockwell, who grew up in a home with traditional values and then in 2011 entered the exclusive Mount Holyoke College in South Hadley, Massachusetts. She wound up "totally indoctrinated" into a woke view that the world was full of toxic patriarchy and that she was an oppressed victim. According to Melinda Rockwell, Annabella's mother, the young woman accused her mother of treating her like a "wind-up toy" and never loving her.[218]

That behavior, evidently, was a product of Annabella's educational experience at Holyoke. She explained that the professors at Holyoke:

...encouraged alienation [from parents] and even offered their homes to stay in. They'd say, like, don't go see them [parents], come stay with us for the holiday. Most of my classmates believed all this stuff, too. If you didn't you were ostracized.[219]

Another example of the amoral cultural influence targeting children is the in-your-face homosexual push, even at Christmastime.

Consider the December, 2022, Florida case of the "Drag Queen Christmas" show that featured sexually explicit material and that was marketed to families and children. Media reports indicate advertising for the event "did not provide notice as to the sexually explicit nature of the Show's performance or other content...[but did state] all ages welcome."[220]

The Florida Department of Business and Professional Regulation's Division of Alcoholic Beverages and Tobacco said the Orlando Philharmonic Plaza Foundation Inc. "promoted the Show using targeted, Christmas-themed promotional materials that did not provide notice as to the sexually explicit nature of the Show's performance or other content."[221]

The foundation did post a notice, printed in small font and taped to the event's front door, according to the complaint filed with the state of

Florida. The notice read: "While we are not restricting access to anyone under [age] 18 please be advised some may think the content is not appropriate for under [age] 18." Nevertheless, the foundation allowed minors to attend the show.[222]

An independent journalist, Tayler Hanson, who attended one of the shows, said:

> I'm thankful to see someone taking action regarding the sexually explicit "all-ages" Drag Queen Christmas Tour that I reported on earlier this month.... Simulated sodomy, exposed fake breasts, and sexually explicit language has no place around children. There is no such thing as a "family-friendly" or "all-ages" drag show.[223]

Satan's Attack

Behind the façade of corrupt progressive politicians and a powerful amoral, woke culture is Satan's attack on the family, the third enemy. Satan and his proxies are advancing against the American family as part of an agenda that dates back to the Garden of Eden.

The Christian is warned in Ephesians 6:10–18 to "stand firm" against the "schemes of the devil." The Apostle Peter describes Satan as our adversary, who "prowls around like a roaring lion seeking someone to devour" (1 Peter 5:8, NIV) and John warns in Revelation 12:9 about the "old serpent" who deceives the whole world.

Satan focuses much of his energy on attacking marriage as a living picture of Christ and the Church. He knows that it is the fabric of a stable society, the foundation of God's work on earth. Therefore, the father of lies seeks to tear down that structure so dear to God's intentions for mankind.

Earlier in this volume, we considered Satan's initial attack on the family in the Garden of Eden, where the Serpent deceived Eve to compel her to disobey God's command. Yes, Satan plunged Eve, her husband, and their relationship into sin. Satan's intent for marriages and families today is the same: total destruction. After all, the signs of Satan's evil work abound; divorce, cultural immorality, same-sex "marriage," destruction of young lives, and much more—all the twisted and perverted work of Satan that deprives us of God's blessings.

Our problem today is that many of us don't understand God's design for marriage and the family. However, the more we recognize Satan's work to change and undermine those institutions, the better we are prepared to resist.

Conclusion

Family is the heart of human civilization. No wonder it is under severe attack by Satan and his divisive proxies.

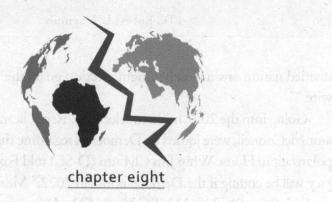

chapter eight

Divided Politics

> I will fight against the division [sic] politics of revenge and
> retribution. If you put me to work for you, I will work to lift
> people up, not put them down.[224]
> —HILLARY CLINTON, former First Lady, US senator,
> and secretary of state

This chapter surveys the political division in the United States and the impact that has for our elections and policies. It concludes with contributors to (causes of) political division, as well as the spiritual component behind our political polarization.

Current State of American Political Division

Shortly after the 2022 midterm elections, Kentucky Senator Mitch McConnell, the US Senate Republican leader, observed from the Senate floor: "When it comes to politics and policy, we are a closely divided nation." He continued: "For the third straight election, our closely divided nation saw a closely fought election go all the way down to the wire."[225]

Going into the 2022 midterm elections, Republican leaders, like Senator McConnell, were joined by Democrats regarding their alarm over our polarization. House Whip Jim Clyburn (D-SC) told Fox News: "Democracy will be ending if the Democrats lose in 2022." Meanwhile, US Senator Rick Scott (R-FL) told NBC News: "The Democrats want to destroy this country, and they will try to destroy anyone who gets in their way."[226]

The alarm over polarization wasn't confined to our political leaders. Just prior to the 2022 midterm election, 57 percent of Americans agreed with the statement: "America is heading toward the end of democracy, where free and fair elections will no longer occur." Fifty-three percent of Democrats and 65 percent of Republicans agreed with that statement.[227]

Political polarization emerges when subsets of the population embrace dissimilar views about parties, ideologies, policies, and their political affiliation. In fact, since the 1990s, Americans have polarized around their political party, rural versus urban, rich versus poor—we've coalesced around polarized national identities as well, and thus have demonized our opponents. In fact, the problem is getting worse, according to a 2022 Pew Research Institute report.

Pew indicates that, in 2016, about half of Republicans (47 percent) and more than a third of Democrats (35 percent) labeled the other party "a lot" or at least "somewhat" immoral. Today, those figures are especially worrisome: 72 percent of Republicans and 63 percent of Democrats believe the other party is immoral. Further, large majorities in both parties believe their counterparts in the other party are "closed-minded" (83 percent of Democrats and 69 percent of Republicans say this).[228]

Political policies often distinguish that polarization. A 2020 Public Religion Research Institute report found that none of the three policy issues popular with Democrats at the time (healthcare, climate change, and foreign interference in presidential elections) overlapped with Republican concerns (immigration, crime, and terrorism). Further, that study found a wide partisan gap on policy issues like immigration (80 versus 32 percent) and climate change (35 versus 79 percent) between Republicans and Democrats.[229, 230]

The political divide reaches beyond policies to issues of party identity, Democratic and Republican. Eighty-three percent of Democrats believe their party "is trying to make capitalism work for the average American." However, 82 percent of Republicans believe the Democrats are "taken over by socialists." By comparison, almost all (94 percent) of Republicans believe their party protects American traditions; eight in ten Democrats argue the Republicans have "been taken over by racists."[231]

Impact of Political Polarization for America

In the 1950s, the American Political Science Association worried that the lack of polarization hurt the country. Evidently, in that post-World War II era, the two major political parties failed to distinguish themselves from the other. The Association wrote: "Alternatives between the parties are defined so badly, that it is often difficult to determine what the election has decided even in broadest terms."[232]

The lack of distinguishable differences between the 1950s-era political parties arguably hurt the country because, according to the political scientists, there needs to be a clear difference in the party positions to incentivize voter interest and participation in the election process.

The worrisome degree of polarization today has the opposite effect. By comparison, current voters are often more motivated by feelings of hatred toward their political opponents than concern about the consequences of policies offered by candidates for office. Also, we are seeing fewer citizens and candidates who straddle the ideological fence. Thus, as a result, we seldom find compromise between opposing political leaders and more strident declarations—and, often, bad policy results.

Evidently, there are costs and benefits to a politically polarized nation—some helpful and others quite destructive. On the beneficial side, polarized citizens tend to more often participate in the political process by voting, protesting, and joining political movements. Polarization and engagement between the parties can ultimately produce more effective government and embrace optimal solutions to societal problems.

The downside to political polarization can challenge the democratic process. After all, when the parties are highly polarized, they often refuse to engage with their opponents, labeling them as radical and their views without merit. This situation results in skewed policy outcomes that ignore minority views.

This outcome is especially dangerous when the half of the society in power embraces a morally corrupt policy, such as we saw with Southern plantation slave owner states prior to the Civil War and the pre-World War II German Nazi regime that embraced an anti-Semitic policy. In those and related situations, only politically skewed, supportive policies—or, at best, suboptimal solutions—were considered by the powerful.

Thus, polarized groups tend to exclude opposing political beliefs and embrace only policies that confirm their partisan preferences, albeit while ignoring facts and flaws in their reasoning. Under such a regime, the democratic process leads to less than ideal outcomes, or even ejects policies that fail to address key social issues.

Causes of Political Polarization

There is a plethora of causes of political polarization. What may polarize me politically may be one issue or a host of issues, but for another it could well be something radically different.

At the time Joe Biden came into the presidency (2021), the US was deeply polarized, according to Ian Shapiro, a political science professor at Yale University.[233] Professor Shapiro said the "transfer of political power to the grassroots has eroded trust in politicians, parties, and democratic institutions, culminating in the rise of divisive, populist politics in the United States and abroad."[234]

The Yale professor cited President Trump to illustrate his polarization point. However, that's a misguided accusation. The fact is, according to Shapiro, Mr. Trump was really a product of bad political institutions and weak political parties. Populists like the former president are too often controlled by unrepresentative voters on the parties' fringes.[235]

Therefore, we need to consider multiple possible "causes" that contribute to America's current political polarization.

Cause #1: Fringe Party Members' Oversized Influence

Fringe party members have always enjoyed a disproportionate influence over the political process because they play an oversized role in primaries. After all, as most voters understand, the problem is that political primaries enjoy very low voter turnout, and political fringe voters participate disproportionately in them. The same is true in states with caucuses. So, when thinking of Mr. Trump's selection as the Republican presidential candidate in 2016, he was selected by less than 5 percent of the US electorate, explained Professor Shapiro.[236]

The same fringe voter plays a disproportionate role in congressional races. That's how the Tea Party took so many Republican Party seats after 2009 because those members accounted for the majority of the 15 percent primary turnout. Of course, the same is true for the Democrats, such as in 2016, when progressive candidate Alexandria Ocasio-Cortez beat incumbent Congressman Joe Crowley, a moderate Democrat, with only an 11 percent turnout.[237]

Cause #2: Ideologically Charged Political Views

Political scientists used to measure the relative ideological positions of members of Congress by considering their voting records. After World War II, the difference in ideology of most Democrats and Republicans wasn't that far apart. At the time, the average Democrat was modestly left of center, and the Republican, on average, was modestly right of the political center. However, today, according to the Pew Research Center, the divide between so-called moderates in both parties increased to the point that Pew indicates there are very few ideological moderates in Congress.[238]

By comparison, most Americans in the twentieth century were not nearly as ideological as their elected leaders. However, there were exceptions to that view. Specifically, the more politically sophisticated, especially the politically elite, did polarize from the norm, and today, with most voters identifying themselves on the political spectrum—liberal to conservative—they tend to be far more polarized than in the past.

Polarization isn't always driven exclusively by our ideological views, however. It can also be an affective phenomenon, which stems from hostility for the political opponent. We see this today in terms of the mutual dislike demonstrated by Republicans and Democrats who have nothing good to say about the other.

Cause #3: Political Tribalism

Affective polarization is like political tribalism, aka identity politics, a cause that impacts both the political left and right. Author Amy Chua explains political tribalism in her book, *Political Tribes* (2018):

> The Left believes that right-wing tribalism—bigotry, racism—is tearing the country apart. The Right believes that left-wing tribalism—identity politics, political correctness—is tearing the country apart. They are both right.[239]

Political tribalism occurs when your affiliation with a political party defines your identity; therefore, you look at the world through a lens of "we" versus "they," whereby collaboration with "they" can be seen by "we" as betrayal to fellow political tribe members.[240]

Cause #4 Media Echo Chambers

The advent of the Internet has fed political polarization. Our new digital media and the First Amendment right to mostly uncensored speech provides platforms for all voices, including those with polarizing views and especially those with the energy to share their perspectives. Also, the proliferation of alternative views on the Internet is compounded in a polarizing way by the decline in journalistic accountability, which results in lower quality and more volume from our "professional" media, blurring the lines between news and opinion, facts and entertainment. The result is more, and more divisive, political polarization.[241]

Cause #5: Geographical Political Polarization

Most observers of America's political landscape know that where we live more often than not reflects our politics. A 2014 Pew Research Center study validates that view.

The study found:

> Conservatives would rather live in large houses in small towns in rural areas—ideally among people of the same religious faith—while liberals opt for smaller houses and walkable communities in cities, preferably with a mix of different races and ethnicities. And sizable minorities of both groups say they'd be dismayed if someone from the "other side" were to marry into their family.[242]

The politically liberal overwhelmingly (76 percent) prefer racial and ethnic diversity when deciding where to live, according to Pew. By comparison, the conservatives place more value on living among people who share their faith (57 percent), as opposed to only 17 percent of liberals who use a faith-based criteria when selecting a home.[243]

Thus, given that Americans tend to live in politically like-minded communities, it's not surprising that self-selection leads to more extreme political beliefs. Authors Bill Bishop and Robert Cushing write in *The Big Sort* (2018):

> Mixed company moderates; like-minded company polarizes. Heterogeneous communities restrain group excesses; homogeneous communities march toward the extremes.[244]

Cause #6: American Exceptionalism

Some Americans embrace an exceptionalist identity that dates to our earliest founders. John Winthrop, an early American pastor, said in his 1630 sermon, "A Model of Christian Charity":

> For we must consider that we shall be as a city upon a hill. The eyes of all people are upon us. So that if we shall deal falsely with our God in this work we have undertaken, and so cause Him to withdraw His present help from us, we shall be made a story and a by-word through the world.[245]

The concept that endures for some American Christians is that these United States are God-ordained as the light of the way for the world. This view is captured by Charles Kupchan, a professor at Georgetown University and a senior fellow at the Council on Foreign Relations. He wrote: "From its earliest days, the exceptionalist narrative has set the boundaries of public discourse and provided a political and ideological foundation for U.S. grand strategy." He goes on to indicate that some Americans, from our earliest days, "embraced a messianic mission: they believed that their unique experiment in political and economic liberty would redeem the world."[246]

Even Thomas Paine (1737–1809), an American political activist and author of *Common Sense*, wrote in 1776 of American exceptionalism that "a situation, similar to the present, hath not happened since the days of Noah until now. The birthday of a new world is at hand." The concept is that America inherited a destiny for greatness so that some, like former President Trump, embraced this uncommon view that has encouraged US political polarization. Yes, this exceptionalism is among some a deeply embedded and polarizing way of viewing our nation's past, present, and future.[247]

Cause #7: Polarization as the American Story

America has always been a mostly Christian nation, which has profound influence over our politics. Professor Alphonso F. Saville, with the Department of Theology and Religious Studies at Georgetown University, argues that to understand our current polarization, we must first appreciate our historical context. He explained:

> The contemporary moment can really be better understood by understanding what the religious foundations of political difference—political ideological difference—are in America's history.

He continued:

> I don't think that this represents a particularly unique moment… [rather,] I think that this [moment], in many ways, crystallizes what is in a microcosm [of] the whole in totality of the American experience.[248]

The professor explained our context *vis-à-vis* the time of American slavery and the origins of the Black church. He wrote that, since our national founding, this country was "forged through often violent and destructive sociopolitical arrangements," markers of our differences— to a large extent thanks to the influence of religion within our society, which is deeply ingrained.[249]

Christianity's influence and the exceptionalist narratives reflect the nation's Puritan heritage, a sixteenth-century religious reform movement that arose within the Church of England, then came to America, where, by the mid-seventeenth century, it had spread across much of New England. The earliest settlers believed in America's Manifest Destiny. Even though liberals often claim our founders separated church and state, religion has always had a pervasive influence on our culture and politics. After all, consider Christianity's influence on early America, as reflected in: our Pledge of Allegiance (1885), which includes the phrase "one nation under God"; our currency, which boasts "In God We Trust"; our presidents' speeches more often than not concluding with the phrase "God bless America"; and our 1776 Declaration of Independence making four references to God.

Christianity's influence began with its Puritan founding, according to French author Alexis de Tocqueville: "Puritanism, as I have already remarked, was scarcely less a political than a religious doctrine." Further, de Tocqueville argued that religion undergirds US culture and society, and it is the "foremost" political institution; it is critical to the sustenance of US democracy and "directs the manners of the community, and by regulating domestic life it regulates the State."[250]

Thus, polarization, given this Christian background, occurs when the values of our past Christian influence clashes with the secular values of our present culture. Those once-dominant Christian views are generally incompatible with contemporary secular, nonreligious/secular adherents who push policies that are an anathema to Christianity, such as abortion on demand and so-called gay marriage. Thus, we find growing polarization over faith-informed past policies. Further, and not surprising, socially and theologically conservative Christians today tend to be overwhelmingly Republican, and modern Democrats tend to include the religiously unaffiliated (secular), as well as mainstream (theologically liberal) Protestants, most non-Orthodox Jews, and nonreligious Catholics.

A similar phenomenon happened to the Roman Empire nearly two thousand years ago when that civilization welcomed foreign people (the

Huns and Barbarian tribes) and their religions. Soon, that inclusion as well as the overreliance on slave labor, overexpansion, and loss of traditional values weakened/polarized the foundations of Roman society and at least partially led to its eventual collapse.[251]

Dark Hand behind All These "Causes"

Behind these causes of political polarization are the evil intentions of the father of lies. We know from 1 John 5:19 that Satan holds authority over all operations of culture and governance. After all, he is the king over this world and uses his powers to create sin and chaos to defeat God's plan.

Satan's tentacles reach broadly across the affairs of mankind. We see the extent of that influence in Revelation 13, where we read that, from behind the veil, Satan (the dragon) is revealed through his various proxies that deceive humans to embrace his agenda for this world.

Conclusion

Political polarization marginalizes the American political process. Today, our process produces suboptimal outcomes, arguably by Satan's design. The causes of that polarization are many and, to a large extent, are thanks to the manipulation by the father of lies, who governs the affairs of sinful people in most cases through his divisive, powerful human proxies. Further, and, to the credit of our broken immigration policy, the inclusion of significant numbers of non-European and non-Christians, the glue that once held America together from the early days, our common Christian faith and ethnic heritage are now failing to hold us together. Mix that with a new potpourri of ideologies, religions, diverse cultural traditions, and more, and America's former melting pot is now a polarized cauldron of discontent poisoning our culture.

chapter nine

Divided Religiously

The world is divided into men who have wit and no religion and men who have religion and no wit.[252]

—AVICENNA, Persian philosopher and writer of the Islamic Golden Age

America was founded by mostly Christian people who guaranteed its citizens liberty from any state-imposed religion. Although we continue to enjoy religious freedom today, much has changed over the past three centuries in America, to include the secularization of government and the addition to our religious landscape of many non-Christian faith groups, mega-churches, storefront churches, and other evidence of significant religious diversity.

Today, most Americans accept our religious diversity. However, in recent decades, our Christian religiosity has declined as the nation has become more religiously diverse and secular. That factor contributes to the current level of religious-inspired political polarization that pits diverse faithful citizens against the growing secular population.

America's Christian Founding

Our colonial forefathers experimented with European-style state religion. However, they became convinced to follow a different course for the United States and selected instead a faith-blind federal republic model, which didn't mean they created a religion-free government. Rather, our founders knew that America at its founding was already a Christian nation (not a theocracy), because the vast majority of the colonial population self-identified as Christian, and their Christian churches were literally at the center of every civil, public, and private activity. Further, though they produced a government without an established religion, America didn't ignore the preponderance of Christian influence. Rather, the pervasive Christian culture at the time was evident across all institutions, as well as in our founding documents. That evidence, albeit subtle in the Constitution—is quite clear in statements by prominent citizens from the period.

The absence of references to God or the Bible in our Constitution drew criticism from significant people like Timothy Dwight, the orthodox Christian president of Yale University. In 1812, Dwight wrote:

> The nation has offended Providence. We formed our constitution without any acknowledgment of God; without any recognition of His mercies to use as a people, of His government, or even of His existence...the convention, by which it was formed, never asked, even once, His direction, or His blessings, upon their labors...thus, we commenced our national existence under the present system, without God.[253]

Even though at the time, most Americans self-identified as Christian, it may surprise the reader that, at our nation's founding, only a third of the population were members of an established Christian body, and only a fifth regularly attended any church. But culturally, those early Americans openly identified with the Christian faith. For example, more than two-thirds of baby boys at the time received Christian names, and before the year 1800, almost all newborns had church baptisms, dedications, or christenings. Further, colonial America was dominated by established religions—the New England Congregationalists (a branch of Puritanism), Virginian Anglicans, South Carolinian Presbyterians, and Maryland Catholics—as well as legal government favoritism for religious groups, which continued into the mid-twentieth century.[254]

By contrast, Americans became more religious after the Revolutionary War. In fact, Alexis de Tocqueville observed in the 1830s: "There is no country in the world in which the Christian religion retains a greater influence over the souls of men."[255] However, our religiosity declined in the early twentieth century to rise again to a peak after World War II.

By the 1950s, America saw itself as a Christian nation thanks in part to the Cold War with the Soviet Union and that regime's atheistic communism. In fact, President Dwight Eisenhower (1953–1961) joined a church after his election, becoming the first president to be baptized while in office. Also, as a further indicator, in 1954, the phrase "under God" was added to the American Pledge of Allegiance to demonstrate the nation's religious stance.[256]

Christian Religiosity Declines, Secularization/Religious Diversity Increases

Until 1960, most Americans (90 percent) perceived themselves as religious (mostly Christian). However, that indicator of religiosity declined from a 1960 peak to about 35 percent of adults attending a religious service in a typical week today. Further, adults claiming membership within any religious group fell from over 75 percent at the time to about 62 percent today. Even the level of religious affiliation fell from 95 percent to about 75 percent over those six decades.[257]

Along with the decline in national religiosity, we've seen a corresponding decline in religion's influence across the culture. Today, a quarter of Americans no longer identify with a faith group, and less than a third are given names associated with any religion. Our legal system is almost exclusively secular, no longer giving special rights to people of faith.[258]

Our transition to a more secular legal system likely contributed to the decline in religiosity. After all, a good indicator of religion's influence in a society is the use of religious words in legal disputes, which in America was quite common until the mid-nineteenth century. However, after the Civil War (1861–1865), courts avoided religious references and stabilized such usage at the current low level by the 1930s.[259]

Research also indicates that "explicitly sectarian governance tends to reduce religiosity because it reduces the competitiveness and diversity of the religious marketplace." Also, and in particular, the expansion of government services—especially secular public education—drive secularization. That's why it would be appropriate to conclude that the decline in religiosity was an "engineered outcome" by secularists overseeing government, and was arguably aided by those in the unseen realm.[260]

The surge in secularism doesn't mean America is all of a sudden an atheist country. The 2014 Pew Religious Landscape Study, the best and most updated effort available at the time of this writing, demonstrates that Americans are still quite religious. The study found that 77 percent of Americans identify with some faith group; an overwhelming number (89 percent) say they believe in God; and almost three in four (69 percent) attend a religious service several times a year.[261]

The Pew findings are also supported by the Gallup organization. In 2022, Gallup found that nearly nine in ten (87 percent) Americans believe in God, three in four (76 percent) identify with a faith group, and 68 percent attend religious gatherings at least occasionally. However, the survey also found that just half (50 percent) claim to be actual members of a specific church, and a third attend regularly scheduled religious services. Also, by 2022, only 45 percent said religion is a very important aspect of their lives.[262]

By comparison, in 2015 (the most recent study), the Pew Research Center looked at Europe's religious forecast through 2050. Pew anticipates European Christians will continue to be the largest religious group by midcentury, but those numbers will drop by about 100 million, down from 553 million in 2010 and, at that point, about a quarter (23.3 percent) of all Europeans will have no religious affiliation. Meanwhile, Europe's Jewish population will shrink from 1.4 to 1.2 million by 2050, and the continent's Muslim population is expected to increase by 63 percent from 43 million in 2010 to 71 million by 2050.[263]

In America, as in Europe, the shift in demographics has an impact on religious diversity but also on religiosity. Specifically, the US reached peak homogeneity in the 1970s, with less than 5 percent of the population being non-native born. Every year since then, the non-native-born number increased. For example, by 2018, the foreign-born population comprised 14 percent of the US population, and in 2023, after two years of President Biden's open-border policy was put into place, the number of non-native-born people in this country is going much higher, although the US Census Bureau has not released the figure in several years. Predictably, such an increase in non-native-born people strains the country's ability to maintain social cohesion on many fronts, including religiosity.[264]

So, even though religion continues to be a significant part of America's cultural landscape, its influence does appear to be declining overall.

Causes of Decline in Religiosity

A number of factors affect religiosity, or a religion's influence across a culture. Lyman Stone with the American Enterprise Institute researched the topic to argue that the primary cause of the decline in religiosity is "secularization." However, America retains a significant minority of energized religious people who influence our culture and especially our politics.[265]

Secular education appears to have played a major role in the decline of religiosity. Research indicates childhood religiosity was significantly impacted by the government's investment in public education. By the mid-twentieth century, public education became thoroughly secularized, and research indicates that the more public money poured into government education, fewer numbers of children are religious.[266]

Another cause for the decline in religiosity is the increase of interfaith marriage. Evidently, World War II impacted the number of marriageable men because of battlefield losses (fewer men were available for marriage), which evidently increased the rate of interfaith marriages. Children from those interfaith families tended to be considerably less likely to affiliate with the faith of either parent, according to research.[267]

By contrast, marriage between spouses of the same faith tends to increase average religiosity. It's also noteworthy that married couples who have children, especially the mothers of those children, are more socially conservative, which has a positive effect on religiosity. Unfortunately, the current decline in marriage addressed in chapter 7 negatively impacts religiosity across the culture as well.[268]

Religion-inspired Political Polarization

Many Americans with high religiosity are quite politically active and motivated by their faith. Robert Putnam and David Campbell write in *American Grace: How Religion Divides and Unites Us* that religiosity, "how frequently you attend church or...how frequently you say grace," is a "pretty strong predictor" of how you vote and "which party you prefer." Mr. Campbell, a political science professor at Notre Dame University, said, "People who are more religious are more likely to be Republican."[269]

This conclusion is supported by a somewhat dated 2014 Pew Research Center survey that juxtaposes the respondents' political party affiliation with whether they self-identify as Christian or non-

Christian. The result won't surprise the astute observer. Specifically, almost a decade ago, 82 percent of Republicans self-identified as Christian, compared to 65 percent of Democrats. Likely, those numbers are more skewed in 2023 and are tracking toward less of a Christian presence in our culture.[270]

Given that trend, today, according to Professor Campbell, there is a "pretty stark political divide [polarization]" based on "the intensity of your religious commitment or the intensity of your religiosity," which no doubt reflects on political party affiliation as well.[271]

These men call out the "growth in conservative religion" in America, especially the "unity that we find along religious lines, that we find people actually coming together of different faiths and different religions" around moral issues. That likely explains the interfaith coalitions on issues of religious liberty and moral issues like abortion, which are mostly dominated by Republicans.[272]

Conservative religious groups, even though diverse, often collaborate when polarized by secular government policies and secular political adversaries. Thus, religion and partisan politics have become increasingly intertwined in America. And, in a growing number of situations, politics even influences Americans' religious views.

There is also the issue of religion becoming mired in partisan politics, because a growing number of politicians routinely appears alongside religious leaders while campaigning or declare their own religious views to appeal for votes. Of course, for some, this overlap of religion and partisanship compels them to abandon religion because it seems to have become an extension of politics—another cause of polarization.

There is also the balance between religion and politics over moral issues, which can be quite divisive. After all, politics often involves moral matters such as equal rights, abortion, drug abuse, and human trafficking, which necessarily are concerns for the religious community. Moral leaders like the late Dr. Martin Luther King Jr. become involved in politics not because they aspire to political office, but because, in King's case, equal rights for Black Americans is a moral issue. Today, many religious leaders are involved in the abortion topic because it has grave moral implications for mankind and our nation. So, in such situations, many in the religious community push back when government promotes a secularist agenda on moral issues.

Ultimately, political polarization really comes down to the moral—religion-based—ecology of the American family. After all, America's moral life is dictated by the culture of our families—in particular, the "parenting style," the socialization system that defines the right and wrong (values) and what the family aspires to instill in their offspring.

Family culture creates within future citizens bedrock values and ideals its members hold sacred—their worldview. Those views are inherently moral and often overlap with political issues like same-sex marriage, birth control, traditional marriage, the role of the mother, and much more. Thus, it shouldn't surprise us that values formed at home result in religious-political issues pursued by those same adult citizens.

In 2012, the Institute for Advanced Studies in Culture at the University of Virginia reported on the "Culture of American Families." That study identified four distinct family cultures: the Faithful (20 percent), the Engaged Progressive (21 percent), the Detached (19 percent), and American Dreamers (27 percent). These groups demonstrate in spades the polarization of contemporary America and why two of these groups—the Faithful and the Engaged Progressive—produce offspring who tend to become engaged against the other in political and cultural battles.[273]

The survey found stark disagreement among the groups over family values. The Institute explains that today's average American family tends to be rather secular and relativistic, believing that there are "few moral absolutes"; "all views of what is good are equally valid"; and "as long as we don't hurt others, we should all just live however we want."[274]

That "average American family" may explain in part our current crop of citizens who either self-exclude or are engaged in our religious, moral ecosystem. Specifically, the report puts aside the Detached families, because they are broken and burdened by poverty, drug abuse, and other social problems. Also, the American Dreamers are not relevant to the religious-political debate, because they are fixated on moving their children up the social ladder, and because they are more often than not immigrant families who work hard to meet expectations and remain aloof from the moral, cultural fight.[275]

The religious-political polarization and cultural battles mostly pit the Faithful against the Engaged Progressive families and their offspring. It's not surprising that, among the Faithful, Republicans outnumber Democrats four to one, and among the Engaged Progressive, Democrats outnumber Republicans four to one.[276]

The study found that the Engaged Progressive family tends to champion "diversity" and "inclusion," and they don't want their children befriending evangelical Christians, people typically part of the Faithful cohort.[277]

So, what we come to understand from this study is that polarization is rooted in an ideological struggle over the values associated with the American religious tradition that are spawned often in the family.

Of course, one strand—the Faithful—is the conservative and populist Protestant tradition that dates back to the Second Great Awakening (early nineteenth century) and joined today by conservative Catholics, Orthodox Jews, and some conservative Muslims.

The other strain—Engaged Progressive—is rooted in liberal Protestantism with Unitarianism, transcendentalism, and aspects of the progressive movement dating back to the late nineteenth century. Of course, these groups became quite secularized by the 1960s, very similar to European secular progressives today.[278]

Therefore, today's religious-political polarization reflects the value-based religious tension that tracks back many years in American history. We've long had a cohort of strong faith-based people who have engaged politically from the founding of this country. Perhaps the difference today, which explains the growing religious-based polarization, is that we have a larger minority of anti-religion progressives who advance a woke culture and use secular government's strong arm against the traditionally Faithful.

Satan Fuels the Left,
Secure Government against the Faithful

Satan and his army of demons are quite busy aiding the unbeliever and the unfaithful Christian church, much less secular government, in their campaign against the Faithful. Of course, Satan's objective in the political sphere is to defeat the Faithful and God's plans.

In that context, Satan turns many people away from political involvement—the Detached and Dreamers—and recruits the anti-Faithful Progressive to use the force of government to push their secular, anti-God agenda. There is also an element within the Faithful community who don't believe in being engaged in the political process, which undermines efforts to attack clear moral issues. Thus, it appears quite clear that the political polarization today has a significant faith-based element, which shows no signs of disappearing.

Conclusion

This chapter demonstrates that America was, at the start, a Christian nation—not in name, but in practice. Of course, the level of religiosity waxed and waned through the country's lifespan, yet today America remains a religious nation with a sizeable minority of faithful people who continue to engage in political activity that tends to be quite polarized—especially against secular government and anti-religious progressives who push amoral issues across the culture.

chapter ten

Polarized Education

If the parents in each generation always or often
knew what really goes on at their sons' schools,
the history of education would be very different.[279]
—C. S. LEWIS (1898–1963), British writer and Anglican lay theologian

America's academia is incredibly polarized with the general population. That polarization is personal for many parents who understand that their role in raising their children is often severely undermined by the ideological indoctrination of government educators.

This chapter examines the growing, significant gap between the government's educational establishment and American families, including a look at the scope of the problem and an examination of some of the underlying causes of the dispute. The problem is especially pronounced across much of America's private and public higher-education establishments—colleges and universities—and there is no indication that a solution is in sight.

141

The Gap (Divide) between US K–12 Schools and Parents

Government schools are battlegrounds pitting concerned parents against school officials, some teachers, their unions, and government leaders. The problem is so pronounced that many parents are pulling their children out of those state-run institutions to give their offspring a fighting chance in this troubled world. Why? They no longer have confidence in the government to educate their children.

Only 28 percent of Americans told Gallup in 2022 they have confidence in US public schools, down from 41 percent in 2020. This view of government education institutions has mostly trended down since 1975, at which time 62 percent of Americans expressed confidence in public schools.[280]

The issue for many parents today comes down to trust in public schools, which, according to the Pew Research Center, is in short supply. Thus, parents disgusted with government schools who have the financial means vote with their feet, moving to different school districts or enrolling their children in private, virtual, or charter schools; even homeschooling skyrocketed to a 54 percent national favorability in 2022 from 45 percent in 2017. Of course, that self-sorting of education venues worsens demographic polarization, which doesn't appear to be abating.[281]

Evidently, the diminished parental trust in the government-education establishment is partially the fault of the reputation-marred medical profession, especially its advice for schools during the COVID-19 pandemic: mandatory masking, vaccination, and the shuttering of the schoolhouse. Not surprisingly, in 2022, the Pew Research Center found a significant drop in the public's confidence in our medical scientists—from 40 percent to 29 percent in 2020. That shift also tracks with a 10 percentage point drop in the belief that medical professionals act in the public's best interests, such as in their advice to school officials to close those facilities.[282]

The parallel lack of parental trust in government schools, and, by association, the advice rendered by some medical professionals, is confirmed by a 2021 survey of 357 school district leaders, which found that three-quarters of those officials agreed with the statement: "Political polarization about COVID-19 or vaccines is interfering with our ability to educate students." So, by extrapolation, the education problem is the parents' fault, not attributable to the coy educators.[283]

The gap between parents and government schools can't all be laid at the feet of COVID-19 protocols, however. Forty-three percent of the school officials agree that the growing polarization with parents is also thanks to objections to the teaching of issues like critical race theory. School officials claim parental objections to such issues interfere "with their ability to educate students."[284]

The divide between parents and school officials is also evidenced in the broader political arena. Specifically, self-identified Democrats tend to favor a lower level of parental involvement and oversight of government schools, while Republicans call for more control.[285]

A fall 2022 YouGov America opinion poll asked Americans their opinions about issues facing public education. It found:

...large gaps in the level of concern expressed by self-identified Republicans and Democrats over many school-related issues. While Republicans are most concerned about liberal indoctrination, a lack of parent involvement, and inappropriate books, Democrats are most concerned about book banning, bullying, and teacher shortages.[286]

Meanwhile, caught in the middle of this public education-based ideological battle are many teachers who report being stressed by the polarizing issues, according to a RAND Corporation study. That study found teachers feel they are "being harassed about political issues and as a result experience lower levels of well-being and worse perceptions of their school or district climate."[287]

Predictably, parents displeased with big government's efforts to stiff-arm their role in local schools are seeking better use of taxpayer funds allocated to public education. Specifically, in states like Arizona, school vouchers are now given to parents for them to decide on the best education venue for their children. Of course, the education bureaucracy in Arizona objects to vouchers, insisting the public's funds belong to them and not to disagreeable parents.[288]

Unfortunately, the growing polarization makes it rightly appear that our nation's public schools are at a "turning point," argues Carl Hermanns, a clinical associate professor at Mary Lou Fulton Teachers' College, Arizona State University. The current parent movement upended the status quo for the government schools, and it is quite possible that public education may not survive in the present form, explains the professor.[289]

In fact, Professor Hermanns openly ponders that "if [public education] atomizes and...public schools as we know them don't exist anymore, what will happen is an open question." Perhaps the emergent alternatives like private schools and homeschooling will step up and actually fill the void by focusing on non-ideological education for the next generation. However, that leaves low-income parents unable to afford private schools or have the ability or willingness to homeschool their children. Thus, those kids are stuck in underperforming government schools.[290]

Meanwhile, most Americans will likely agree that the public education franchise is a foundational element of our democracy, a view shared by Derek W. Black, a professor at the University of South Carolina School of Law. Our founders, according to Professor Black, "believed that there was a common good, and that they'd find the common good together, through education."[291]

Evidently, we've arrived at the point that education's "common good" is in serious trouble. Big government is in league with the professional education establishment to include the bankrupt, politically driven teachers' unions that are engaged in fighting parents for the right to have a say over their children's education. That role should be welcomed, not rejected, by government education officials and teachers. However, today there is an arrogance demonstrated by the education establishment that it alone knows best and therefore ought to have the freedom to push even more radical ideologies on our innocent children, a viewpoint many taxpayers and especially concerned parents reject.

Causes behind Polarization of the K–12 Government Schools and Parents

A 2022 American Family Survey (AFS) found a number of issues/causes that explain the polarization between schools and parents. Unfortunately, many people on the ideological left are blind to the threat. A few of the issues identified by the survey and a couple others not part of the poll are highlighted below.

Cause #1: Objectionable material: Material in school libraries has become a polarized political issue. Liberal Democrats, according to a 2022 national survey by YouGov, mostly support diverse library collections (89 percent), compared with Republicans who support that view at 46 percent.[292]

Some parent groups, such as Moms for Liberty, demand that schools remove objectionable books, such as those that are sexually explicit, from libraries. In Brevard County, Florida, that group called on the local school board to remove "racially divisive," LGBTQ-themed books, those critical of Christianity, and others with explicit sex scenes from the school library shelves.[293]

The AFS survey found that 12 percent of Americans agree that parents should have a say about books placed on school library shelves.[294] However, the education establishment predictably disagrees in the name of diversity. Specifically, American Library Association president Lessa Kanani'opua Pelayo-Lozada claims the growing number of challenges fueling polarization about library books are "coordinated, national efforts to silence marginalized or historically underrepresented voices." She said such efforts "deprive all of us…of the chance to explore a world beyond the confines of personal experience."[295]

Cause #2: Transgender push in schools: Even though many public schools are behind the transgender push, the AFS survey found low levels of national support for transgender students in government schools. In particular, most people said transgender athletes should "only be able to participate in high school sports as the gender they were assigned at birth." So far, eighteen states have enacted laws limiting transgender sports participation at public schools.[296]

The AFS also found only 39 percent of Americans support teachers who insist on using students' preferred pronouns, and half disagreed with allowing public school students to decide which bathroom to use. Not surprisingly, liberal Democrats expressed a majority support for the pronoun and bathroom-choice issue.[297]

Cause #3: Pushing race-related curriculum: The AFS explored Americans' views about public education instruction regarding the history of racism in America. Two-thirds (64 percent) agreed that government schools ought to teach the history of racism. However, the issue for many parents is the actual content of that curriculum, such as the push for so-called critical race theory (CRT), which some parents say indoctrinates pupils with un-American revisionist, racist history.[298]

The Goldwater Institute, a conservative think-tank that opposes CRT, described the "theory" as a mechanism that insists all events and ideas must be viewed through the lens of racial identities. Further, according to the Heritage Foundation, a conservative Washington, DC-based think tank, 43 percent of teachers are familiar with CRT, but only 30 percent view it favorably.[299] However, the National Education Association, America's largest labor union, endorses CRT, and many public school principals, according to a University of California study, called parental alarm over CRT "mass hysteria" that is "fueled by disinformation about schools' curricula."[300]

Republicans and most conservatives argue that students ought to be taught an optimistic interpretation of American history, not one that is purposefully divisive, like CRT. "Critical race theory is destructive because it advocates for racial discrimination through affinity groupings, racial guilt based on your ethnicity not your behavior, and rejects the fundamental ideas on which our freedom is based," said Matt Beienburg with the Goldwater Institute.[301] Our freedom, according to former President Franklin D. Roosevelt, is based on four ideas: freedom of speech and expression, freedom of worship, freedom from fear, and freedom from want.[302]

Pushing aberrant curriculum in public schools is not a new problem, however. In the 1930s, Harold Rugg, a progressive education professor at Columbia University, pushed his Marxist textbook as a means to focus on American social ills. Then again in the 1990s, President George H. W. Bush's administration promoted voluntary national history standards, which some conservatives, like Lynne Cheney, the wife of former Vice President Dick Cheney, said were all about "political correctness" because they ignored white male representation in the curriculum. At the time, the US Senate passed a resolution condemning the voluntary standards.[303]

Recently, in January 2023, Florida Governor Ron DeSantis (R) and the Florida Department of Education rejected an advanced-placement (AP) African American Studies course taught in public schools. The state of Florida complained the course "lacks an educational purpose" and pushes a "political agenda." The concern expressed by the state educators was over lesson plans about "Intersectionality and Activism," "Black Queer Studies," the "Black Lives Matter Movement," "Black Feminist Literary Thought," the "Reparations Movement," and "The Black Struggle in the 21st Century."[304]

The Florida Department of Education elaborated on its complaint by citing concerns over "intersectionality being central to [critical race theory]," as well as material advocating reparations for past slavery and abolishing prisons. Further, the material included readings by Gloria Jean Watkins (1952–2021), aka her pen name "bell hooks," who wrote about "white supremacist capitalist patriarchy." Her writing explores intersectionality of race, capitalism, and gender, and she described that as producing and perpetuating systems of oppression and class domination.[305,306]

Not surprising, the Biden administration rejected Governor DeSantis' calls to scrap the course. White House Press Secretary Karine Jean-Pierre said the Biden White House found Florida's removal decision "incomprehensible" and "concerning." Evidently, that view was shared by others identified as "faith leaders" and "civil rights leaders" across Florida.[307]

Fortunately, on February 1, 2023, the College Board announced that it revised the curriculum for its AP African American studies course to include "the removal of topics like Movement for Black Lives, scholars associated with critical race theory and the Black queer experience." That decision was seen as a victory for DeSantis in the culture wars. Evidently, officials like DeSantis can push back on the left's radical agenda and enjoy success.[308]

The bottom line for many parents is they want oversight of the materials presented to their children. At this point, one-third of Americans support parents having a final say about books in public school English classes, while one-quarter (24 percent) believe it is the teachers' right to decide. Further, only 4 percent favor leaving that decision to government representatives.[309]

Cause #4: Underperforming students: Parent satisfaction with public schools is also declining in part because of COVID-19 classroom closure, which significantly impacted student performance, according to the National Center for Education Statistics. The Center found a dramatic decline in test scores among American nine-year-olds since the start of the pandemic, the largest decline in reading scores since 1990, and the first ever drop in mathematics scores.[310]

The decline in student performance isn't just the fault of COVID. Frankly, our education establishment is no longer world class and hasn't been for some time. Specifically, the US is losing its advantage when academic test scores are compared with other countries, according to the Program for International Student Assessment tests, which are administered by the Organization for Economic Cooperation and Development (OECD). In 2018, the last time the test was widely administered, the

US placed eleventh out of seventy-nine countries in science and placed thirtieth in math.[311]

Some government schools are worse than others. Baltimore City public schools are arguably the worst in the nation, and it's really scary how that public school system fails the taxpayer at $21,000 per student per year.

Project Baltimore, an investigative reporting initiative by Sinclair Broadcast Group Inc., analyzed the 2022 test scores of two thousand Baltimore City school students to find that "not a single student is doing math at grade level."[312]

Baltimore resident Jovani Patterson, who filed a lawsuit against the city's schools, said, "We're not living up to our potential." The lawsuit claims the Baltimore school "district is failing to educate students and, in the process, misusing taxpayer funds."[313]

Mr. Patterson continued, "We, the taxpayer, are funding our own demise." And, he said, "My immediate reaction is, take your kids out of these schools."[314]

Thousands of Baltimore public school children took the state math test and not one could do math at grade level, Patterson said. He continued:

> These kids can't do math. You're not preparing them to buy groceries. You're not preparing them to do accounting, to count their own money. You're not preparing them to read contracts and negotiate salaries.[315]

No wonder a growing cohort of parents is concerned about the decline in academic performance. Yes, many noted that government schools' poor performance during the pandemic was especially appalling, as evidenced by packets of take-home worksheets, unimpressive Zoom lessons, and—once back in the classroom—the forcing of kids to mask up and view their teachers behind Plexiglass shields. However, the problem of underperforming schools and their students is a national emergency.[316]

Cause #5: Big government's anti-parent overreach: The Department of Justice under the Biden administration, at the request of a school board union, sought to designate parents who publicly object to leftist ideology in their children's schools as domestic terrorists. This issue, which captured significant national media attention at the time, was understandably a lightning rod for concerned parents.

In 2021, Attorney General Merrick Garland denied that the Justice Department labeled parents as "domestic terrorists" in a memorandum he signed and sent to Justice Department employees about intervening in incidents of violence or intimidation targeting school board officials. According to Fox News, Garland issued the memorandum in response to a request from the National School Boards Association asking the Biden administration to use the terrorism-related PATRIOT Act to deal with disruptive parents at school board meetings.[317]

In testimony before the US House of Representatives, Mr. Garland said he supports and defends the First Amendment right of parents to complain about the education of their children and curriculum taught in public schools. He insisted, however, that his memorandum does not use the words "domestic terrorism" or "PATRIOT Act." However, the memo begins with mention of a "disturbing spike in harassment, intimidation, and threats of violence against school administrators, board members, teachers, and staff who participate in the vital work of running our nation's public schools." Neither Garland nor the Department of Justice ever defined "harassment" or "intimidation."[318]

Cause #6: Hyper-partisan involvement in education: The partisan divide over public education fuels the parent-public school polarization. Consider a view expressed in the *Washington Post* and a University of California study of the issue.

Jennifer Rubin, who wrote for the *Washington Post*, blames MAGA (former President Trump's followers known by the label "Make America Great Again") "culture warriors" for the current level of polarization between parents and government schools. Rubin bases her analysis on a joint study by the University of California at Los Angeles and the University of California at Riverside.[319]

That study claims it found that the "virulent stream of hyperpartisan political conflict" has had "a chilling effect on high school education." It alleges teachers are "pulling back on teaching lessons on civics, politics, and the history and experiences of America's minority communities" because of "verbal harassment of LGBTIQ [lesbian, gay, bisexual, transgender intersex, and queer or questioning] students."[320]

The California report includes a survey of 682 public high school principals that confirmed to the researchers the intimidation of public schools that forced "changes to align with right-wing ideology." Further, the authors of the study claim that "political conflict over a set of hot button issues occurred at more than two-thirds (69%) of public schools across the nation during the 2021–2022 school year." Apparently, nearly half of those challenges to school policies were related to LGBTIQ student rights.[321]

No doubt there are more issues and causes that contribute to the polarization of many parents and the public education establishment. However, these by themselves are extraordinary and very concerning, and explain the growing divide.

Issues/Causes behind Polarization in Higher Education

Many higher education institutions have become incredibly biased against conservatives. For example, Turning Point USA president Charlie Kirk's late-2022 voluntary discussion on the US Constitution event at the University of New Mexico, Albuquerque campus, was shut down by an organized protest. Kirk, a conservative, said on Fox News' *Tucker Carlson Tonight*: "It's really interesting when you try to show up on a college campus and do an optional voluntary event how angry the other side gets."[322]

"But this," he added, "is a very important moment for people to recognize and understand that the other side—the left, the radical left—they're acting like the very same domestic violent extremists that the entire federal government is now organized to go after."[323]

America's higher education establishment is filled to the brim with intolerant liberals. A Harvard *Crimson* (the university's student newspaper) 2021 survey of incoming students found that 87 percent voted for Joe Biden and only 6.3 percent voted for Donald Trump in the 2020 presidential election. It would seem the Boston-based university selects students whose political views are heavily skewed to the left of the national average.[324]

Yale University surveyed its student body in 2022 and found that "nearly three-fourths identify as 'very liberal' or 'somewhat liberal,'" as opposed to only 11 percent who identify as "conservative."[325]

Those two top-tier universities are joined by many other highly rated schools that evidence an overwhelmingly progressive milieu. After all, selecting a majority liberal student cohort fits well into the typical higher education environment. In fact, higher education tends to push people further to the left ideologically, and the problem is even worse among graduate students. That results in too much moral relativism and not enough critical thinking by graduates, a mindset now becoming all too common across our culture.[326]

It is no surprise that those university faculties are deep left. A National Academy of Sciences (NAS) report in January 2020 studied the campaign contributions by college professors. The study found an 8.5:1 ratio in favor of Democrats. Further, the NAS report found the higher the ranking on the national pecking order of universities, the more campus culture is skewed ideologically left.[327]

We shouldn't be surprised that higher education is so polarized from the American population, because it is an old issue. Recall that, in the 1960s, campuses were very politically charged, thanks in part to leftist professors who infiltrated those institutions beginning in the 1930s, such as the Marxists brought to this country escaping Nazi Germany.

I address the infiltration of our higher education institutions by Marxists in my 2021 book, *Give Me Liberty, Not Marxism*. In the chapter dedicated to the education issue, I explain how radical socialist Fabians joined the Frankfurt School Marxists, who then impacted our educational establishment.

In the early 1930s, the Frankfurt School's true "research" was focused on destroying Western civilization. That agenda came to the US thanks to the rise of Adolf Hitler and John Dewey, the American father of progressivism and "modern education."

I write in *Give Me Liberty, Not Marxism*:[328]

> Evidently, Dewey raised the necessary financing for the relocation of the Jewish Frankfurt School philosophers from institutions like the Rockefeller Foundation to place them on the faculties of top American universities: University of California, Berkeley; Princeton, Brandeis; and Columbia University's Teachers College.
>
> These immigrant cultural Marxists used their new American academe perches to advance radical views about the destruction of Western civilization, and soon the effects were being felt. Ralph de Toledano wrote in his book *Cry Havoc!: The Great American Bring-Down and How It Happened* that the Frankfurt School immigrants advanced teachings that led to "tearing down campuses, vilifying decency, glorifying violence and pornography, and nazifying the spelling of 'Amerika.'"[329]
>
> Quickly, cultural Marxists became respectable in the US because, according to [Professor Paul Gottfried, an American philosopher and historian at Elizabethtown College] …the Frankfurt School immigrants fought fascism [the Nazi influence] "as a cultural and emotional danger and for advocating for a progressive democratic society." A significant aspect of that "fight" was the legacy of Nazi anti-Semitism, which motivated a key aspect of

cultural Marxism, prejudice. They castigated and extrapolated prejudice not just against Jews, but also "blacks, social revolutionaries, homosexuals, and women who were revolting against what they viewed as the patriarchal family."[330]

Even as the Cold War started (1947), cultural Marxism "made powerful inroads" in America. "Leaders of the Frankfurt School were sent back to Germany by the American state department to 'reeducate' the former subjects of the Third Reich and to make them 'good anti-fascists,'" explained Professor Gottfried. Meanwhile, Frankfurt School pioneers like Eric Fromm became popular thanks to their books on psychological well-being (a Marxist ruse), which were all the rage through book-of-the-month clubs.[331]

Given the significant Marxist influence across our higher-education establishment, we can begin to appreciate why those institutions have long been a polarizing thorn in our national side. Recall that, in the 1960s, many campuses were very political because of the Vietnam War and their leftist faculties cheering from the sidelines. However, that polarization never really faded, and by the 1980s, and especially in the last decade, every leftist issue found a welcome mat across our higher education enterprise.

Unfortunately, higher education is also polarizing because it has become a pasture for retired politicians, especially the left-leaning variety. For decades, we've seen the top billets at numerous major universities assumed by rank politicians like Janet Napolitano, a former Arizona governor and President Obama's secretary of homeland security, who is at the helm of the University of California system, even though she had no experience in education. Purdue hired former Indiana Governor Mitch Daniels as president, and the University of North Carolina brought on Erskine Bowles, President Bill Clinton's former chief of staff. The list of politicians who have become top educators is long and storied.

You might anticipate that this metamorphosis of campus leadership doesn't stop with the top position at our leading education institutions.

Boards of regents are often filled with politicians, attorneys, bankers, and other well-heeled non-educators—too often bringing their liberal bias to the nation's leading universities.

No wonder that, long ago, these institutions lost sight of their purpose: preparing America's students to contribute to our society. However, today's woke-based college campus world is all about those who "win" and "lose," and far less about gaining experience and knowledge to contribute to a bright future.

Therefore, it shouldn't be surprising that, according to the Pew Research Center, only half of American adults believe higher education has a positive effect on the country, and four in ten (38 percent) believe it has a negative impact. Specifically, many Americans are skeptical about the way admission decisions are made by universities and the "extent to which free speech is constrained on college campuses." Predictably, these views are linked to partisanship, especially among Republicans and Independents who tend to see the negative effect of the experience.[332]

Conclusion

The American education establishment is a vital player for our future society. However, today's government educational institutions tend to be polarizing, thanks to their leftist agenda that, in the long term, fails the best interests of the country. Therefore, it's understandable why education at all levels has become such a polarizing issue for many Americans.

chapter eleven

Polarization of Investments and Workplaces

ESG is a scam.... It has been weaponized by
phony social justice warriors.[333]
—ELON MUSK, billionaire founder, CEO of SpaceX, Tesla, and Twitter

Progressives are trying to gain control of governments, financial markets, and ultimately all workplaces using their corrupt, polarizing strategy known as "ESG," an acronym standing for "environmental, social, and governance."

This chapter traces the origins of the divisive ESG by defining the term, identifying who is behind its use, and their agenda, exposing some of the dangers of the movement and summarizing some of the anti-ESG responses.

Origins and Definition of ESG

The craze associated with the ESG strategy started in 2004 with the meeting of representatives from twenty major financial institutions that, at the time, managed $6 trillion in assets. That group published a study with the United Nations' help, "Who Cares Wins: Connecting Financial Markets to a Changing World." That study focuses on recommendations that target different financial sectors, which address the issue of integrating drivers in the financial world. A year later in Zurich, Switzerland, numerous financial market actors (institutional investors, asset managers, research analysts, consultants, government regulators, and the United Nations) met to endorse the view that a for-profit firm's bottom line is affected by ESG factors other than products and services, and the conferees wanted to require all firms to embrace ESG guidance.[334]

Gavin Power, a senior officer with the UN's Global Compact Office of the Secretary-General, said of the outcome of the ESG conference:

A powerful and historic convergence is clearly under way, between the objectives and concerns of the United Nations and those of the private sector, including—crucially—the financial markets. Peace, security, and development go hand-in-hand with prosperity and growing markets. As finance, trade and investment deepen the connections between people and societies, companies and investors are increasingly faced with global— and potentially material—ESG issues. The Global Compact stands ready to support efforts to advance understanding and implementation in this rapidly evolving field.[335]

The announced idea behind ESG is that a company's bottom line, a view endorsed by the UN, is ultimately affected by factors other than their products. Therefore, firms with so-called socially conscious ESG practices are really advancing good practices for their business and the bottom line. *Forbes*, an American business magazine, explained the ESG rationale:

This might include how corporations respond to climate change, how good they are with water management, how effective their health and safety policies are in the protection against accidents, how they manage their supply chains, how they treat their workers and whether they have a corporate culture that builds trust and fosters innovation.[336]

Once narrowed down to its essence, ESG is about "sustainability" and "corporate responsibility"—old concepts. Those notions call for the efficient use of natural resources and efforts to reduce harm to our environment. They also include "doing the right thing," which includes ethical business practices and commitment to the "greater good," even before focusing on profit.[337]

Most people will agree with these factors. However, ESG advocates go much further. They claim business leaders must develop a strategy that integrates ESG risk management into their financial models, which really becomes a mandate for the entire ESG agenda. After all, ESG proponents claim a firm's performance is closely correlated to its share price and its ability to raise capital. Further, investors and even consumers ought to make their purchasing decisions based on ESG standards, according to supporters.

When drilling down on each of the components of ESG, one begins to discern the true scope of the initiative, which is quite expansive and arguably pretty sinister.

The "E" for "environmental" factors includes the firm's impact and risk management practices. ESG advocates want to know: Does the company limit its greenhouse gas emissions, and does it perform carbon monitoring? Is management a good steward of our natural resources like energy usage and water management? What is the company's plan against climate change, such as alleged byproducts like floods and fires?

The "S" is for "social," which refers to the firm's relationship with its stakeholders. How fair is the company with its employees in terms of wages and benefits, and what impact does the firm have for the communities in which it resides? Does the company promote diversity, equity, and inclusion—the political left's social justice mantra? This aspect of ESG extends outside the firm to include supply-chain partners, the impact on developing economies, and even labor standards.

Finally, the "G" is for corporate "governance," which measures how a firm is managed. This is beyond what a fiduciary might monitor before making an investment decision like the firm's internal controls, transparency, and accountability. The "G" also considers business ethics, tax transparency, as well as board composition and executive compensation.

Behind the ESG Veil

On the surface, ESG appears to be about responsible financial and manufacturing behavior. Advocates argue that using ESG as a basis for deciding on investing is a moral duty for those who care about good stewardship of natural resources and human rights. However, we must pull back the veil to find the true goal.

The primary problem with ESG is the assumption undergirding the theory. There is no validity for many of the proponents' ESG-related claims in rigorous empirical evidence. Rather, it reflects nothing more than the priorities and biases of the politically progressive interest groups promoting it; yet, like critical race theory in public schools, it has grabbed headlines and recruited government and private support.

Some political scientists lend their credentials to support ESG initiatives. However, in doing so, they stand on thin ice, because, for the most part, there is "little statistically significant and repeatable experimental rejection of carefully formulated hypotheses," argues a 2022 article in *Trends*, an e-magazine backed by a network of business experts, inside information, privately distributed reports, speeches, and more.[338]

The "science" behind ESG is little more than "scientism," a term that refers to the "beliefs and opinions" of some scientists, claims *Trends*.

However, real science is based on the scientific method, and much of the foundation for ESG fails that metric. Yet, the push for ESG across the world is very important for us to understand, because what its proponents seek will have enduring policy implications.[339]

The *Trends* article eviscerates the foundation of ESG by explaining that we saw the same type of misguided "scientism" in the nineteenth century. People at that time relied on the consensus of noted "scientists" who insisted on the validity of what are now completely debunked theories. Specifically, according to *Trends*, those nineteenth-century, credentialed scientists dared anyone to refute their view that "the universe has always existed;" "like sound, light is transmitted via a universal medium called the ether;" and "living cells are simple packages of liquid called protoplasm."[340]

We face the same situation today with ESG. Even though there is sketchy empirical science, if any, behind much of the strategy, proponents have gained credibility from a gullible public.[341]

Such blind acceptance of ESG scientists' advocacy is especially dangerous because much of that promotion is pushed by social media—and a lot of it is truly fake news. Consider the following illustration of the distorted ESG scores for firms in the Russian Federation.

A study by Jurian Hendrikse at the Tilburg School of Economics and Management and published by the Harvard Law School Forum on Corporate Governance indicates that ESG ratings often don't deliver on their promise. Specifically, that study focused on companies with operations inside Russia, a country known for disregarding ESG. Logically, then, if the ESG ratings are reliable, a Russian company ought to have a lower score than ESG-compliant firms, say, in Europe.[342]

The Tilburg study compared average ESG scores for firms with significant Russian activities, a country well known for corruption, human-rights abuses, and a terrible environmental record. Yet those firms earned scores of 78 out of 100 compared to other similar-sized, nonfinancial European companies that just earned a score of 64. Higher ESG scores are supposed to reflect more socially responsible corporate behavior.

What "scientists" awarded Russian firms high scores while ignoring fla-grant corruption, human-rights abuses, and significant pollution?[343]

Long ago, we were warned about this type of threat from "scientism." Peter Drucker (1909–2005), a management consultant and author, and Alvin Toffler (1928–2016), a futurist and businessman, according to *Trends*, said the "control of knowledge is the primary source of power in the digital era." Therefore, the knowledge existing on social media platforms like Google, Facebook, and TikTok work behind the scenes to push "information" that complies with their technocratic overlords, the powerful ESG-promoting elite. Truth, after all, is relative, and it's an inconvenience for those who seek control.[344]

We certainly saw evidence of this regarding Elon Musk's purchase of the social media platform Twitter for $44 billion. After taking over the firm, the billionaire and CEO of Tesla released inside documents that demonstrated rank malpractice and government collusion by Twitter regarding the 2020 presidential election and, more specifically, the cover-up of the explosive Hunter Biden laptop story. Therefore, we should be equally suspicious of the proponents pushing ESG as a panacea for private firms, because they, too, can manipulate both social media and mainstream outlets with fake facts to fit their agenda to sway the public.[345]

We've seen how some ESG proponents push their "fake science" on social media platforms like Twitter. However, perhaps more disturbing, some advocates of the idea successfully leverage government bureaucra-cies to advance ESG-favoring regulations, as demonstrated in the follow-ing pages. Further, proponents also recruit like-minded subject-matter experts in the name of "science" to advance ESG policies that ultimately trample on our civil liberties and truth.[346]

We saw that kind of "science" or "scientism" on full display dur-ing the COVID-19 pandemic when some scientists and health offi-cials made assertions about the virus that were not based on empirical science. At best, those officials were guessing based on experience—"scientism"—and the result was tragic for many older Americans, millions of people who lost their jobs, and children who lost years of important education.

The same "scientism" and fake news appears to be supporting ESG, which is tethered to four ideological constructs that are popular among the powerful progressive elite, according to *Trends*. Specifically, those progressives seek a world defined by globalism, socialism, social justice, and environmentalism.

Globalism is a debunked idea that argues we shouldn't have national borders, and that all cultures are inherently valid, a view embraced by many of the so-called elite in academia but demonstrably false for anyone with experience across this world. Globalism's archnemesis is nationalism, which explains why ESG proponents viscerally hate former President Trump's campaign slogan, "Make America Great Again," a clear call for renewing America's nationalism and not depending on other nations like communist China for key products like antibiotics. At present, the US manufactures virtually no antibiotics. Rather, China controls roughly 90 percent of the global supply of inputs required to make the generic antibiotics that treat ailments like bronchitis and pneumonia, and life-threatening illnesses like sepsis.[347]

Socialism is the dream of eighteenth-century Karl Marx to remove all class distinctions, which has never succeeded in the history of man from the former Soviet Union, Cuba, North Korea, and China, which, to survive, inserted capitalist practices in its economy. Unfortunately, a segment of naïve politicians and a plurality (42 percent) of our population—mostly youth educated in leftist, mostly public institutions view the choice with a bankrupt and historically inept simplistic slogan: "Capitalism bad, socialism good."[348]

Social justice, aka "wokism," is quite the rage among leftist elite, an issue within our public education establishment that's now making inroads into our workplaces. Wokism's advocates tap into our consciences to shame traditional views by calling for moral relativism in our decision-making, anti-racism programs, support for LGBTIQ (homosexual) identities, and secular humanism. They use government to promote collective guilt through regulation, and insist that socially responsible, for-profit companies must share this view and foster the same within their workforce.

Radical environmentalism is the mostly pseudo-scientific belief that humans are destroying the earth because of our use of carbon-emitting fossil fuels. Some elite environmentalists, like former Vice President Al Gore, push their so-called Green New Deal mantra, acting like violence-threatening terrorists forcing on corporations and government alike insane alternatives to fossil fuels, such as battery-operated electric cars, windmills, and solar panels—all in the name of saving the planet.

Who Is behind the ESG Agenda?

ESG has infiltrated many aspects of American life, which is why it's critical to become aware of the political nature of this strategy. Unfortunately, a growing number of retirement-fund companies like BlackRock Inc., the world's largest asset manager, with $10 trillion under management, often uses hardworking Americans' savings to pursue managements' ESG interests with little regard for their duty to protect investor aims.

These management firms invest our retirement savings in so-called ESG-compliant firms, even though some of those companies don't necessarily protect the climate, promote social equality, or exercise good corporate governance. No, they just adopt the guidelines because of outside pressure, which raises the question: What are the ESG proponents really after?

The ESG proponents are after control—and, ultimately, they use our investment funds with the help of government's administration/ deep state via regulations to advance their agenda and with little to no accountability.

Understand that ESG is truly an anti-free market strategy, according to Our Money, Our Values (OMOV), an anti-ESG nonprofit organization. For example, according to OMOV, ESG promoters attack our energy independence, small businesses, and even family farms while seeking to ban clean coal mining in West Virginia and oil drilling in Texas. They even use the strong arm of big government to mandate abortion on demand and attack our Second Amendment rights.

Let's drill down a bit further to consider each of the factors in ESG, and how they are abused.

Much of the objection to pro-ESG efforts is based on the "E" component, the environment. Specifically, ESG-embracing, large-asset companies pledge to invest our assets only in firms that promote carbon-neutral initiatives, which means they deny investments in nuclear energy and fossil fuel-driven energy enterprises. However, they never explain why going "cold turkey" on these available sources of cheap energy now is in our best interests. After all, solar and windmill-produced energy are many years, at best, from addressing our true needs and becoming cost-effective.[349]

Meanwhile, as we've seen in recent years, so-called green energy has a bankrupt track record. Remember solar panel start-up Solyndra that collected $535 million in US government-backed loans from Obama's 2009 stimulus bill—the American Recovery and Reinvestment Act (ARRA)? Solyndra misled the US Department of Energy in its application, and a couple of years after receiving the funds, it filed for bankruptcy, laid off its employees, and shuttered operations.[350]

Abound Solar, a solar cell start-up firm, received $401 million in US federal government-backed loans from the Department of Energy in 2010 to manufacture in Colorado and India. By June 2012, the firm filed for bankruptcy, leaving 405 people unemployed, and it abandoned its production facilities. Then the taxpayers had to clean up after the venture at the cost of an additional $3.7 million.[351]

The list of government-endorsed green energy projects is long and includes mostly losers. Evidently, the government does a poor job of picking winners in the marketplace, because it seldom properly vets the firms and then fails to audit performance. Besides, the underlying "science" is, at best, suspect.

The "S" in ESG, the "social" factor, is used to grade firms based on how they comply with progressive priorities, often established by unelected government administrators or non-government interest groups. For example, these priorities often use their government-supported platforms to attack our First (speech and religion) and Second (bear arms) Amendment rights.[352]

The social aspect is especially egregious for Americans concerned about religious liberty. ESG advocates often promote abortion on demand and the latest expressions of the homosexual community on issues like transgenderism and "gay" marriage. Unfortunately, this push is having considerable success with large corporations like Starbucks and Walmart, which have already pledged to pay for employee abortions and/or their travel to obtain the procedure. As a result, those firms score higher on ESG, which makes them eligible for favorable financial treatment from asset-management firms and now from big government.[353]

ESG proponents also pressure firms to create diversity, equity, and inclusion (DEI) policies, which results in wokish "continuing education" programs for all employees, such as indoctrination on radical issues like critical race theory and transgenderism. Even small businesses aren't immune to the DEI push, because they work with larger ESG-compliant companies that mandate virtue signaling in order to do business with them.[354]

Citizens concerned about their Second Amendment rights need to consider the impact of the social factor as well. Specifically, arms and ammunition manufacturers are often financially disadvantaged when retail companies like DICK'S Sporting Goods pull guns and ammunition off their shelves because of "social" mandates—and, of course, investors in those firms lose the financial profit associated with such sales.[355]

The "G" aspect of ESG has to do with decisions such as compliant asset-management firms using our money to force obedience among private firms. Besides, big government is more often than not part of the ESG advocacy campaign. Specifically, the Biden administration and many within the Democratic Party's establishment join the asset-management firms to push ESG. For example, in 2022, the Biden administration unleashed the Securities and Exchange Commission (SEC), an independent federal regulatory agency that allegedly protects investors, to mandate ESG disclosures, particularly around climate risks, and pushing for companies to monitor and then report their ESG metrics. Some of these initiatives will be enforced by regulation and executive order and others by acts of Congress.[356]

Biden's Department of Labor (DOL) uses regulatory authority to push ESG as well. In late 2022, the DOL issued a new rule "that allows retirement plan fiduciaries to consider climate change and other ESG factors when they select retirement investments and exercise shareholder rights, such as proxy voting."[357]

This change reverses two Trump-era rules, which Biden's DOL said "unnecessarily restrained fiduciaries' ability to weigh environmental, social, and governance factors when choosing investments, even when those factors would benefit plan participants financially." Thus, Biden is greenlighting politically driven asset managers to invest in firms aligned with the administration's ESG agenda, and, by association, to deny capital to companies like fossil fuel producers while at the same time pushing investment in wind- and solar-power developers.[358]

This regulation also protects progressive fiduciaries that invest in ESG and allows them to put our retirement savings into ESG-favoring funds without our knowledge and/or consent.

Unfortunately, on March 20, 2023, President Biden issued his first veto, rejecting a bipartisan measure to block the Labor Department's rule that advances "woke" ESG policy that will harm retirees' pocket books. Mr. Biden claimed to the contrary that striking down Congress' resolution "made sense" because it would "put at risk the retirement savings of individuals across the country."[359]

House Speaker Kevin McCarthy (R-CA) responded to Biden's veto with a statement: "President Biden's veto is against a bipartisan bill that protects retirement savings from political interference."

He continued:

It is clear that President Biden wants Wall Street to use your hard-earned money not to grow your savings, but to fund a far-left political agenda. That will hurt seniors and workers, especially after President Biden's reckless spending caused record inflation and rapid interest rate hikes.[360]

No Appreciable Financial Benefits

ESG proponents claim we can make a profit while transforming our world to comply with their guidelines. At this point, that doesn't appear to be true.

A Bloomberg report found that eight of ten of the largest ESG funds by total assets held in 2022 underperformed the benchmark Standard & Poor's 500, a barometer of the overall stock market's performance. That's the cost of being ESG woke. Even a Harvard Law School forum on corporate governance on ESG fund performance found no support for progressive claims that investing in "social good" benefits the investor's bottom line. At best, ESG financial-related performance is "uncertain," claimed the Harvard study.[361]

It may be true that some investors with asset-management firms don't mind sacrificing financial returns for better ESG performance. However, it appears that those funds don't even deliver better ESG performance, either.

In early 2023, roughly $2.7 trillion was invested in "sustainable" funds that publicly set ESG objectives. Many of those funds are doing poorly, according to a study in the *Journal of Finance*. That paper considered the American financial services firm Morningstar Inc.'s sustainability ratings of more than twenty thousand mutual funds representing over $1 trillion in savings, but none of the high sustainability funds outperformed the lowest-rated funds.[362]

A joint study by researchers at Columbia University and the London School of Economics considered ESG records for 147 ESG-compliant fund portfolios as opposed to 2,428 US firms with non-ESG portfolios. They found that the ESG portfolios performed worse for both labor and environmental rules. The same outcome is true when comparing US ESG-compliant firms with non-ESG companies in Europe. Specifically, the nongovernment and nonprofit European Corporate Governance Institute conducted a similar comparison, between 684 US institutional investors that signed the United Nation's Principles of Responsible Investment (PRI), an ESG initiative, with 6,481 institutional investors that did not sign the PRI. They detected no improvement in the ESG scores of companies with ESG ratings, and their financial returns were lower, and risk was higher for the ESG-compliant firms.[363]

Why are ESG firms doing so poorly? One explanation is the ESG guidelines are redundant. In other words, in competitive markets, managers try to maximize share value, and the responsible thing is to pay attention to the ESG-related issues. Therefore, setting artificial ESG targets may distort managements' decision-making.

Likely, a better explanation of poor performance by ESG firms is they are using the mandate as an excuse for poor business performance. Ryan Flugum with the University of Northern Iowa and Matthew Southern of the University of South Carolina explained in their 2022 research paper, "Stakeholder Value: A Convenient Excuse for Underperforming Managers," that "when managers underperformed the earnings expectations (set by analysts following their company), they often publicly talked about their focus on ESG, according to a 2022 article in the Harvard Business Review."[364]

Pushback against ESG

There is a growing anti-ESG movement. In 2022, Elon Musk called it a "scam," and said, "It has been weaponized by phony social justice warriors." Evidently, Musk was upset that Tesla, his electric-car company, had been dropped from a Standard and Poor's 500, or S&P's ESG

index. However, his statement reflects what some conservative politicians describe as "woke capitalism."[365]

Former Vice President Mike Pence is fighting the pro-ESG forces as
well. In 2022, Mr. Pence attacked the Biden administration for pushing
"capricious new ESG regulations that allow left-wing radicals to destroy
American energy producers from within."[366]

The biggest pushback against ESG comes from Republican-domi-
nated states that target ESG with policies to counter "woke capitalism."
Specifically, these states pass policies to deny investment managers access
to retirement funds if they use ESG-related strategies and at the same
time refuse to invest in fossil fuel and firearms firms or in companies that
fail to embrace social-justice issues.[367]

Some state governments have already pulled billions in retirement
funds out of Wall Street asset-management corporations like BlackRock
Inc. and Vanguard, because those companies are giving their clients poor
returns while bowing to left-wing ESG pressure. In fact, Texas legislators passed a law that prohibits that state's agencies from investing or
doing business with firms that "boycott" fossil fuel firms by "taking any
action…intended to penalize, inflict economic harm on, or limit commercial relations" with the entities.[368]

Everyday taxpayers are hurt by the ESG dictates, because when state-
invested ESG funds lose, the taxpayers often have to backfill the void.
That explains why Florida Governor Ron DeSantis is pushing back
against politicized firms like BlackRock. "If Larry [Fink, the chief executive officer of BlackRock] or his friends on Wall Street, want to change
the world—run for office. Start a non-profit. Donate to the causes you
care about," says Florida's chief financial officer Jimmy Patronis. However, don't use Florida's retirement funds for "social engineering."[369]

The ESG push isn't just about return on investment for retirement accounts. Some state officials write the big credit-rating agencies
to caution them against using ESG factors in their credit scoring. For
example, S&P's global ratings began including ESG factors in their
credit ratings in March 2022. That pro-ESG decision caught the atten-

tion of Kentucky State Treasurer Allison Ball, who wrote that the new factors unfairly politicize credit ratings and put in place subjective judgments that should be solely based on financial factors. Specifically, she stated: "It creates a dangerous framework for state borrowing mechanisms, whereby state creditworthiness will fluctuate wildly based on ever-changing political tides."[370]

Ms. Ball also supported legislation that requires financial companies that do business with Kentucky to cease boycotts of the fossil fuel industry. Failing to do that will lead to the state divesting all public investments from any offending firm.[371]

Kentucky's treasurer also told the S&P that the new ratings system hurts Kentucky's economy, which is reliant on fossil fuels:

A reduction in coal, oil, and gas production would cause increased unemployment, higher fuel costs, and a decrease in overall tax revenue, thereby negatively impacting Kentucky's overall creditworthiness and causing undue hardship and suffering for the people of this state.[372]

West Virginia barred major financial institutions like BlackRock from new state business because they boycotted the fossil fuel industry. West Virginia State Treasurer Riley Moore said his state took this action after reviewing policies of firms that limit "commercial relations with energy companies engaged in certain coal mining."[373]

Finally, author Michael Shellenberger, who focuses his writing on the intersection of politics and climate change, argues that progressivism is linked to many of society's ills, such as homelessness, drug addiction, and mental illness. Mr. Shellenberger told Fox News that President Biden's green energy push is an "environmental nightmare" and called on the administration to restore our energy independence. He explained the negative impacts of renewables on the environment and economy.

Mr. Shellenberger described the ESG push on climate as an "environmental nightmare." He continued:

It's one of the biggest scams of maybe the last 50 years, the idea that renewables are good for the environment. They're absolutely terrible for the environment. Solar and wind require three to four times as much land to make the same amount of electricity as natural gas or a nuclear power plant. You just read the huge quantities of materials and mining that's required for solar, wind, electric cars. The problem is the energy is too diluted from sunlight and wind. It's not energy-dense enough. So, you have to grind up all of this nature, all the natural environment to be able to produce sufficient amounts of energy. It's not going to happen. Right now, about 10% of minerals on earth are used for energy. If you go to renewables, it's going to go up to 50%. That is inflationary. That is going to cause inflation in two ways by making the energy itself more expensive, and then also by making electricity in particular more expensive because of the unreliable nature of sunlight and wind.[374]

Conclusion

Progressives are pushing their nightmarish ESG agenda on the world, which is based on some corrupted "scientists" and mostly fairytale wishes backed by little empirical data. This radical agenda costs millions of citizens good returns on their retirement accounts, turns private companies into tools of the radical left, undermines the critical fossil-fuel industry, robs us of our civil liberties, and ultimately grants more control to big government.

ESG is all about division, which grants control to the powerful few and is a tool in the hands of Satan, who uses it to advance his agenda.

chapter twelve

Media's Polarization of Our Culture

> If people in the media cannot decide whether they are in the business of reporting news or manufacturing propaganda, it is all the more important that the public understand that difference, and choose their news sources accordingly.[375]
> —THOMAS SOWELL (1930), author, economist, and political commentator

Much of the polarization in America's culture can be laid at the feet of the media, and most people recognize that reality. Unfortunately, the Biden administration and its Democratic Party allies weaponized many of those outlets to divide us with the intent of manipulating the country to serve their crass interests.

We begin this chapter by acknowledging the media's role in polarizing the American people along ideological and, by association, issue lines. We've seen similar efforts in history that didn't end well. In fact, today, our media-saturated culture is once again being used by ideologues and big government alike to push a mostly radical, anti-truth agenda. I'll conclude the chapter with three case studies to demonstrate the media's danger: one on the Iraq War; another on the abuse of social media platforms to divide us; and a third, which addresses the divisiveness associated with the government's role in the COVID-19 pandemic.

Media's Role in Polarizing America

The Information Age demonstrates the miracle of technology, which allows a large swath of the world's population to know in an instant about breaking news. It is also a dangerous medium in the wrong hands—the hands of those who can distort the truth and lead people to do some rather unconscionable deeds. No wonder most Americans long ago lost confidence in traditional (mainstream) media and began seeking alternatives.

A late 2022 survey of Americans found less than a third (32 percent) trust the mass media "to report the news fully, accurately and fairly," according to Gallup polling. In just one year (2021 to 2022), the level of Americans trusting the media sank 8 percentage points.[376]

It wasn't that long ago (1976) when almost three in four Americans (72 percent) trusted investigative journalism regarding breaking news at the time, such as the Vietnam War and the Watergate scandal. That's no longer the case.[377]

Trust in the media started a serious nosedive among the American public with the 2016 US presidential election. At the time, many conservatives claimed the Democratic Party candidate for president, Hillary Clinton, received overly positive media attention compared to the mostly negative reporting granted Republican candidate Donald Trump. Of course, following that election, the mainstream media didn't let up on Mr. Trump; in fact, it launched a host of politically motivated scandals: Russiagate; the proven fake Steele dossier; and, more recently, the COVID-19 fiasco. Each media-pushed campaign of misinformation/fake news demonstrated traditional media's growing unreliability and bias. It's little wonder that, today, Republicans say their trust in media is at the lowest confidence level in twenty years (18 percent), according to Gallup.[378]

A paper published by the Pardee School of Global Studies at Boston University echoes the view that "an essential driver of this [America's widespread] polarization is the media, particularly cable news and social media." The author of that 2022 paper, Flavia Roscini, argues: "Traditional and social media channels have exacerbated political polarization by spreading disinformation to their viewers, posing a threat to American democracy." However, Ms. Roscini fails to identify the appropriate authority to decide what is and isn't disinformation.[379]

The partisan media divide became especially pronounced among the cable news networks, says Ms. Roscini. She cites Margaret Sullivan, the former media columnist for the *Washington Post*, who supports Ms. Roscini's view about cable channels. Ms. Sullivan wrote that Fox News and MSNBC are the "birthing centers for polarizing rhetoric." That may be true and a reflection of the transformation of the cable news business, which depends on viewer ratings to drive advertisement income. So, it is perhaps also understandable why cable networks tend to blur the lines between news/fact-based reporting and entertainment.[380]

The divisive tone evidenced by most cable news outlets, according to Ms. Roscini, is the appeal for viewers of both the ideological left and right. Further, this type of programming tends to harden polarization, because "the more political media one consumes, the more warped [off-balanced] their perspective of the other side becomes," a view expressed by Tom Jones, a senior media writer with the Florida-based Poynter Institute for Media Studies, a nonprofit journalism school and research organization supported in part by Facebook and a federal government grant.[381]

Meanwhile, just as traditional media like cable news channels morphed into an ideological mouthpiece, social media gained influence and became perhaps a bigger contributor to polarization than mainstream outlets. Why? Social media's technology differs from traditional media, because it provides an attractive interactive tool: two-way communications for those using a platform capable of reaching a global audience. The frequent criticism laid at the feet of social media is accuracy and reliability of the information, which often earns the label "fake news," especially when it comes to elections. However, the popularity of social media is significant and growing.

A July 2022 report by Datareportal indicates that more than half (59 percent) of the world uses social media, an estimated 4.7 billion people. That figure grew a whopping 227 million new users in the twelve-month period ending July 2022. Further, the average daily time spent by an individual on a social media platform is two hours and twenty-nine minutes.[382]

Thus, it's clear that the advent of cable news, social media, and the pervasive Internet, which is open to all opinions except where it is censored like in communist China, radically altered the modern world and continues to significantly contribute to polarization.

Marxists Using Media to Garner Control

The power of media in the wrong hands can be incredibly dangerous. Communists have historically seen media outlets as a tool to manipulate entire societies. That view reflects the writing of nineteenth-century communists Karl Marx and Frederick Engels in their book *Rules of the Communist League*, which calls for "revolutionary energy and zeal in propaganda." They referred to media as the "party battlefield," "political center," and a "tool for public opinion."[383]

A disciple of Marx and Engel was Vladimir Lenin (1870–1924), the founder of the former Soviet Union, who used mass media to promote Marxism leading up to the 1917 Russian Revolution. After toppling the tsar from power, Lenin used the state's media outlets for political indoctrination inside Russia and for promoting his ideas abroad.[384]

Years later, in Moscow, former Soviet Prime Minister Vyacheslav

Molotov explained that the Soviets used media outlets overseas to advance their political agenda among non-communists:

> Who reads the communist papers? Only a few people who are already communists. We don't need to propagandize them.... We have to influence non-communists if we want to make them communists or if we want to fool them. So, we have to try to infiltrate in the big press.[385]

The Chinese Communist Party (CCP) has long used mass-media outlets as a tool to manipulate its citizens as well as those outside China. Before Mao Zedong took the reins of the People's Republic of China in 1949, he expressed a simple media principle: the CCP newspaper "has to carry through the party's viewpoints and understandings in all articles, every essay, every news report, and every newsletter."[386]

Once Mao took over the country, he imposed strict control over Chinese media. The CCP retains rigid control over all Chinese mass media even today; the relationship is best described with the Chinese phrase: "I [media] am the Party's dog, sitting by the Party's door. I'll bite whomever the Party tells me to bite and however many times I am told."[387]

Marxists brought their radical ideas to America by infiltrating our media between the two World Wars. Specifically, the Frankfurt School Marxists immigrated to the US and then settled into our mainstream media—especially our film industry in California.

I wrote in *Give Me Liberty, Not Marxism.*[388]

> Willi Münzenberg, one of the Frankfurt School faculty that [American progressive educator] John Dewey brought to America in the 1930s, introduced his communist ideology in Hollywood by saying his goal was to make "the West so corrupt; it stinks. We're going to rock them from within, and we're going to teach immorality to the young people. We're going to try to push pornography and we're going to try to increase alcoholism."[389]

Mr. Münzenberg found fertile ground in California's Beverly Hills to realize his goal of corrupting America. He joined other Marxists in Hollywood, where they followed much the same script outlined by Lenin and Stalin in Soviet Russia. They used the entertainment business to spread their ideology. That cabal of communists included pro-Soviet artists like Yip Harburg, a songwriter best known for his work on the Wizard of Oz. Harburg and other communists used their talents to psychologically manipulate the gullible American population by producing films that contained favorable portrayals of communism and socialist ideals, while denigrating capitalism and American morality.[390]

During the pre-World War II era, Soviet spies also worked their way into prestigious American media outlets like *Time Magazine*. Whittaker Chambers, the publication's former editor (1939–1948), was a Soviet spy, as detailed in his book *Witness*. Mr. Chambers went on to become the editor at *National Review* and turned on his previous allegiance to the Soviet Union.[391]

Also, in *Give Me Liberty, Not Marxism*:[392]

The broader problem of Marxist infiltration was chronicled in a novel. Scottish-born novelist Helen MacInnes wrote twenty-one novels describing the struggle against totalitarianism, first at the hands of Nazi Germany prior to and during the Second World War, and later, after the war, she turned her attention to the Russian communists and their infiltration of America's media.[393]

Ms. MacInnes wrote in her 1951 novel, *Neither Five nor Three*, a description "of the methods the left used to take almost complete control of a once-noble institution: the American media." American David Jenkins, photographer and writer, summarized Ms. MacInnes' view on how Marxists took over

America's media: "By undermining, discrediting, and marginalizing honest reporters, writers, and editors, the left gradually replaced them with people who would oh-so-subtly (and sometimes not so subtly) parrot the [communist] Party line."[394]

Media and Government Collaborate

In recent years, left-wing media outlets created an initiative to control the narrative on presidential elections, including the 2020 election between President Trump and then-former Vice President Joe Biden. That narrative control effort is known as the "Trusted News Initiative" (TNI), which was launched by the government-controlled United Kingdom's British Broadcasting Network (BBC) in 2019.

Jessica Cecil, the director for the TNI, explained in 2020 how big tech collaborated with most mainstream media outlets to "alert each other to the most dangerous false stories, and stop them spreading fast across the Internet, preventing them from doing real world harm."[395]

Ms. Cecil wrote:

A year ago the BBC convened partners across the world in an urgent challenge: at times of highest jeopardy, when elections or lives are at stake, we asked, is there a way that the world's biggest tech platforms—from Google, YouTube, Facebook and Instagram to Twitter and Microsoft and major news organisations [British spelling] and others—from the European Broadcasting Union, the Wall Street Journal and The Hindu to Reuters, AFP, The Financial Times, CBC/Radio-Canada, First Draft, The Reuters Institute for the Study of Journalism - can alert each other to the most dangerous false stories, and stop them spreading fast across the internet, preventing them from doing real world harm?[396]

Ms. Cecil explained how the TNI went on to control the narrative on elections:

> We have been sharing alerts over COVID-19, and before that, over falsities which posed a threat to democratic integrity during the UK and Taiwan Elections. And now we are sharing alerts over the most serious disinformation in two very different elections—in the US and in Myanmar. And because different news organisations are most relevant in different regions, we are working with a wide and expanding group of publishers. In the US we are also working with the Washington Post, AP and the LA Times.[397]

The *New York Times* was a TNI partner, which claims the initiative was devised as "a shared early warning system of rapid alerts to combat the spread of disinformation during the upcoming U.S. presidential election." However, it's not clear who, if anyone, appointed the *New York Times* and the other TNI partners to be the arbiter of so-called fake news, much less of the standards applied.[398]

Ultimately, the real purpose of TNI was to control global information and protect the interests of the big media conglomerates. Understand that even though there are thousands of mainstream television channels, they are mostly owned by just six companies: Time Warner, Viacom, CBS, Disney, National Amusements, and News Corporation. We have the 1996 Telecommunications Act to thank for that consolidation. With only six entities governing most broadcast television, it is much easier to control the narrative on any issue.[399]

Thus, TNI was created based on the notion that media conglomerates favored preventing foreign interference in the 2020 US elections, especially given the 2016 storied "foreign collusion and interference." So, the 2019 TNI project sounded like a noble idea at the time, but it soon became something quite different.

TNI's intent has always been to neutralize information mainstream media overlords don't want shared. It also led to the introduction of the so-called fact checkers, a now widespread effort meant to contradict information the TNI conglomerate wants you to ignore. That included denying even expert opinions that dared to contradict the mainstream view. Thus, the term "doxed" emerged, a term that meant you were publicly identified, or your private information was published as a form of revenge by a social media platform like Facebook for being a disinformation spreader, even if the information was true but didn't match the approved narrative.

TNI was joined by the Google News Initiative (GNI), a $300 million funding commitment to ensure advertisers don't push "false or misleading news." Evidently, early in the COVID-19 pandemic, TNI and GNI collaborated on editorial standardization to control the narrative on the pandemic. Those controls include four standards:

- The pandemic threatens the survival of all humanity.
- There is no therapy to cure the sick.
- It is necessary to confine the whole population, and
- The delivery will come only from a vaccine.[400]

Dr. Robert Malone, an American physician and biochemist, wrote in a Substack article, "Propaganda, Corporatism and the Hidden Global Coup," that "TNI uses advocacy journalism and journals to promote their causes. The Trusted News Initiative is more than this though; if you go back to Hitler's basic principles, the members of the TNI are using these core principles to control the public." Specifically, Hitler's basic principles were:

- Avoid abstract ideas—appeal to the emotions
- Constantly repeat just a few ideas. Use stereotyped phrases
- Give only one side of the argument
- Continuously criticize your opponents
- Pick out one special "enemy" for special vilification.[401]

As if TNI and GNI weren't enough, the Biden administration tried to pile on the message—control the bandwagon by creating within the US Department of Homeland Security a bizarre organization dubbed a "Disinformation Governance Board" to combat what they labeled as "misinformation." For those unfamiliar with George Orwell's book *1984*, Orwell wrote about a "ministry of truth." The main role of that fictitious ministry was to rewrite history to correspond with the party's claims. Members of the ministry revised and recreated journals, articles, and periodicals by relying on approved government propaganda.

Rewriting "history" to comport with a political agenda isn't that unusual today. In 2022, the Chinese Communist Party (CCP) put this approach on full display. Prior to the 20th Party Congress in October 2022, the CCP amended the party constitution and rewrote the party's history to enshrine Mr. Xi as the "core" leader and reinforce his iron grip on power. The CCP, twice before Mr. Xi, rewrote party history to fit their changed agenda and to usher in new leaders.[402]

The fact that the Biden administration has so far failed to create a ministry of truth is surprising. Perhaps the administration hasn't succeeded because there are still enough people who recognize what they are doing; therefore, opponents of this dangerous idea are working to stop that initiative. Further, like TNI and GNI, there is an element among our political and otherwise powerful elite who intend to control public information, not unlike what the CCP and the Nazis before them did. The media is their key weapon to garner and maintain control.

Three Cases of Media Manipulation of the Public

The following three case studies illustrate the power of media and the role government often uses to harness our media when public approval is part of their effort or to polarize us. The first case is very personal, and the second and third are still works in progress.

Justifying the Go-to-War Decision in Iraq

I was at the center of the Bush administration's efforts to manipulate the public regarding the decision to go to war in Iraq. I share this personal perspective to demonstrate how government and big media may collaborate, or not, to influence public opinion.

In October 2002, I received an official letter from then-Secretary of Defense Donald Rumsfeld inviting me to a meeting at the Pentagon to review the situation regarding Iraq.

Leading up to that point, I frequently provided news analysis for cable networks, as well as for other broadcast and print news outlets. Meanwhile, by late 2002, the Bush administration began making the public case that Iraq's Saddam Hussein was a threat to American interests, and on numerous occasions, I appeared on cable networks to address that situation.

I accepted Mr. Rumsfeld's invitation and, on the appointed day—October 30, 2002—I was among perhaps fifteen other cable-network retired military analysts seated opposite Secretary Rumsfeld, who was flanked by the Chairman of the Joint Chiefs of Staff, General Richard Myers, and other Pentagon notables.

That initial meeting opened the door to many briefings and opportunities over the next few years to understand the Bush administration's intentions regarding Iraq. And, once the war started, those meetings and even two trips to the war zone continued.

The entire group of military analysts invited to those Pentagon meetings was rather large; one estimate indicated seventy-five personnel were involved in what came to be known as the Pentagon's "military analysts" program. The *New York Times* explained the initial idea for the Bush administration was to recruit "key influentials" to help sell the public on "a possible Iraq invasion."[403]

"Internal Pentagon documents repeatedly refer to the military analysts as 'message force multipliers' or 'surrogates' who could be counted on to deliver administration 'themes and messages' to millions of Americans 'in the form of their own opinions'," wrote David Barstow, a reporter with the *New York Times* who won a Pulitzer Prize for his reporting on the topic.[404]

The Bush Pentagon, according to Barstow, made a strategic decision in 2002 to make the analysts the "main focus of the administration's public relations push to construct a case for war."[405]

One of our initial Pentagon meetings was with then-assistant Secretary of Defense for Public Affairs Victoria Clarke. A group of us met in her office to listen to Iraq-related briefings and to ask questions about the threat and US military plans. None of the briefings were labeled "classified," however.

Over the months leading up to the Iraq war, I frequently called a Pentagon point of contact identified by Ms. Clarke and quickly got fact sheets, what some call "talking points," about the latest-breaking news on the war. Those documents were generally helpful as background when preparing for media interviews. Of course, just reading the Pentagon's official take on a particular story naturally colored my understanding, but I never relied on that single source for interview preparation. Further, I was often quite skeptical about the information the Pentagon provided the analysts. Let me illustrate.

In the fall of 2002, I became acquainted with a former Iraqi general living in the United States, a man brought here allegedly by our intelligence community. Lieutenant General Fawzi al-Shammari at the time was the founder of the Iraqi Officers' Movement, which tried to prevent the US from going to war with Iraq. On a number of occasions, Fawzi helped me better understand that Mideastern country, especially its dictator, Saddam Hussein. Further, Fawzi maintained contact with friends in the Iraqi army who insisted that the country no longer possessed weapons of mass destruction (WMD).

General Fawzi's accounts about Iraqi WMD dramatically disagreed with what the Bush Pentagon kept insisting: that Hussein had a massive arsenal of WMD. On multiple occasions, I asked senior Pentagon officials, including Secretary Rumsfeld, about the administration's public claims about the WMD threat and was always assured the threat was real.

A month prior to our invasion of Iraq, I arranged for General Fawzi to meet with an official in our intelligence community to outline his contradictory information about the WMD threat. Unfortunately, at that point, it was too late, because a decision was made, and the Bush administration took us to war on March 20, 2003.

Years later, Mr. Barstow's article accurately reflected my concern about the decision to invade Iraq. The *New York Times* article states:

> Maginnis, a retired army lieutenant colonel who...attended the same [Iraq pre-invasion] briefing and recalled feeling "very disappointed" after being shown satellite photographs purporting to show bunkers associated with a hidden weapons program. Mr. Maginnis said he concluded that the analysts were being "manipulated" to convey a false sense of certainty about the evidence of the weapons.[406]

My conclusion from participating in the Pentagon's program is that the Bush administration in fact used us to present their message to manipulate—divide—the public. They used our credibility as military experts to communicate to the American people their justification for the Iraq War and then to continue that undertaking that ultimately cost 4,487 service member lives, with another 32,000 wounded in action. The challenge for me at the time was always to discern truth from the administration's spin and then decide on just what to communicate in my interviews.

Clearly, the Bush administration's strategy worked; we carried their water, to a certain extent. They gained the American public's support to go to war, albeit based on no credible evidence about WMD. Then, after the invasion, sentiment in America for the war shifted, as did many of the analysts' opinions about the ongoing sacrifice.

The record of the go-to-war effort is well documented. The Department of Defense Inspector General conducted a thorough investigation, and I was interviewed twice. There were investigations carried out by the Federal Communications Commission as well. Evidently, according to the FCC's letter to me, members of Congress asked the agency to examine the Bush administration's media program.

Would I have participated in the program had I known it was a set-up to manipulate the American public? No. However, at the time, like other retired military analysts, I firmly believed that I could sort out fact from fiction and present a clear picture to the American people. We were mistaken.

Social Media's Finger on the Scales of Free Speech

Many Americans have long suspected that social media platforms are divisive and clearly biased—especially against conservatives and Christians. However, the proof wasn't publicly documented until 2022, thanks to Elon Musk, who purchased social media giant Twitter and granted reporters access to expose the platform's divisive history.

Twitter emerged in 2004 due to people with a Google Inc. background. Not wanting to compete with Google and Apple, they hired engineer Jack Dorsey, a future Twitter CEO who proposed a short message service (SMS) for blog-like communications among friends. By 2006, the enterprise took the name Obvious Corp., which soon morphed into Twitter, Inc.[407]

Twitter was always primarily a free SMS with a social-networking aspect, but early on it lacked a clear revenue stream from advertising or membership dues. In 2010, Twitter announced "promoted tweets," its advertising arm, to provide a revenue stream. But it wasn't until the 2008 presidential election that the social-media sphere took off in a big way, in terms of users and revenue.[408]

Still, the platform wasn't a key news source until the events of January 15, 2009. On that day in New York City, a ferry passenger, Janis

Krums, broke the story of the US Airways Flight 1549 making an emergency landing on the Hudson River. Soon, her tweeted pictures of passengers standing on the downed, floating aircraft wing exploded across the social media platform. At that point, Twitter had arrived as an emergent news platform.[409]

Soon Twitter's utility as a source of breaking news became a mainstay. Later in 2009, Twitter users in Iran used the platform to report on protests in the wake of the Iranian presidential election. Authorities in Tehran banned foreign journalists, which gave an opening for the social media platform to fill the void.

By 2017, Twitter became a public company, growing with a significant revenue stream and realizing 330 million monthly users.

Then by 2022, the platform's divisive, political role, which was long suspected, was exposed. In that year South African-born American entrepreneur Elon Musk purchased the social media outlet and facilitated the exposure of Twitter's past use of the platform to manipulate public opinion about political issues.[410]

When he purchased Twitter, Mr. Musk promised full disclosure about the platform's past misconduct arguing, the "public deserves to know what really happened." He continued: "This is a battle for the future of civilization. If free speech is lost even in America, tyranny is all that lies ahead."[411]

Twitter became especially divisive and political in the run-up to the 2020 presidential election when it censored the *New York Post's* Hunter Biden laptop story. Evidently, according to media reports backed by revelations hosted by new owner Mr. Musk, a small group of top-level Twitter executives decided to label the *Post's* Hunter Biden story as "hacked material" and removed references to the story from the platform.[412]

After taking the reins of Twitter, Mr. Musk decided to clean house and expose the platform's secret actions to advance a divisive political agenda. Therefore, he gave a number of reporters access to Twitter files, and soon the truth saw the light of day.[413]

Independent journalist Matt Taibbi was one of those reporters given access to Twitter files. He wrote the decision to censor the Hunter Biden laptop story was made "at the highest levels of the company." Taibbi indicated "damning emails and comments from former Twitter employees showed that 'everyone knew' the social media giant's suppression of *The Post's* scoops about Hunter Biden's infamous laptop 'was f---ed.'"[414]

Twitter's rationale for banning the Biden story was that it violated the company's "hacked materials" policy, wrote Taibbi. However, "Hacking was the excuse, but within a few hours, pretty much everyone realized that wasn't going to hold. But no one had the guts to reverse it," said an ex-Twitter employee.[415]

Other revelations about Twitter's bias became public because of Musk's efforts. Evidently, company emails responding to requests by the 2020 Biden presidential campaign showed a real political bias and suppression of free speech on the platform.[416]

Mr. Taibbi wrote:

Both [political] parties had access to these tools. For instance, in 2020, requests from both the Trump White House and the Biden campaign were received and honored.

However, as a former *Rolling Stone* writer said, the Twitter "system wasn't balanced." He continued:

Because Twitter was and is overwhelmingly staffed by people of one political orientation, there were more channels, more ways to complain, open to the left (well, Democrats) than the right.[417]

In addition to the *Rolling Stone* article, John Davidson, a senior editor at *The Federalist*, identified three significant examples of divisive actions by the collusion of social media and the deep state.[418]

First, Mr. Davidson wrote that the concept of "content moderation" by Twitter and other outlets is a "euphemism for censorship by social media companies that falsely claim to be neutral and unbiased."

He continued, that social media companies' "content moderation policies are at best a flimsy justification for banning or blocking whatever their executives do not like."[419]

Second, he points out that "Twitter was taking orders from a deep state security apparatus that was created to fight terrorists not to censor or manipulate public discourse." He labels this subverting of the First Amendment "information psy-ops on the American public" and the players became "malevolent government actors."[420]

Third, Mr. Davidson writes, "The administrative state [federal bureaucracy] has metastasized into a destructive deep state that threatens to bring about the collapse of America's constitutional system within our lifetimes."[421]

Mr. Davidson concludes with a poignant question: "The question we face now is whether the American people and their elected representatives will fight back. The fate of the republic rests on the answer."[422]

Manipulating the Public about COVID-19

History provides many examples of those with power using whatever means to control those without influence. Today, big government and big tech (media) exercise significant power to control the public narrative. However, that was never our founders' intent, and the Supreme Court agrees that the First Amendment prohibits private companies from abusing the public square for their profit. Unfortunately, beginning in 2020, big government and its ally, big media, censored the world of science, medicine, and academia in the name of protecting the public from COVID-19.

When dealing with a skeptical public, the media is a useful mechanism to help mitigate resistance to a particular policy position. That was very true thanks to the widespread confusion, skepticism, and doubt about the threat posed by COVID-19.

At the early stages of the pandemic, our media and government took their lead from public health organizations, including the World Health

Organization. Those early messages were clear, frightening, and broadcast by media, such as the following:

1. The pandemic threatens the survival of all humanity
2. There is no therapy to cure the sick
3. It is necessary to confine the whole population, and
4. The delivery will come only from a vaccine.[423]

TNI's role, identified earlier in this chapter, in suppressing the truth about COVID-19 is documented quite well by Elizabeth Woodworth in her 2022 *Global Health* article, "COVID-19 and the Shadowy 'Trusted News Initiative.'"[424] Her article begins with a revealing statement:

> What do the inventor of mRNA technology; the lead author of the most downloaded paper on COVID-19 in the *American Journal of Medicine*; a former editor of the *American Journal of Epidemiology*; renowned epidemiologists at Harvard, Stanford, and Oxford; and France's leading microbiologist—have in common? They have all been censored by a repressive media network that most people have never heard of. This network has outrageously conceived and conveyed a "monopoly of legitimate information."[425]

The consistency of the media's message (propaganda) about the COVID threat was rather frightening, but not an accident. We can rightly blame the collaboration of government and big media for dressing up propaganda about the virus, especially the global censorship network spawned by TNI.

Keep in mind the COVID pandemic was TNI's first major test. In July 2019, months before word of the rising pandemic was made public, the United Kingdom and Canadian governments hosted the FCO Global Conference on Media Freedom. At that conference, BBC director-general Tony Hall said:

Last month I convened, behind closed doors, a Trusted News
Summit at the BBC, which brought together global tech platforms and publishers. The goal was to arrive at a practical set of
actions we can take together, right now, to tackle the rise of misinformation and bias…. I'm determined that we use that [BBC]
unique reach and trusted voice to lead the way – to create a
global alliance for integrity in news. We're ready to do even more
to help promote freedom and democracy worldwide.[426]

Arguably, the TNI network was created with reasonable motives,
but their actions vis-à-vis the pandemic came to prove it a dark effort.
By March 2020, as the pandemic was officially recognized across the
Western world, TNI announced plans to "tackle harmful coronavirus
disinformation."[427]

It launched a verification technology labeled "Project Origin" to
identify news accounts to suppress. By July 2020, Eric Horvitz, the
chief scientific officer for Microsoft, stated: "We've forged a close relationship with the BBC and other partners on Project Origin, aimed
at methods and standards for end-to-end authentication of news and
information."[428]

By December 2020, the alarm over "disinformation" about COVID
was already gaining momentum, according to the BBC, which reported
it was "spreading online to millions of people," including efforts to
impugn the motives of the vaccine developers.[429]

The nexus between TNI "disinformation" efforts and government
is quite revealing. From the start of the pandemic, TNI relied on the
world's major public health agencies as their source of legitimate information: the World Health Organization, US Centers for Disease Control, and US National Institutes of Health. That information was passed
to the media through government representatives, which too often put
their "scientism" spin on the news.

There were plenty of examples of corrupted news sifted through government, such as National Institute of Allergy and Infectious Diseases

Director Dr. Anthony Fauci's contradictions about the protection value of face masks.

One of the most misleading pieces of information pushed by the collective public health community was their denial of effective COVID treatments. In fact, in late 2020, the only recommended option for those suffering from COVID was to stay home until they couldn't breathe, then go to the hospital.[430]

TNI suppressed all early treatment reports that included hydroxychloroquine (HCQ), ivermectin (IVM), quercetin, zinc, budesonide, or vitamins C and D. The denial of the efficacy of these treatments even convinced many US state pharmacy boards to ban outlets from filling HCQ prescriptions to treat outpatient COVID-19 patients.[431]

By August 2020, news came of the pre-licensure, emergency-use authorizations for the various mRNA vaccines. At the time, the media embraced that news, and there was little widely publicized investigative journalism about the efficacy of the vaccines.

The Global Research study considered seven acts of suppression of COVID-related information by mainstream media. Those suppressions are outlined below:[432]

Suppression #1: The source of SARS-2. TNI aggressively suppressed any blame for the virus attributed to the Wuhan, China, biosafety labs. In January 2023, a group of national security experts sent a letter to the "editors, authors, and contributors" of *The Lancet, Nature Medicine, The New York Times,* and *Time* magazine accusing major media outlets and scientific journals of censoring dissenting voices regarding the origins of the COVID-19 pandemic. Those experts included Representative Michael McCaul (R-TX), the chairman of the House Foreign Affairs Committee, and former National Security Advisor Robert O'Brien.[433]

The letter, signed by forty-three national security experts, stated:

Leading scientific journals censored dissenting voices; many science writers at major news outlets promoted narratives or asserted conclusions unsubstantiated by evidence; reporters failed to make even cursory attempts at surfacing potential conflicts of interest of their sources.

The letter continued:

This served to hamper national and international policy discussions about how to mitigate against future pandemics of any origin—natural, accidental, or deliberate.[434]

At the time of this writing, additional information demonstrated the truth about the suppression. Specifically, in late February 2023, the US Energy Department wrote that with "low confidence" the virus that causes COVID-19 most likely leaked from a Chinese laboratory. That acknowledgment came a year after the Federal Bureau of Investigation (FBI) concluded a lab accident in China was the origin of the disease, a decision made with "moderate confidence."[435]

In March 2023, Dr. Fauci acknowledged the virus that causes COVID-19 could have come from a Chinese laboratory. The former director of the US National Institute of Allergy and Infectious Diseases admitted to CNN: "A lab leak could be that someone was out in the wild maybe looking for different types of viruses in bats, got infected, went into a lab, and was being studied in a lab, and then came out of the lab."[436]

Suppression #2: Early treatments. TNI suppressed evidence of some treatments by ignoring peer-reviewed studies showing the value of readily available drugs. Who can forget that Dr. Fauci said there was no evidence to support the claim that ivermectin was effective against COVID-19? However, just visit ivmmeta.com and find at least seventy international clinical trials on ivermectin's efficacy.[437]

Suppression #3: Dissenting expert voices. TNI listened to mostly government "experts" and silenced many eminent public health professionals who provided alternative, sometimes refuting, views about the virus. Dr. Robert Malone, the founder of the mRNA technology, was silenced and his videos were removed from social media platforms because he had a contrary view about the mainstream media and government's approved COVID-19 messages.[438]

Suppression #4: Silence about vaccines' side effects and deaths. The dangers associated with the vaccines were well established by the health community, but that information was suppressed by most of the media.

Post-vaccine side effects and deaths were reported by the US Centers for Disease Control (CDC) VAERs (Vaccine Adverse Effects Reporting system). For example, in the US, VAERs reported 491,218 adverse effects and 11,405 deaths from February 10 until July 24, 2021.[439] Based on that level of harm, British Dr. Tess Lawrie of the Evidence-Based Medicine Consultancy wrote a letter to Great Britain's Medicines and Healthcare Regulatory Agency (MHRA) chief executive showing that "the MHRA now has more than enough evidence on the yellow card system to declare the COVID-19 vaccine unsafe for use in humans."[440]

Suppression #5: Strength of natural immunity rejected. The mRNA vaccines produced temporary immunity against the original SARS-2 spike protein, but was less effective against the follow-on, altered viruses. Meanwhile, according to Jon Sanders, an economist and director of the Center for Food, Power, and Life at the John Locke Foundation in Raleigh, North Carolina:

> Natural immunity comes from battling and defeating an actual infection, then having your immune system primed for the rest of your life to fight it off if it ever shows up again. This immunity is achieved at a sometimes very high personal price.[441]

The mRNA vaccine-induced "immunity is to prime your immune system with a weaker, non-threatening form of the invading infection, so that it's ready to fight off the real thing should you ever encounter it, and without your having first to risk severe illness or death," explains Mr. Sanders in his article, "Why Is There Such Reluctance to Discuss

Natural Immunity?" published by the American Institute for Economic Research (AIER).[442]

"Immunity is immunity, regardless of whether a particular person has it naturally or by a vaccine," states Mr. Sanders in the AIER article. Not so, according to Dr. Fauci, who told people early in the pandemic that natural immunity was no more than 70 percent effective. However, over time, as more Americans were vaccinated, Dr. Fauci admitted that he started "publicly cinching those numbers up: 75 percent, 80 percent, even 90 percent…. He is quoted in the *New York Times* admitting to doing so deliberately to affect people's behavior."[443]

As Dr. Fauci was "cinching" up natural immunity's effectiveness, TNI and its surrogates, at the encouragement of government, pushed the profitable vaccines, even for those people with natural immunity.

Suppression #6: Vaccine evidence of antibody dependent enhancement (ADE). Serious side effects for the vaccinated were known early but suppressed. Peter Schirmacher, director of the Pathological Institute of the University of Heidelberg, cited on August 3, 2021, and based on autopsies of dozens of people who died within two weeks of the COVID vaccination, that he found "rare, severe side effects of the vaccination—such as cerebral vein thrombosis or autoimmune diseases."[444]

The government and complicit media failed to warn people receiving the mRNA vaccines about the ADE risks, in spite of considerable medial science attesting to the liabilities.

Suppression #7: Role of comorbidities. People were most at risk for serious health issues if they contracted COVID and at the same time had preexisting conditions. Government and the medical profession failed to address issues such as being overweight and having a vitamin D deficiency, in spite of evidence at the time that 78 percent of US COVID hospitalizations were among the overweight[445] and 59 percent of hospital admissions were those who were deficient in vitamin D.[446] Where were the warnings?

Remember that TNI formed allegedly to eradicate "disinformation." However, the COVID-19 pandemic demonstrated the utter failure by the media to warn the public—and, in fact, it acted as an agent for government "misinformation" and arguably as a front to advance the financial interests of big pharmaceutical companies.

The showing by most media during the pandemic failed its mission and, at worst, is partially responsible for spewing fake news. Dr. Piers Robinson, a British researcher and the codirector of the Organization for Propaganda Studies, said: "It wouldn't be an underestimation to say that this [the COVID-TNI-government collaboration campaign] is probably one of the biggest propaganda operations that we have seen in history." Further, he concluded: "What happens is down to how people resist and how much force and coercion the authorities use."[447]

Big media shuttered any dissenting information about COVID not approved by the public health community. That denied the public the opportunity to learn about contrary, expert views to inform their personal health decisions that might have saved many more lives. Unfortunately, Big Pharma's oversized voice influenced not only the government, but a complicit big media, and the common people paid a high price for Big Pharma's self-enriching propaganda campaign.

Conclusion

The media is a powerful tool, and it's especially dangerous in the wrong hands. Every freedom-loving American ought to be outraged by the media's arrogance and its complicity with ideologically driven government, especially when the powerful elite are seeking to gain more control for themselves.

chapter thirteen

The Federal Government as a Polarizing Agent

It's not tyranny we desire; it's a just, limited, federal government.[448]

—ALEXANDER HAMILTON (1755–1804), founding father who served as US Secretary of the Treasury

How does the US president and, by association, his administration divide/polarize the country, and why? Clearly, we've had an assortment of dividers-in-chief in our history—men who used the office of the presidency to employ the levers of government to push their ideology and, as a result, polarized a segment of the American people.

This chapter will review the polarization history of America's federal government and, in particular, will outline some of the dangers for the nation when our presidents use the office to divide the country. I'll take special note of the current occupant of the White House, President Joe Biden, and his actions that polarized much of the country rather than, as he promised after being elected, were the actions of "a president who seeks not to divide, but to unify."[449]

197

Divided Government became Polarizing

America's federal governing process is messy by design. The three parts of government—executive, legislative, and judicial—are purposely intended to interact, to act as a check on one another. However, the nature of those checks is often disorderly and, unfortunately, subject to abuse if not properly controlled.

Therefore, when government is politically divided, there is the opportunity for abuse—and polarization can result. For example, if the president (executive) is a member of the Republican Party and Congress is controlled by the Democratic Party, then we have a divided government. This is contrasted with a unified government, whereby both the executive and legislative branches are controlled by the same political party. The US has had a divided government thirty-two times since the Civil War (1865).[450]

There are a number of causes of a divided government in our system, such as on a presidential election year when a candidate from the party opposite to that in control of the Congress is elected. Another example is during a midterm election, such as 2022, when half of the Congress was won by the Republicans, albeit with a Democrat remaining in the White House and the Senate staying under a Democrat majority control.

We experienced a divided government in 1984, when President Ronald Reagan, a Republican, faced a Congress controlled by Democrats in the 1984 midterm elections. There are a variety of explanations why this happens, such as the citizens using their vote to express discontent with the party in control of the executive branch and the policies of the federal government.

A divided government does not necessarily polarize the electorate, however. For many years, although the major political parties often had different visions for America, they worked together in a bipartisan manner by compromising to find solutions to address national challenges such as world wars, economic depression, poverty, race issues, and much more.

American Historical Warnings to Avoid Polarization

Once the Republican Party entered America's national political scene with the election of President Lincoln (November 6, 1860), the course of our government became influenced by the two major political parties, Democratic and Republican. However, over the life of our country, we've had other parties and different names for the current parties, such as Federalists, Anti-Federalists, Whigs, and more.

For the majority of the time from the post-Civil War era until the mid-twentieth century, most voters registered with one of the two main political parties. However, today, almost half of the US electorate rejects that political template, and now independent voters are a significant power (42 percent) in American politics.[451]

The problem for those seeking office in the twenty-first century is discerning what independent voters think and want from their government, said Thom Reilly with the Arizona State University School of Public Affairs. "What exactly is on the minds of independent voters is difficult to know," he said. "Sometimes they elect liberals, sometimes conservatives, sometimes moderates, all in the same election." Mr. Reilly is the codirector for the Arizona State's Center for an Independent and Sustainable Democracy (CISD).[452]

A 2022 study documented voter discontent with the rise in the number of American voters self-identifying as Independents. The Partnership for Public Service study found that 56 percent of voters surveyed said "they do not trust the federal government, and 65 percent believe the government does not listen to the public."[453]

Mr. Reilly attributed that level of skepticism of the current two-party system to the polarization of the electorate and the widespread view that our federal government is dysfunctional. He continued:

We at the Center [CISD] are seeking to learn whether a viable pathway to nonpartisan governance exists, whether major reform to our political structure is possible and if we are able to remake the terms of self-governance.[454]

What Mr. Reilly seeks, "remaking the terms of self-governance," was warned about by our founders long ago. George Washington, our first president, cautioned about the dangers of polarization in his 1796 Farewell Address to the nation. In that speech, the president called for unity by putting aside regional interests for the good of the nation: "You have in a common cause fought and triumphed together." He continued, "Your union ought to be considered as a main prop of your liberty and…the love of the one ought to endear you to the preservation of the other."[455]

President Washington pointed out the chief danger for our nation, which is letting regional (political) loyalties dominate loyalty to the nation. He believed that would lead to factionalism, the problem addressed by James Madison in *Federalist* Number 10. Further, President Washington warned that when we vote according to party loyalty rather than in the best interest of the whole nation, we foster a "spirit of revenge" and promote the rise of "cunning, ambitious, and unprincipled men" to political office who "usurp for themselves the reins of government; destroying afterwards the very engines, which have lifted them to the unjust dominion."[456]

America's second president, John Adams (1735–1826), wasn't especially sanguine about America's chances of surviving as a democracy. He wrote in a letter to his wife, Abigail:

Remember, democracy never lasts long. It soon wastes, exhausts, and murders itself. There never was a democracy yet that did not commit suicide.

Then he explained why:

When clear prospects are opened before vanity, pride, avarice, or ambition, for their easy gratification, it is hard for the most

considerate philosophers and the most conscientious moralists
to resist the temptation.[457]

Abraham Lincoln, our president during the most polarized period
in America's history, the Civil War, wrote to Congress on December
1, 1862, one month prior to signing the Emancipation Proclamation,
which freed the slaves. At the time, Mr. Lincoln called for unity of purpose regarding the war and the nation:

> As our case is new, so we must think anew and act anew. We
> must disenthrall [set free] ourselves, and then we shall save our
> country.[458]

Fortunately, America hasn't yet committed "suicide" as Adams suggested might happen, but our representative republic has had its share
of tough, polarizing times like the Civil War. We've also had many char-
acters who rose to political prominence over the past two-plus centuries who fit the descriptions warned about by Washington and Adams:
"cunning, ambitious, and unprincipled men" who couldn't "resist the
temptation."

Fortunately, up to the mid-twentieth century, most of our federal
government's political class consistently demonstrated, in spite of their
many differences and some terrible situations, that, even though we
often had "divided" government and not a few arguably unprincipled
"leaders," we still managed to find a way through the ideological jungle
to address national problems in a mostly bipartisan manner.

That consensus effort in governance especially started to deteriorate
in the late twentieth and early twenty-first centuries. Today, our two
major political parties have become very polarized, an issue I addressed
in the "political" chapter (chapter 8). The Republican and Democratic
parties no longer accommodate the other, much less compromise, on
significant issues for the good of the country, as founder Washington
encouraged.

Perhaps the parting of the bipartisan ways began in earnest with the 1994 Republican Revolution, or the "Gingrich Revolution," named after the Georgia congressman and House Republican whip Newt Gingrich, who became the speaker and led the Republicans behind a single national legislative program. At the time, the Republicans' success in the 1994 US midterm elections resulted in their taking the House of Representatives and growing the party's control of the Senate by picking up eight additional seats.

Arguably, that election victory was the beginning of a significant polarization between the two political parties in their congressional voting patterns, and in the wake of that election there was far less bipartisan legislation. Of course, fault for the decline in bipartisanship could be found on both sides of the political divide. However, and separately, fueling the partisan divide was the separate states' accelerated, politically rigged system of redistricting congressional seats, which reduced the number of truly competitive elections and thus drove our congressional election system into an extremist situation.

Soon, total political war between the parties became the norm—fueled by the extremists on both sides of the political aisle. At the same time, as the political class abandoned bipartisanship, our democratic republic began to be drained of trust for the American people. The electorate soon came to believe that our national-level challenges were less likely to be resolved through bipartisan compromise.

Just as bipartisanship declined across the political spectrum, our news media contributed to the chaos by fueling polarization as a business model by feeding their mostly politically aligned viewers with red-meat-like news analysis that fit their ideological perspective and arguably made worse by the advent of cable news and the twenty-four-hour news cycle. Of course, the emergence of social media, as addressed in the previous chapter, further balkanized the electorate by exaggerating some of the arguments of the strongest political proponents on both sides, which tended to skew the public's views about both political parties and the issues, as well as their respective views of their political opposition.

Today, that political and media balkanization explains why 73 percent of Americans believe the Republicans and Democrats seemingly can't agree on anything. That's a recipe for disaster and, as former President Adams warned, it could lead to the nation's "suicide."[459]

Although most Americans want the political parties to find a way to work together in our best interest, most (60 percent)[460] conclude that both major parties are out of touch with the country. That may explain why more than half (57 percent)[461] now favor the establishment of a third political party, providing an alternative to the Democratic and Republican parties.

Dangers Associated with a Polarizing Presidency

We must be very concerned by polarization encouraged by a politically charged federal government because it threatens our way of life. David Blankenhorn, founder of the New York City-based Institute for American Values, wrote for *The American Interest* to explain that polarization is not really just the fault of bad politicians. Rather, he quotes Larry Sabato with the University of Virginia, who states: "So often blamed just on the politicians, polarization actually has its roots in us, the electorate." Thus, polarization is not all political Washington's fault, but the blame rests with all of us, because we allow the political bickering to influence our views, shaped by the media.[462]

James Q. Wilson (1931–2012) was an American political scientist and professor at Harvard University. Dr. Wilson defined polarization in a political way that helps us view its influence on everyday Americans, especially from a federal government-influencing perspective. He wrote:

[Polarization is] an intense commitment to a candidate, a culture, or an ideology that sets people in one group definitively apart from people in another, rival group. Such a condition is revealed when a candidate for public office is regarded by a competitor and his supporters not simply as wrong but as corrupt or wicked; when one way of thinking about the world is assumed to be morally superior to any other way; when one set of political beliefs is considered to be entirely correct and a rival set wholly wrong.[463]

Let's apply Wilson's polarization definition by considering some common consequences associated with the phenomenon. Specifically, Blankenhorn enumerates polarization harms associated with the federal government that address what Wilson identifies as "corrupt or wicked… when one way of thinking about the world is assumed to be morally superior to any other way;" and "when one set of political beliefs is considered to be entirely correct and a rival set wholly wrong."

Public Policy Polarization

At the federal level, partisan disagreement about public policy on a host of issues feeds polarization. Some of those matters include so-called abortion on demand, immigration, and homosexual rights. The political divide at the national level on these and other issues is evidenced by "permanent political warfare," states Blankenhorn. It results in governance paralysis, which feeds more polarization, with both sides arguing that they have the moral high ground.[464]

Illegal immigration is one of the country's most polarizing political issues, according to a 2022 Gallup poll. Almost four in ten (38 percent) of respondents want the number of immigrants entering the country to decrease. Two years ago, 28 percent called for immigration levels to decrease.[465]

Gallup reports that those favoring a decrease in immigration are mostly Republicans. Nearly 70 percent of self-identified Republicans, the highest percentage this century, call for less immigration according to Gallup. Further, more Republicans than Democrats view illegal immigration as an important issue, with 15 percent saying it is the most important problem facing this country.[466]

Illegal immigration is very much a polarizing partisan issue at the grassroots, and for good reason. For example, Texas Governor Greg Abbott (R) is fighting with the Biden administration over the federal government's failure to enforce our immigration laws, which has resulted in a massive surge of illegals entering this country accompanied by some suspected terrorists and a flood of deadly fentanyl, an addictive drug responsible for more than one hundred thousand deaths a year in the United States, according to the Drug Enforcement Administration.[467]

Public Policy Polarization: Public Discussion Especially Incendiary

Too often when polarized policy talking heads (news analysts) meet on cable channels to "debate" federal issues, there are fireworks, because the cable network news producers select advocates who present the most extremist positions. They are not just contradictory on the program, but are too often hostile, raising the viewers' blood pressure and fanning the flames of further polarization. Compromise and a calm demeanor by the debaters are seldom evidenced; the broadcasters want controversy because it sells, and the viewers tune in to reinforce their polarized perspectives. This is what Wilson argues is evidence that one's political beliefs are "entirely correct and a rival set wholly wrong."

I fell into this trap as well. For many years, especially in the 1990s, I was a frequent guest on CNN's *Crossfire*, a prime-time program that hosted "debates" on controversial issues. Of course, at the time, I was with the Family Research Council, and we stood for a biblical worldview on moral issues. The CNN producers would always confirm my position on the issue via "pre-interviews" to make certain I was strident enough and therefore "entertaining" for their viewership. Frankly, we seldom disappointed, because verbal fireworks on cable network programs sells.

Public Policy-Engendered Inequality Contributes to Polarization
Economic and social inequality contribute to polarization, claims Blankenhorn. This has a federal nexus because government tax and social policies often widen the gap between the rich and poor, which tends to become a contentious political issue.[468]

In other words, there seems to be a relationship between polarization and inequality, states Blankenhorn. Polarization seems to have a socio-economic dimension such that the gap between prosperous Americans and the rest of us contributes to some of the nation's most disturbing social problems. Therefore, as Wilson argues, one side tends to assume they have the "morally superior" perspective because they support either economic or social equality.

Polarizing Government Policy Undermines Trust

Trust in government institutions is perhaps at a record low. Certainly, in the wake of the Trump-era Russia collusion scandal and the Biden administration's weaponizing of the Federal Bureau of Investigation (FBI), both situations undermined trust in federal law enforcement and thus encouraged more polarization. This is important, because, according to research, high-trust societies do better than low-trust societies, and unfortunately the US electorate's trust in our federal government, especially federal law enforcement, is on the decline—and at the same time, that mistrust magnifies polarization.[469]

The growing mistrust is attributable to factors Professor Wilson would likely label as "corrupt or wicked." Specifically, many Americans label as "corrupt" the actions of our Department of Justice (DOJ) and the FBI targeting parents by labeling them domestic terrorists because they dare to speak out against local school board decisions that promote critical race theory or transgender issues in public schools. Below are a few examples of trust-robbing, big-government actions.

DOJ targets parents as domestic terrorists. Although this issue was previously addressed in the education chapter (chapter 10), it fits here as well because it undermines trust. You will recall that, in late 2021, Biden's attorney general, Merrick Garland, issued a memorandum to DOJ employees about intervening in incidents of violence or intimidation targeting state and local school officials. Evidently, according to Fox News, Garland issued the memo days after the National School Boards Association asked the Biden administration to use the terrorism-related PATRIOT Act to address these free-speech confrontations. That memo begins by calling out a "disturbing spike in harassment, intimidation, and threats of violence against school administrators, board members, teachers, and staff who participate in the vital work of running our nation's public schools."[470]

Evidently, the DOJ and the FBI may have stopped targeting parents after all the adverse publicity, but now they appear to take aim at pro-life activists.

FBI targets pro-life activist. The case of Roman Catholic pro-life activist Mark Houck also illustrates the weaponization of federal law enforcement along political lines. In 2022, fifteen FBI agents stormed Mr. Houck's home while pointing their weapons at his wife and seven children. His "crime," according to federal charges, was the violation of the Freedom of Access to Clinic Entrances (FACE) Act. Evidently and allegedly, Mr. Houck assaulted an abortion clinic volunteer in Philadelphia, Pennsylvania, by using "force with the intent to injure, intimidate, and interfere with anyone because that person is a provider of reproductive [abortion] health care."[471]

Mr. Houck was found not guilty of the federal charges, however. "This is a win not just for the pro-life movement and Mark but for free speech and every single American," 40 Days for Life's general counsel, Matt Britton, told the *Daily Caller*. He continued:

> The federal government trumped up charges months after a
> local case had been dismissed. If the feds had prevailed, every

argument in front of every abortion facility, no matter the subject, could result in federal charges.[472]

Evidently, the Virginia-based FBI office thought certain Catholics are extremists worth targeting as well.

FBI targets Roman Catholics in intelligence report. In January 2023, the FBI's Richmond, Virginia, division issued an internal intelligence product entitled "Racially or Ethnically Motivated Violent Extremists (RMVE)." Evidently, that "intelligence" product was intended to protect Virginians from the threat of "white supremacy," which the Richmond FBI office believes is found among Catholics who prefer the Latin Mass, according to Kyle Seraphin, a former FBI agent and author of the article that broke the story, "The FBI Doubles Down on Christians and White Supremacy in 2023."[473]

The FBI document, posted with Mr. Seraphin's article, assesses with "high confidence" that it can mitigate the alleged threat of radical-traditionalist Catholics (RTC) "by recruiting sources within the Catholic Church." Further, a footnote on the FBI document indicates that RTCs are "typically characterized by the rejection of the Second Vatican Council." Then the FBI writer makes the unsubstantiated claim that the RTC's religious views can amount to an "adherence to anti-Semitic, anti-immigrant, anti-LGBTQ and white supremacist ideology."[474]

The FBI Richmond chief division counsel, the office's top lawyer, approved the document, which also includes an article, "Appendix D," authored by the far-left, anti-Christian group Southern Poverty Law Center (SPLC), entitled "Radical Traditional Catholicism Hate Groups." The SPLC article describes this "hate group" as perhaps "the largest single group of serious antisemites in America."[475]

The FBI product also cites the far-left online magazine *Salon* and *The Atlantic*. Specifically, the *Salon* article includes the statement: "Traditional Catholics and White Nationalist Groypers[476]

Forge a New Far-Right Youth Movement" and "White Nationalists
Get Religion: On the Far-Right Fringe, Catholics and Racists Forge
a Movement." The author of the article exposing the FBI memorandum states:

> The *Salon* writer makes the wild leap that using a photo of
> someone at a church indicates the pictured individual or his
> beliefs are relevant within a religious institution with 70 mil-
> lion adherents in the United States alone and over 2000 years of
> tradition and history.[477]

The former FBI agent author notes that "documents like these can
be used to drive the FBI's priorities in specific regions and boost the vis-
ibility of non-existent threats." Further, such products "help focus on
alleged 'hostility towards the abortion-rights advocates,' which the FBI
has used to justify significant enforcement actions tied to the FACE Act
(18 USC 248)," such as the case against Mark Houck, who was acquit-
ted on January 30, 2023.[478]

The former FBI agent warns that such products can also be used to
open "the door to associating white supremacists with traditional religious practices based on common Christian positions on abortion and
the LGBTQ political agendas is a dangerous step." He continued that
such analysis could lead to a similar decision to pursue so-called "Radical
Traditional Baptists, Radical Traditional Lutherans, and Radical Traditional Evangelicals."[479]

On February 8, 2023, the Richmond FBI office retracted the offending intelligence product, stating the memo "does not meet the exacting
standards of the FBI." This episode further sullies the FBI's already seriously compromised reputation and raises fresh concerns about its political bias—and this came just a year after the agency bungled efforts to
treat Northern Virginia parents protesting at school board meetings as
domestic terrorists.[480]

Finally, the federal government also undermined trust with its COVID-19 mandates (addressed in the previous chapter) that disrupted most aspects of our lives, which in some cases seemed contrary to our best interests and medical science. In time, these draconian overreach incidents by our government in the name of "science" and law enforcement will expose government agents and elected officials as truly anti-freedom and acting without sufficient justification, which validates our skepticism about their trustworthiness.

Polarizing Government Distorts Our Thinking.

When government favors one group over another, the result is more polarization. Why would big government pass laws or institute regulations that favor someone because of their sexual orientation, race, ethnicity, or heritage that benefits them over another group?

In 2021, a federal judge issued a preliminary injunction preventing the Biden administration from discriminating based on race or ethnicity when distributing federal funds from the American Rescue Plan to farmers. Agriculture Secretary Tom Vilsack tried to justify the discrimination by arguing that we must "acknowledge the cumulative effect of discrimination."

Secretary Vilsack argued: "We must discriminate against people now to address discrimination in the past." On a similar vein, Biden's Small Business Administration allocated COVID relief funds to only nonwhite or women restaurant owners. Evidently, Biden's logic was the same as with the farmers; "past discrimination mandates present-day discrimination."[481]

The idea of so-called social justice-related empathy polarizes people who are discriminated against, such as white males, the target of so much discrimination in our nation today—and, in some cases, by our federal government, as demonstrated above. This type of policy, according to Wilson, is likely viewed as "entirely correct" by some on the political left but considered "wholly wrong" by those being discriminated against, mostly on the political right.

America: A History of Polarizing Presidents

We turn to Confucius (551–479 BCE), the Chinese philosopher and politician, for wisdom regarding the importance of the head of state. In the book, *The Wisdom of China and India*, specifically the chapter entitled "The Aphorisms of Confucius," we find the section on "Government," which states:

> Tsekung asked about government, and Confucius replied: "People must have sufficient to eat; there must be a sufficient army; and there must be confidence of the people in the ruler." "If you are forced to give up one of these three objectives, what would you go without first?" asked Tsekung. Confucius said, "I would go without the army first." "And if you were forced to go without one of the two remaining factors, what would you rather go without?" asked Tsekung again. "I would rather go without sufficient food for the people. There have always been deaths in every generation since man lived, but a nation cannot exist without confidence in its ruler."[482]

Americans generally respect their presidents and give them the benefit of the doubt. However, as Confucius indicates above, confidence in our ruler is critically important. Unfortunately, a number of former presidents have squandered the opportunity to build confidence and were rejected, while others enjoyed Americans' support.

The Great Depression (1929–1939) presented a significant challenge to President Herbert Hoover (1874–1964), and his failures sapped Americans' hopes and dreams, which scuttled his chance of reelection, because most citizens at the time lost confidence in him.

Hoover was beaten by Democrat Franklin Delano Roosevelt in 1932, a time of considerable polarization among the electorate. Robert Dallek, an American historian who specializes in presidents and the author of *Franklin D. Roosevelt: A Political Life*, wrote that, at the time of the Roosevelt election, there "was the deep cultural divide between urban and rural Americans, or modernists and fundamentalists, as they were described."[483]

President Roosevelt did what Hoover failed to do, said Dallek. He restored America's confidence in the presidency and sustained that trust by instilling within the citizens pride in themselves and a hope for a bright future. Other Democratic Party presidents weren't so fortunate, however.

In the wake of the assassination of President John F. Kennedy, Lyndon B. Johnson came to office. That Democrat leader began his term with the nation stalwartly behind him, but that trust quickly vanished and dissuaded him from seeking a second term, mostly thanks to his support for the Vietnam War, which, prior to the election, seemed stalemated thanks to anti-war protests that rocked the country at the time.

President Jimmy Carter (1924) served as the thirty-ninth president (1977–1981). He never captured the confidence of the American people because of the Iran hostage crisis and a poor economy. He lost his reelection bid to the far more charismatic and unifying Ronald Reagan.

Decades later, President Donald Trump was a polarizing figure to many citizens, especially those on the left, because of his callous disregard for democratic norms and personal habits, which included demonizing anyone who tried to hold him accountable or was critical. It's notable that, until his term in office, Mr. Trump was the only president in history to never have rated above 50 percent in job approval, according to Gallup polling.[484]

Although Mr. Trump remained especially popular among his polarized base, that cohort wasn't large enough to help him win the 2020 reelection bid. Further, during the campaign, Mr. Trump never tried to win over some of his opposition, but tended to demonize them, which only further polarized that portion of the electorate.

Joe Biden the Extreme Divider-in-Chief

In 2021, President Joe Biden came to the Oval Office promising to unify the country, but he quickly polarized the electorate. It didn't help that his election, by many accounts, was seriously tainted by allegations of massive voter fraud, ballot-harvesting, unclean voter rolls, and a lack of voter identification, which raises serious doubts among many within the electorate about whether he is legitimate (then, by association, neither would be those he appointed and the policies they now promote.) Thus, the voters who felt disenfranchised by an alleged faulty election were understandably polarized, as was the case in the 2016 election between Mr. Trump and former Secretary of State Hillary Clinton as well.

Once Mr. Biden was ensconced in the presidency, he wasted little time further polarizing the country thanks to a host of radical leftist policies. For example, he quickly pumped untold billions of our tax dollars into climate-change activism. He lost more of our confidence in his unequal application of the law through the weaponization of the Department of Justice, not only in the administration's campaign to discredit former President Trump and by going after pro-life supporters, but also by the department's ignoring the well-publicized contents of Hunter Biden's laptop, which likely implicates the entire Biden family and puts into question President Biden's personal corruption and vulnerability to foreign manipulation.

Certainly, the FBI's raid on Mar-a-Lago, former President Trump's Florida estate, in August 2022 in search of classified documents appears to be evidence of the weaponization of the Justice Department's authority and an abuse of the law. Juxtapose that action with the 2022/2023 discovery of classified documents at Mr. Biden's Delaware homes and at a think tank bearing his name, some dating as far back as 1974.[485] The differences in the treatment between the two men, Trump and Biden, on this classified-document matter is night and day. Then, there is also the matter of the January 6, 2021, so-called attack on the US Capitol and the Democratic Party's partisan select committee's use of the incident to fuel further distrust in government. All of these actions fueled polarization, undermining trust in our federal government.

If that isn't enough to polarize the electorate, the Democratic Party's use of the Internal Revenue Service (IRS) to target the Tea Party during the Obama administration and the Environmental Protection Agency's (EPA) regulations that harass farmers and ranchers over questionable climate threats sends many voters over the polarized edge. Recently, under Biden, the Democratic Party-controlled Congress accelerated its campaign to target the average American when it passed in 2022 the Inflation Reduction Act that included a cool $72 billion to hire eighty-seven thousand more IRS agents, auditors, and other staff—over the period of a decade—to target hard-working Americans rather than wealthy individuals and corporations. We'll see whether the new Republican-controlled House of Representatives can overturn the IRS hiring frenzy.

Mr. Biden's radical climate campaign weaponized the EPA as well. In August 2022, the US Supreme Court ruled that Biden's EPA overstepped its authority to control how America generates electricity. The EPA also tried to bypass the states and force oil and gas out of the market entirely by unilaterally changing policy to force Biden's Green New Deal on states.[486] Meanwhile, the Biden administration's campaign against fossil fuels caused pump prices to skyrocket, forcing some Americans to choose between eating and heating. All these actions pumped up polarization.

The administration's handling of the COVID-19 pandemic also polarized much of the nation, thanks to what Biden both did and failed to do. He oversaw, with the help of the Democrat-controlled Congress, passage of trillion-dollar spending bills allegedly for COVID relief aid that mandated, contrary to the science, the closure of our schools and workplaces and forced many out of work. Meanwhile, Mr. Biden was silent about "gain of function" experiments, likely in part funded by American tax dollars at the Chinese lab in Wuhan, China, that may have leaked the virus, which claimed the lives of more than one million Americans.

Mr. Biden's policies at our Southern border further polarized the country. His open-border policies allowed, by the end of 2022, more than five million illegal immigrants into the country, along with tons of poisonous illicit drugs like fentanyl, which, as stated earlier, kills at least a one hundred thousand Americans each year. Then there is the issue of massive human trafficking and sex slavery, more than a million "gotaway" immigrants who crossed the US border but evaded capture and many thousands of unaccounted-for children who came into this country and immediately became financial wards of the state, further burdening our economy that was already in recession.

On top of these challenges, Mr. Biden and his congressional supporters outspent all past presidents together by putting our country more than $32 trillion in debt. No wonder, given this growing list of radical actions, that much of the country is now polarized against this president and his political proxies.

On the foreign policy front, Mr. Biden's record has fueled mistrust and polarization as well. In particular, Mr. Biden ordered our hasty withdrawal from the twenty-year war in Afghanistan that needlessly cost thirteen American service member lives and brought into the US many tens of thousands of unvetted Afghans while leaving others with legitimate claims of asylum behind. Meanwhile, Mr. Biden and his Democratic colleagues in Congress tolerated Chinese malfeasance at our expense and are draining our arms arsenals and pushing massive amounts of aid to support Ukraine in its war with Russia without explaining our national interests in that fight.

Mr. Biden also pushed a radical agenda on our military that included COVID-19 mandates that contributed to hollowing out our force by undermining recruiting. Meanwhile, Biden's secretary of defense, Lloyd Austin, pushed mandatory COVID vaccinations while denying exemptions, even for religious reasons. That policy hurt retention and recruiting, and forced out of the ranks many thousands, in spite of the fact that the vaccine remained experimental. Like Senator Rand Paul of Kentucky said, "The United States simply cannot afford to discharge our brave men and women in uniform and lose the investments we have made into each and every one of them due to an inept bureaucratic policy." Of course, at the last minute, in December 2022, the Democrat-controlled House compromised with the incoming majority Republicans regarding the 2023 National Defense Authorization Act to remove the vaccine mandate over Secretary Austin's ongoing objections.[487]

There is also the matter of the Biden administration's "wokism" push within the military, all in the name of diversity, equity, and inclusion, which operationalizes the dysfunctional critical race theory. This effort forces the military to see the world through a lens of skin color, gender, and sexual orientation, which destroys unity and trust by creating suspicion and division (polarization) in our ranks.

The Biden administration's abuse of the military also drains popular trust in the institution. A November 2022 Reagan National Defense survey of the American people found a significant decline in trust for our armed forces. Five years ago, 70 percent of Americans said they had a great deal of confidence in the military. However, in 2022, only 45 percent of Americans had the highest level of confidence in the armed forces, a loss of 22 points, arguably thanks to Mr. Biden's woke abuse of our military.[488]

The top concern (62 percent) expressed by surveyed Americans about our military is that it has become overly politicized. It's noteworthy that 60 percent blame the president for the decrease in confidence, and 55 percent blame Biden's civilian Pentagon appointees like Mr. Austin for the decrease.[489]

Not only are Mr. Biden's actions and those of his proxies terribly divisive, but the president's public statements are equally polarizing.

Even though he called for national unity and bipartisan cooperation in his inaugural address and most recently in his 2023 State of the

Union address, his track record on divisive remarks already has had a polarizing effect.[490]

In his 2023 State of the Union address, President Biden called the US "a nation that embraces light over darkness, hope over fear, unity over division. Stability over chaos." Yet, during the course of his address, he made some pretty outlandish and divisive claims.[491]

For example, he claimed that "some Republicans want Medicare and Social Security to sunset." He continued with that allegation: "I'm not saying it's a majority of you." However, according to Fox News, "even left-leaning outlets have said Biden's characterizations of the GOP's ["Grand Old Party," the Republican Party] plans for Social Security and Medicare is misleading."[492]

Mr. Biden repeated his often gross exaggeration about the total number of jobs "created" since he took office in 2021. "Two years ago, our economy was reeling," he said. "As I stand here tonight, we have created a record 12 million new jobs, more jobs created in two years than any president has ever created in four years." However, according to the Bureau of Labor Statistics, the economy under Biden has only added 2.7 million jobs overall; the rest were lost during the COVID-19 pandemic. Presidential lying undermines trust and encourages further polarization.[493]

Now briefly consider Mr. Biden's record on divisive statements over the past two years. Back in 2021, President Biden called a voting law enacted in Georgia a "blatant attack on the Constitution and good conscience," likening it to "Jim Crow in the 21st century." The Georgia law in question changed how that state voted, such as expanding early voting, requiring voter identification for absentee ballots, and restructuring the State Elections Board to exercise more oversight of local offices.[494]

President Biden alleged that Georgia election law was used by former President Trump "and his supporters...to suppress your vote, to subvert our elections." They want "to disenfranchise anyone who votes against them," said Mr. Biden, without providing a shred of evidence to support his allegation.[495]

He continued the attack, stating:

That's the kind of power you see in totalitarian states, not in
democracies…. Will you stand against election subversion? Yes,
or no? Will you stand for democracy? Yes, or no?… Do you want
to be on the side of Dr. King or George Wallace? Do you want to
be on the side of John Lewis or Bull Connor? Do you want to be
on the side of Abraham Lincoln or Jefferson Davis?[496]

Recall that, on multiple occasions in 2022, Mr. Biden painted
his Republican opponents as Trump's "Make America Great Again"
(MAGA) supporters as extremists who threatened democracy. Evidently,
Biden's advisors studied that messaging for months with the help of the
leftist group Center for American Progress Action Fund to arrive at that
polarizing line. Mr. Biden kept using it throughout the year.[497]

In May 2022, Mr. Biden denigrated what he called the MAGA
movement. He told reporters: "This MAGA crowd is really the most
extreme political organization that's existed in American history, in
recent American history." Then, months later, Biden described the
MAGA movement as fascist.[498]

"What we're seeing now is the beginning or the death knell of an
extreme MAGA philosophy," he told Democrats at an August 2022
fundraiser in Bethesda, Maryland. He continued: "It's not just Trump,
it's the entire philosophy that underpins the—I'm going to say something, it's like semi-fascism."[499]

Perhaps the most astonishing example of Biden's MAGA hyperbole
took place in September 2022 in Philadelphia, with a backdrop of a
couple of US Marines standing at parade rest in front of Independence
Hall all draped in the glow of red lights. At that setting, Biden said,
"Donald Trump and the MAGA Republicans represent an extremism
that threatens the very foundations of our Republic." Perhaps not surprisingly, most Americans disapproved of Biden's Philadelphia speech as

divisive, dangerous, and going too far, according to surveys taken just after the speech.[500]

As Confucius was quoted earlier in this chapter, "A nation cannot exist without confidence in its ruler." Today, a growing cross section of Americans have lost total "confidence" in Mr. Biden, who—through his actions and words—has polarized this nation unlike any former president. That isn't to say prior presidents weren't also guilty of abusing the office of the presidency to undermine trust and thus polarized the nation as well.

Conclusion

A divided government does not necessarily polarize the electorate. However, as we've seen in this chapter, certain policies and personalities that rob the American people of confidence and trust in the president and his administration most often result in rejection. Certainly, the current occupant of the Oval Office, President Biden, and his administration are arguably the most polarizing of any of his predecessors—to include Mr. Trump. At this point, his reelection is very much in doubt.

STRATEGIES FOR OVERCOMING DIVISION

What is important is that we make sure to
work together, that we understand our
strength comes from unity and not division.[501]
—BARACK HUSSEIN OBAMA, forty-fourth president of the United States

Our journey to this point has traced a path through the roots of division, its place in history, and, more specifically, division at home across critical institutions in twenty-first-century America. We now turn to strategies to overcome division across the seven institutions addressed in the previous section: family, politics, religion, education, work, culture (media), and government.

Chapter 14 considers how those who came before us dealt with division/polarization. I use three case studies to identify lessons on mitigating polarization that might be instructive for us today and employed across our many critical institutions.

Chapter 15 addresses some strategies that are personal (for us to embrace in our various roles) and others that apply in our workplaces. It also presents strategies for nations to consider when faced by division/polarization today and how best to overcome those challenges.

chapter fourteen

Strategies to Overcome Divisions across History

As every divided kingdom falls so every mind divided between
many studies confounds and saps itself.[502]
—LEONARDO DA VINCI (1452–1519), Italian painter, draftsman,
sculptor, and engineer

There are lessons from history that can help us address the current level of division/polarization across America's society. I've selected three short case studies with that objective in mind. Two were spawned here in the United States and one in the Kingdom of the Netherlands. All three historic examples identify lessons for overcoming polarization, which may be instructive for America's current state of division.

Case Study #1: Founder James Madison's Useful Insights

"How do we get beyond the hyper-partisanship?" asked Dr. Lynn Uzzell, an American politics and rhetoric assistant professor at the Washington and Lee University and the former scholar in residence at the Center for the Constitution at James Madison's Montpelier, the plantation of the Madison family located in Orange County, Virginia. Ms. Uzzell argues in her essay, "Madison's Five Lessons for Overcoming Polarization," that the former president "not only lived through one of the worst epochs of American partisanship but also helped lead the country past that unruly epoch and into greater harmony."[503]

President Madison wasn't an icon of hospitality and a congenial soul. In fact, as Dr. Uzzell writes, Madison wrote in the *Federalist* Number 10 that humans are irritable by nature; therefore, we must accept "the spirit of party and faction in the necessary and ordinary operations of the government." Further, Uzzell notes, Madison succumbed to partisan fervor as well.[504]

Even though Madison was flawed like the rest of us, Dr. Uzzell explained that "he knew that factions could not be removed from free government that he actively sought ways to defang them to render them less destructive." Thus, Madison's life experiences taught him how to get beyond polarization.

Ms. Uzzell identified five lessons from Madison's efforts that helped him and perhaps others in his company overcome polarization/faction that goes beyond the pluralism mentioned in the preface of this volume.

Lesson 1: "Teach classical rhetoric to America's youth."

Ms. Uzzell argues that Americans have forgotten the purpose of free speech, and, as a consequence, speech we disagree with tends to polarize.[505]

Madison provides an example of how to tolerate those with contrary views because he was trained in classical rhetoric. The future president attended the College of New Jersey (now Princeton University), where he enjoyed an education in classical rhetoric, which included lectures by John Witherspoon, a clergyman and Princeton's sixth president, such as "Moral Philosophy, Rhetoric, and Eloquence." Much later in his life,

Madison was known to have studied eighteenth-century Scottish minister Hugh Blair's "Lectures on Rhetoric and Belles Lettres," which contributed to his ability to think and speak accurately.[506]

Evidently, Madison was equipped with the rhetorical ability to cope with those with whom he disagreed because he was immersed in classical rhetoric. The lesson is that America's education establishment should start teaching our students how "to engage logically with speakers expressing diverse viewpoints," then perhaps there would be less polarization.[507]

Lesson 2: "Find creative ways to encourage both sides of every argument."

Mr. Madison was a big supporter of the power of the freedom of the press. He acknowledged abuses but believed "the world is indebted [to the press] for the triumphs which have been gained by reason and humanity, over error and oppression." He reasoned, according to Uzzell, that if one paper published "falsehood," then a rival paper could make the correction.[508]

The lesson from Madison, according to Dr. Uzzell, is that instead of promoting free speech by "inviting the most polarizing or even inflammatory speakers," we should encourage more bipartisan debates, which would be less polarizing. Of course, when applied to today's cable networks, which embrace a business model based on conflict, this suggestion will likely be rejected.[509]

Lesson 3: "Socialize with your (political) enemies."

In Madison's day, members of different political parties kept separate; they only met to wage political battles. Evidently, during President Thomas Jefferson's term in office, he would host a dinner with only Federalists one evening and then invite only Republicans (Anti-Federalists) the next, according to Uzzell.[510]

President Madison chose a different path, one that helped mitigate the political polarization. In fact, that new path is attributed to First Lady Dolley Madison, who instituted regular Wednesday "drawing room nights" at the White House for people of all parties. One guest, according to Uzzell, said: "By her [Dolley Madison's] deportment in her own house [the White House] you cannot discover who is her husband's friends or foes."[511]

The lesson is that too often we are polarized by politics and thus rarely socialize with our political opposition. We need to take a lesson from Dolley Madison's nonpolitical social graces and socialize more with those with whom we disagree.

Lesson 4: "Never allow political disagreements to get personal."

"In his public speeches, Madison could be a forceful voice for his political party," said Uzzell. However, "he never allowed his criticisms to get personal." She continued: "It was taken for granted that gentlemen [in Madison's day] did not cast personal aspersions against their adversaries." Dr. Uzzell added: "Contemporaneous newspapers were infamous for their personal invective," but the "ruling elite tended to hold itself to a higher standard than the scandalmongers."[512]

The lesson is to avoid all personal affronts, including political disagreements. Ms. Uzzell explained that "ad hominem is listed among the logical fallacies for a reason: it never improves our political understanding but invariably poisons our political atmosphere." And, I would add, it tends to further polarize us.[513]

Lesson 5: Avoid accusing adversaries of "malevolent intent."

Evidently, according to Uzzell, Madison came to regret his youthful excesses, such as when he "stooped to accusing his political adversaries of malevolent intent."[514]

Later in life, Madison criticized himself for the contents and an exchange with Alexander Hamilton in his 1793 *Helvidius* essays:

> I ought not perhaps to acknowledge my having written this polemic tract, without acknowledging at the same time my consciousness & regret, that it breathes a spirit which was of no advantage either to the subject, or to the Author.[515]

There is no excuse for vitriolic behavior, because it only produces excitements that tempt well-meaning people into misbehavior, explained Dr. Uzzell. That's a good lesson and something we all need to take to heart.[516]

Dr. Uzzell's five lessons from President Madison's life on fighting polarization have application for all of us today. However, the most hyper-partisan, polarized period in our history was not Madison's era, but the time beginning in the 1850s, which ended with the Civil War. That's when partisanship truly got out of hand.

Case Study #2: President Lincoln's 1858 House Divided Speech

On June 16, 1858, Abraham Lincoln delivered what's known as the House Divided speech, his acceptance of the Illinois Republican nomination for the US Senate. That speech marked not only his official entrance into politics, but offered then and offers today some timeless lessons about the costs of polarization.[517]

Bradford Vivian, professor of communication arts and sciences and director of the Center for Democratic Deliberation, Pennsylvania State University, uses Lincoln's speech to call out the costs of "deep-seated political polarization." Professor Vivian identifies several important lessons on polarization in his article, "Lessons on Political Polarization

from Lincoln's 'House Divided' Speech, 160 Years Later," published by
the History News Network.

Professor Vivian indicates that, at the time of Lincoln's speech,
America was more divided than it is today and there were no easy solutions. In the speech, Lincoln anticipated calamity, if not outright war:

> If we could first know where we are, and whither we are tending,
> we could then better judge what to do, and how to do it.... I
> believe this government cannot endure, permanently half slave
> and half free.[518]

"The alternative to bitter polarization that Lincoln offered didn't prevent the Civil War," explained Professor Vivian. However, as he wrote:
"It shaped postwar understanding of the territorial political and even
armed conflicts that led to it and the lessons to be learned from it."[519]

Some of those lessons are summarized below.

Lesson #1: "A house divided against itself cannot stand."

Lincoln emphasized that America faced "a crisis" over slavery and asked
his fellow citizens to "choose the common purpose that would best serve
their Union" either to be a country with all slave states or an all-free
country. His point was that the Union of states was "perpetual," and no
state was free to exit it. Or in other words, according to Vivian: "Lincoln
held that Americans belong to the Union before they belong to political
parties [or, by association, to the individual states]."[520]

Lincoln's warning, "A house divided against itself cannot stand,"
implied that the Union should also rest "on a firm moral foundation: a
bedrock dedication to equality." It was not a "compact of convenience
or a loose-knit confederation," said Professor Vivian. Thus, the moral
purpose of the Union was to "extend conditions of equality to as many
people as possible."[521]

The lesson on polarization is one of purpose. First, answer: Who are we as a nation, and what is the glue that holds us together? We must focus on those answers and not dwell on extraneous issues that might pull us apart.

Lesson #2: Compromise sustains, not resolves, polarization.

There were a number of bipartisan compromises on the issue of slavery at the time—the Missouri Compromise of 1820, the Compromise of 1850, and the Kansas-Nebraska Act of 1854. These compromises kept slavery in place and passed any final solution to the next generation. Lincoln argued that such compromises made the conflict more inevitable:

> We are now far into the fifth year, since a policy was initiated, with the avowed object, and confident promise, of putting an end to slavery agitation. Under the operation of that policy, that agitation has not only, not ceased, but has constantly augmented.[522]

Lincoln also cautioned of "false political prophets" who won applause for the compromises that evaded the true problem—the inequality of the slave. He said the compromisers avoid a strong union, and warned: "Our cause, then, must be intrusted [sic] to, and conducted by its own undoubted friends—those whose hands are free, whose hearts are in the work—who do care for the result."[523]

The polarization lesson is to avoid the "snake oil" salesmen or the "false prophets" who, through their efforts to find a temporary compromise, only delay solving the underlying problem(s).

Lesson #3: Eventually, polarization will end.

Early in his speech, Lincoln acknowledged that polarization would eventually end and the Union would survive. He said:

I do not expect the Union to be dissolved—I do not expect the house to fall—but I do expect it will cease to be divided. It will become all one thing, or all the other.[524]

The obvious danger of this view is, given enough time, one side will win the struggle and the entire Union will be united around one outcome. Fortunately, the polarization that led to the Civil War and the devastating losses of that conflict ended with equality for all, to include those captured in the tyranny of slavery.

Both Madison and Lincoln had much to say about the polarization of their day. The lessons they gave us about that scourge may be helpful. Now, consider another polarized situation, this time from a European country that may offer applications for us today as well.

Case Study #3: Dutch Lessons

Matthijs Tieleman, a historian with Arizona State University, wrote an article, "Dutch Lessons for Political Polarization in the United States," for the *Journal of Applied History*. In it, he states that, in the eighteenth century, the Dutch Republic was terribly polarized—to the point of civil war. However, by the twentieth century, the Netherlands found that pluralism could dispel most polarization. Therefore, the Dutch experience may have lessons for the United States to help create a society of *E pluribus unum* ("out of many, one") to mitigate some of the effects of polarization in contemporary America.

Dr. Tieleman suggests the history of the Netherlands provides both a warning and an opportunity for America given its current polarized condition. After all, the Netherlands was deeply divided both culturally and politically in the eighteenth and nineteenth centuries, a situation that seemed insurmountable at the time and pressed that country to the point of civil war.[525]

The former Dutch Republic, the predecessor to the current Kingdom of the Netherlands, had political parallels to America's two lead-ing political parties (Democrats and Republicans), the Patriots and the Orangists. Those parties grew out of the divisions that dated back to the Dutch Revolt in the late sixteenth century, when the States Party (*staats-gezinden*) and the Orangist Party (*prinsgezinden*) wrestled for control at every level of government.[526]

The States Party was representative of the urban merchant class, which tended to favor provincial sovereignty over the centralized power of the *stadtholder*, the Dutch Republic's elective executive/chief magis-trate from the fifteenth to late eighteenth centuries. The States Party's preference for provincial power, according to Dr. Tieleman, was a cover for the ambition to dominate the Dutch Republic through the central government. That leverage meant the *stadtholder* could dictate both defense and foreign policy.[527]

By contrast, the Orangist was an urban working-class party. It sought a more centralized government through the office of the *stadtholder* and for a strong land force as opposed to the States Party's preference for a strong navy to protect the country's maritime and commercial inter-ests. Specifically, the Orangist wanted a large ground force to protect the Republic from possible overland invasions from neighbors France and Germany.[528]

The political polarization between the States and Orangist parties continued through the eighteenth century, which saw the Dutch econ-omy decline as nepotism and self-enrichment increased among the rul-ing elites. Gradually in that century, the country lost much of its prestige and geopolitical heft, providing the French and British the opportunity to exploit Dutch political divisions for their own benefit.[529]

Meanwhile, while dealing with polarization in America at the time, James Madison portrayed the struggles facing the Dutch Republic in his *Federalist* papers as evidence of "imbecility in the government; discord among the provinces; foreign influence and indignities; a precarious existence in peace, and peculiar calamities from war."[530]

Many Dutch at the time likely agreed with Madison's assessment of their situation. Meanwhile, the Dutch States Party, also known as the Patriots, watched the progress of the American Revolution against the oppressive British monarchy and saw a template that might apply to them as well. Just perhaps the American revolutionary model could help reverse the Dutch decline. However, by contrast, the Dutch Orangists remained loyal to the *stadtholderate* and aligned themselves with the British monarchy as opposed to the upstart Americans.[531]

Dutch political quarrels and culture wars intensified in the late eighteenth century between the Orangists and Patriots, who believed their polarization was at the root of the nation's overall decline. Finally, the parties agreed that only unity (*eendract*) could restore the nation's former stature. But the way ahead was difficult, because the parties couldn't agree on the path to unity.

The Patriots favored copying the American model with state constitutions that favored local elections and a weak *stadtholderate*. However, they wanted to limit suffrage to membership in citizen militia in order to vote or run for local office. At the time, the militia were key for the Patriots, because they dominated those forces.[532]

Meanwhile, the Orangists thought unity could be achieved through deference to the *stadtholderate*, which favored their position at the time. Unfortunately, the Patriots never agreed to a government dominated by the *stadtholderate*, thus unity remained elusive.[533]

By the mid-nineteenth century, the Dutch found a path to solving their polarization problem. They established a parliamentary democracy in 1848 under the guise of the Kingdom of the Netherlands that was quite diverse in politics and culture, unlike the Patriot-Orangist divisions of the previous century.[534]

The new constitution allowed previously disenfranchised Catholics to participate alongside Protestants in Dutch politics, and the new guidelines provided civil liberty protections for all. The government addressed working class concerns and welcomed strong labor protections. Also, socialists of all flavors gained traction—especially among the working class in the late nineteenth century—and liberalism became a potent political force that brought about expanded suffrage and the abolition of child labor.[535]

The Dutch found that acceptance of political pluralism through compromise worked to ease tensions among their previously fragmented political and social geography. That helped overcome differences between the confessional parties, the Protestants and Catholics, and the socialists regarding issues like funding public schools. Soon, equal funding for both Christian and secular schools satisfied all camps.[536]

Those compromises created in Dutch society the process known as "pillarization," which became the cultural foundation of political pluralism in the Netherlands today. Broadly, "pillarization" means that different social factions can peacefully coexist by respecting the others' "sovereignty," a term attributed to the Dutch politician Abraham Kuyper, a former prime minister of the Netherlands (1901–1905) and an influential Calvinist theologian.[537]

"Socialists, various Christian denominations, and liberals each formed their own civil society in which they practiced their beliefs and shaped their political ideas," explained Professor Tieleman. He continued:

> In the 20th century especially people of different faiths and worldviews created new institutions and organized their social lives almost entirely based on their respective pillars. Each faction, for example, created their own broadcasting organization on the Dutch public—first radio and then later television—networks. They were provided with equal government funds if they met certain membership targets.[538]

The Dutch concept of pillarization created reliable constituencies with very few so-called swing voters. And in fact, voters became less loyal to political parties and more open-minded to voting for new parties and ideas.[539]

Now, in the twenty-first century, the Dutch period of pillarization is gone, but the cultural political pluralism continues. Today, the Dutch parliament has more than a dozen political parties, and the largest one has no more than 30 percent of the seats. This political splintering results in a better representation of the complex array of opinions and reveals the pluralistic political landscape of the country.[540]

Does the Dutch pillarization template have application for America in the twenty-first century? After all, compromise and pluralism eased Dutch tensions between warring political factions while preserving societal diversity. America has a similar political divide today. Further, the dueling Dutch political parties faced likely destruction of their country had they not put aside their stark differences to compromise and insist on national unity. Only then did they find the means to accomplish their policy goals.

On a personal note, I've spent considerable time in the Netherlands over the decades—in Dutch homes and churches, and traveling with Dutch citizens. It's my opinion that the Dutch created a host of parallel mini-cultures that coexist while remaining rather insular from one another. You find in the Netherlands today considerable diversity that includes a rich, vibrant Christian culture astride a rather spiritually dark, parallel culture. Those insular political-aligned subsocieties have limited interaction except in the commercial and the political coalition spaces. Yes, pluralism is very real in Holland, and political polarization isn't that obvious because of the parallel subcultures that stay to themselves.

Perhaps this approach works because the Netherlands is a small country in terms of both population and geography. It does have a diverse population as far as religion and ethnicity. Whether that model would work for the United States to mitigate against the current level of polarization is the pregnant question, and one worthy of consideration. However, I acknowledge that, in order to do this, the US would have to move from a national structure now limited to essentially two parties to one more like a parliament that would force coalition-building, which tends to be, according to the historic record, one marked by significant instability.

Conclusion

This chapter considered three case studies on how to overcome polarization. Each had a unique set of circumstances, and the outcomes appear to have helped mitigate the consequences of polarization. They offer insights that Americans ought to consider as we wrestle to put aside polarization to find unity.

chapter fifteen

Strategies to Address Division

Unity is strength, division is weakness.[541]
—Swahili proverb

Division/polarization happens at all levels of life; we see it within the primary building block of society, the family, but also more broadly in politics, religion, education, the workplace, culture, and government. I outlined some of the impact of division/polarization for each of these venues in section III of this volume. Of course, there are mitigation strategies that apply for each of these settings. However, those strategies are not generally prescriptive across the board, because each situation is unique.

This chapter presents general strategies to address polarization at three levels: personal/family group; company/organization; and macro or national. Clearly, these strategies are derived from the works of a host of scholars, experts—albeit from a secular perspective—to address social interactions that encourage cohesion, teamwork, and cooperation, and that generally produce harmony, not polarization, at those levels. The next section will address the Christian principles that apply to division and how, in a spiritual context, they can work against polarization.

I come to this chapter with some trepidation, however. I have an advanced degree in organization development and many years of experience as a leader in military and civilian, government and nongovernment (for- and not-for-profit) organizations. However, I doubt anyone can with certitude guarantee they have a truly effective strategy to address division/polarization at all three levels addressed in this chapter, primarily because the phenomenon requires an understanding of a host of sciences like psychology, sociology, and anthropology. At best, I'm presenting alternative approaches/strategies in this text that ought to be considered and then altered if they don't work.

Strategy to Overcome Divisions in Small Social Groups

We live in a society torn by polarization on issues like abortion, race, government, politics, religion, lifestyle, and much more. Division/polarization is especially delicate when we meet as a family unit because there can be dramatic differences of opinion on such divisive topics. Most often at such gatherings, we know to remain silent about certain matters; otherwise, those discussions could be explosive and further polarize the family. So, we avoid those topics like the plague.

There are things we can do to avoid those no-go discussion zones. Specifically, to prevent the infrequent family get-together from deteriorating into an awkward or heated discussion and resulting in hurt feelings, there are strategies that might help. After all, we often come to those gatherings already warned by prior explosive occasions when Aunt June or Uncle Ted were ideologically charged on very sensitive issues that we find morally or otherwise misguided.

Below are four approaches that might prove useful to help maintain peace in situations where there are issues and/or political divisions within the immediate and extended family. So, the objective is to maintain harmony while perhaps sharing our perspective without being attacked.

I like Nick Cady's suggestions in his article, "4 Strategies for Families Divided by Politics," at nickcady.org. At first, these suggestions may seem rather stilted or programmatic. However, based on personal experience, they can work, given the opportunity.[542]

Establish Ground Rules

Although that may sound rather uncomfortable, agreeing up front on some simple ground rules for family discussions can help avert much potential conflict. For example, don't accuse the other person; rather, make "only perception-based statements." Mr. Cady suggests examples of how to use this strategy, such as: "Rather than, 'You people are…' say something like, 'This stance comes across to me as….'" That takes the onus of blame off the other person and the focus becomes your "perception" of the issue. That opens the door for the other party to outline their view about the issue, which could inform your understanding, but not necessarily change your mind.

Another aspect of this strategy is to "discuss issues, not identities." Instead of beginning a conversation with an accusation: "You pro-life people are…," a better approach is to express an affirmative view, such as by saying: "I disagree with the abortion policy because…". Express that view in a non-condescending, non-judgmental manner that includes words that welcome further discussion.

Don't allow the discussion to begin with a negative tone. That's no way to build bridges, which should be your objective when you sincerely care for the other person. If the conversation starts that way, then take a break and avoid further discussion on the issue or find common ground that allows for a civil discussion. It's not worth dividing your family gathering and perhaps forever soiling unity. However, you should find a way to discuss your concerns without trampling on the others' feelings.

It's important to mention a necessary caveat here. There are principled positions on issues that shouldn't be compromised away. Stake your ground, present the facts in a non-judging manner, and make suggestions for further consideration by the family member who disagrees, such as by recommending a book that provides a thorough analysis of the value-charged issue.

Begin with a Focus on the Big Picture

This is an especially helpful strategy when talking about divisive political issues. Mr. Cady illustrates this approach by making a distinction between the marketing of politics that portrays the opposition as "dangerous and evil," as opposed to the everyday political interactions. The political campaign is designed to be polarizing; it is a means of marketing the candidate and selling a particular political view. Of course, as we've all seen, once the political campaign with its incendiary rhetoric is behind us, the politician's tone inevitably changes to something more conciliatory.

We've seen this scene play out in virtually every political campaign. For example, in 2016, outgoing President Barack Obama said the Republican candidate for the presidency, Donald Trump, was "very dangerous" and "a threat to democracy." Those are fighting words for some Republicans. Trump wasn't any less attacking. He called Obama "a disaster," "the founder of ISIS [a Mideastern terrorist group]" and the "most ignorant president in our history." So much for hyperbole. However, as the 2016 campaign wound down and Trump's victory appeared virtually certain, President Obama became far more conciliatory. He said: "Trump will be his president," they were "on the same team," and he was "committed to helping Trump succeed." In time, Mr. Trump said of Obama after the campaign: "He is a very good man."[543]

That's quite a contrast between comments made in the heat of the campaign and those made after the votes were counted. After all, politics is a contest much like a football rivalry between two state schools. Sometimes we say things at the pep rally or seated among other fans in the stands on game day that would otherwise not come out of our mouths.

The tone of our comments inevitably changes after the game, however. I've been to a number of Army-Navy football games, the annual classic matchup between the two service academies. The rhetoric leading up to the game is often harsh, and on the day of the game, we say things about the opponent we don't really mean. However, once the game time lapses and the score is final, the Middies and the Cadets meet in centerfield to exchange handshakes. Then they move to opposite corners of the field, win or lose, to sing their respective alma maters.

The same approach to rivalries—whether sports, political, or other issues—ought to go no further. Understand that the nature of the political campaign, the pre-game pep rallies, and the issue debates on school campuses or community school boards are much the same. Don't allow those artificially created rivalries—especially within the family—to be more than temporary. Acknowledge their purpose and return to the point that, although you favor one side, you can still have a relationship with your disagreeing family member. Harmony is paramount.

Affirm Values Undermining Others' Views

I agree that, on certain issues like abortion, affirming the other person's perspective may be hard to do. Why? Because you care for the other person—a family member. Perhaps they believe as they do because "they want to make things better," Mr. Cady writes. Yes, the family member may in fact be passionate, caring, and thoughtful. Perhaps they really believe they are opposing evil and advancing the interests of others.

You can only ascertain the motivation behind their support for a particular position by discussing the underlying rationale. Take that opportunity to affirm some of the values behind their reasoning and, if possible, acknowledge whether you share the same values.

An illustration of this approach might be a discussion of the life issue. You might say, "I'm pro-life because I believe the child conceived in the woman's womb is a real human being who deserves the opportunity of life just like anyone else." In response to the discussion point by the opposite view—it's a woman's right to abort (kill) the child—you can affirm that the view stems from compassion for the woman, especially if she is poor, has no spouse, or already has other children. Don't attack the family member but affirm the shared view that the hypothetical pregnant woman considering abortion may face some serious challenges. Do express compassion for her situation, and perhaps more specifically express compassion for her economic plight. At that point, you might need to step in to recommend alternative strategies that might lead the woman to keep the child, such as helping her financially. Then the discussion becomes less emotional, not as morally charged, and more focused on helping her keep the child or give the infant to a family who seeks to adopt.

Invite Others to Share Their Views

Invite others to talk about their views on the topic. After all, most people enjoy talking about themselves, and your listening is an expression of respect. Just hear them out and don't interrupt—a real challenge for those of us who may be highly-verbal people.

Good listening is a cultivated art. We read in Hebrews 12:2 that Jesus suffered on the cross for our sake in order to repair our broken relationship with Him. For much the same reason, to restore a relationship, we can "suffer" through listening to our disagreeing family member(s). Mr. Cady notes that listening intently and without interrupting may affirm "the good values and principles in their views. You might just find that the other person is so surprised and honored that you took the time to hear them out that they are most open to listening to you in return."[544]

This approach changes a potentially toxic, divisive discussion in your family into a healthy and amiable discussion that potentially could change minds about contentious issues.

Strategy to Overcome Divisions in Large Groups

Division in the public sector, workplaces, and other types of organizations is mitigated by building trust and overcoming biases among the workers/fellow members.

Consider some alternative strategies to overcoming division/polarization in those settings.

John Maxwell offers some helpful ideas about overcoming polarization in team situations—from two-person small businesses to giant corporations. Mr. Maxwell is well positioned to address this topic. He has decades of working with corporate leaders to inspire, challenge, and equip organizations to reach their potential. He's the author of more than one hundred books, including several *New York Times* bestsellers. He has also taught what he knows about organizations, culture, and leadership to Fortune 500 company leaders and university staffs, as well as to church and community leaders.[545]

I subscribe to these same ideas because I taught them to infantrymen at Fort Benning, Georgia, where I served three years as the chief of leadership and ethics instruction for the US Army's Infantry School and Center.

Mr. Maxwell wrote an article outlining these practices, "Leading in Polarizing Times," in which he said: "All over the world, we are now defined largely by what separates us." He wrote that this makes a challenging culture to navigate, and leaders "are tasked with finding what unites [as opposed to polarizes] people in order to get things done."[546]

There are "five practices which leaders must embrace in order to bring people together," writes Mr. Maxwell, and he begins with the practice of "clarity."

Clarity: "A leader who can't be clear is a leader that can't bring a group of people into a functioning team," writes Maxwell. He states that, first, leaders must make clear their values and vision, the foundation of their leadership style. Values are the basis of our integrity and create trust in our leadership. A clear vision is critical so that everyone is moving in the same direction, and that's key because, as Maxwell writes, "When you know what you stand for and where you're going, you have a greater chance to rally people to your side."[547]

Connection: Good leaders get to know their people and don't just assume their physical presence means they agree. Too often, new leaders expect employees to come to them with issues. That's naïve. You must be intentional about getting to know them—and make it a daily practice. Further, often informal, one-on-one, ad hoc encounters with employees is far more productive than town halls, where you bring everyone together to talk at them and dare them to ask questions.[548]

Compassion: Leaders must recognize that the world includes many views, not just those that are in your realm. Good leaders sacrificially set aside their own desires and agenda and throw themselves into someone else's view/perspective. Yes, this means leaders must demonstrate humility and empathy by taking time to look employees in the eyes and try to understand them.[549]

Candor: Don't believe sugar-coating everything helps. Sometimes leaders have to be perfectly candid with employees, because that's often best for the organization and the employees. As Maxwell writes: "Leaders cannot lead well if they can't or won't speak the truth to their team." Be truthful and at the same time express genuine concern and understanding when discussing issues with employees. That helps build trust and solid, cohesive teams.[550]

Courage: As a US Army infantry leader, I found that setting the example by being near the danger point often emboldened my soldiers. The same is true in the civilian context: Demonstrating courage by stepping into the middle of a situation often brings people together.[551]

Mr. Maxwell writes about a company leader who, once every few months, brings his entire company together for a voluntary meeting. He also provides them lunch—a good incentive—and then, once everyone is seated and eating, he intentionally brings a topic of conversation to the gathering. Then he grows quiet and listens to the conversation.

The selected topic for discussion is usually a hot-button issue he knows people are already discussing. Soon the conversation takes off, and he hears a diversity of views and perspectives. The leader purposely never puts his opinion into the mix; rather, he sits back and learns. Yes, as Maxwell argues, this approach takes courage, and some of the issues are in fact quite divisive. However, the byproduct of such lunches is that it creates a safer culture for the people in the company. They get to know one another, and they are reminded that not everyone thinks the same way.

Yes, leadership can also be polarizing at times, which means we must work especially hard to achieve unity in the team. It is a difficult and sometimes unpleasant effort, but a necessary one. As Maxwell wisely states: "We can't run from it, so that means we must run to it—with clarity, connection, compassion, candor, and courage."[552]

Three Recommendations

Martin Reeves, chairman of Boston Consulting Group's BCG Henderson Institute in San Francisco, is the lead author of the article, "How Business Leaders Can Reduce Polarization," a 2021 piece in the *Harvard Business Review*. His thesis is that "by taking a selective and strategic approach, CEOs can reduce the harm of polarization first within their own companies, and then within their broader communities by focusing on issues and situations where they have self-interest, credibility, and influence." The article offers strategies to bridge the divide.[553]

Polarization can have a significant impact on the bottom line for companies, a major reason for companies to attack the problem. However, Mr. Reeves warns that companies that take a public position on controversial issues risk alienating their employees and customer base.[554]

Corporations can find themselves at financial risk if they fail to address polarizing issues in the marketplace of ideas. However, taking a public position on potentially controversial issues can be a two-edged-sword, because some customers will view the corporation's stance as a litmus for winning or keeping their business. Thus, Reeves argues that CEOs ought to practice "corporate statesmanship" by being visible on social and political issues.[555]

Reeves outlines three major actions associated with addressing polarization for the large corporation: bridge the divide, influence the ecosystem, and inspire broader impact. The *Harvard Business Review* article details each recommendation. I summarize each area below.

Bridge the divide: Mr. Reeves encourages CEOs to understand and address the context of the rising polarization problem in a strategic manner. He begins by calling on CEOs to first get their own houses in order.

Address polarization within your own organization to create a stronger foundation for external influence, Reeves argues. The workplace is the social setting that draws a cross section of people who don't necessarily share the same values and views about issues. Thus, creating connections among the diverse workforce can prove to be valuable and a reliable source of social cohesion, marginalizing polarization.[556]

There is a key bottom-line purpose for marginalizing polarization in the workforce. A survey of workers found that a quarter (24 percent) said a divisive political workplace can impact work outcomes, including yielding lower productivity. That's why leaders must bridge those gaps to foster cooperation, writes Reeves.[557]

Influence the company's ecosystem: Business leaders have influence over others in their ecosystem: customers, suppliers, and other business stakeholders. The anti-polarization role enables business leaders to broaden their influence on issues of common interest. Reeves makes the point that "a strong ecosystem can amplify the expression and realization of a company's purpose and afford expanded possibilities to address the context of polarization."[558]

Inspire broader impact: Mr. Reeves believes that businesses can build public trust just as there is a general decline in confidence in public institutions. The article cautions business leaders to focus on only a few specific areas related to the firm's expertise that are also consistent with the company's beliefs and actions. He argues such leaders might have "more ability to shape emerging issues than those that are already highly polarized."[559]

Mr. Reeves develops each of these recommendations in his article, then concludes that "polarization is unlikely to disappear anytime soon, and it can have severe ramifications for businesses," a clear caution for the public sector. However, taking an appropriate strategic approach by focusing on only a few issues at once may help mitigate polarization while serving the organization's best bottom-line interests.[560]

Strategy to Overcome Divisions at the National Level

National-level division/polarization is mostly about politics, ideology, and divisive issues. That's the focus of this strategy. We turn to three British scholars for some key insights: Lee de-Wit, a political psychologist at Cambridge University; Sander van der Linden, an assistant professor of social psychology at Cambridge; and Cameron Brick, also a social psychologist and research associate at Cambridge. Their 2019 article, "What Are the Solutions to Political Polarization?" is published by *Greater Good Magazine*, a product of the University of California at Berkeley.[561]

The article provides recommendations on the drivers behind political polarization. More specifically, the authors' thesis is that "we can build bipartisan support for specific policies by focusing more on their boring nuts and bolts."[562]

The authors call out a number of studies that suggest "people like policies proposed by members of their own in-group—and they don't like ideas generated by out-groups."[563] They explain that, for decades, social psychologists have attempted to understand the opposition between groups, and their findings are the basis for the recommendations in their article.[564]

Further, the article indicates that the most divisive topics tend to be deeply rooted in moral beliefs, such as those about responsibility, like,

"People's outcomes in life are determined largely by forces out of their control," or "People are largely responsible for their own outcomes in life." Also, the authors illustrate that ideological liberals and conservatives tend to differ on common issues like parenting and a host of other human efforts.[565]

The Cambridge colleagues cite a study with an intriguing hypothesis. Specifically, a 2019 study, "Voters' Partisan Responses to Politicians' Immoral Behavior," presented two thousand participants with "examples of different moral violations by different actors." What they found was that "it wasn't the nature of the moral violation that was most important. Instead, it was the political allegiance of the violator. Democrats in the study were prone to giving Democrats a pass; the same was even more true of Republicans."[566]

Thus, this partisan influence on policies juxtaposed with moral judgments provides insight for addressing polarization at the nation-state level. The authors suggest political seeds that drive polarization are exacerbated by psychological processes "that shape how we interpret identity and groups." In turn, to reverse polarization, the authors argue, we need to identify political solutions grounded in understanding social psychology.[567]

The article introduces five political solutions that might in fact affect polarization at the national level. These are worthy of consideration.

Intergroup Contact

The underlying idea is that getting to know contrary groups can reduce prejudice and polarization. Doing so, according to the authors, means that "many conditions have to be met for contact [with the contrary group] to reduce prejudice," polarization. Specifically, they suggest the communication must be "with more than one member [of the contrary group]" that includes "a genuine exchange of ideas, and between individuals of similar social rank."[568]

Perspective Taking

Another strategy is to get to know the others' perspective. Evidently, this approach has some merit based on an experiment cited by the article, whereby exchanges of perspective actually altered people's attitudes on a controversial topic. Interestingly, the authors also indicate the revolution in communication technology, especially the advent of social media with government oversight, has accelerated polarization. Therefore, introducing the masses to contrary perspectives may in fact mitigate some cultural polarization.[569]

Superordinate Goals

Evidently, psychological literature indicates that identity-based conflicts tend to require a "superordinate" sense of identity "to bring people back together." Therefore, to make this happen, "we need a large sense of ourselves that is able to bridge smaller differences." We've seen this in history, whereby a sense of who we were as Americans was a driver that spawned great nationalism to face the challenges of World War II. Then again, there is a serious downside to such an approach.[570]

Richard Dawkins, a British evolutionary biologist, author, and professor of a course titled Public Understanding of Science at the University of Oxford, tweeted:

> National pride has evil consequences. Prefer pride in humanity. German pride gave us Hitler, American pride gave us Trump, British pride gave us Brexit. If you must have pride, be proud that *Homo sapiens* could produce a Darwin, Shakespeare, Mandela, Einstein, Beethoven.[571]

The risks of "superordinate goals" can be polarizing itself. It can be used to advance destructive nationalism, if left to populists like Adolf

Hitler rather than keeping it more abstract. After all, as former British prime minister Theresa May said about a "universalist perspective": "If you believe you are a citizen of the world, you are a citizen of nowhere."[572]

Proportional Voting

This is a concept used elsewhere, but not in the United States, and it warrants further consideration. We must understand the context in which political decisions are made. Specifically, in the US, the political community is dominated by just two parties: Democratic and Republican. Therefore, the outcome of all elections is a process that exacerbates polarization, because the "winner takes all." Alternatively, some countries use a proportional system, which means if a party gets "5 percent of the popular vote, they will receive 5 percent of the seats in a given representative body." However, in the US, where, generally speaking, only two parties compete for votes, the loser gets no representation—"which could worsen the us-and-them dynamic of the U.S. political system."[573]

Another positive outcome of the proportional system is countries with that system tend to realize higher levels of voter turnout.[574] Higher voter turnout and earning a share of the seats in a representative body correlates "with citizens being more likely to report feeling that their vote makes a difference." Therefore, politics isn't nearly as polarizing.

Voting for Policies, Not Parties

The final recommendation to mitigate national political polarization is to "hold direct referendums on specific issues." Countries like Switzerland regularly use referendums to address complex policy topics. In fact, I participated as an ally with my Swiss friends in the late 1990s, helping them fight the pro-drug referendum in that country. While serving as the Vice President for Policy at the Family Research Council, my staff helped produce in Swiss German a documentary on the harms associated with drug use and called for defeating the referendum to liberalize that nation's drug policy that included heroin give-away clinics. We failed in that effort, but at least we had the opportunity to help our friends voice their opposition.[575]

"The psychological impact of more direct voting systems is worthy of further enquiry," states the article. I agree. Well implemented referendums can cut across existing polarized political lines and "help establish a new social norm that can move a country forward."

Conclusion

This chapter addressed three distinctive venues for mitigating polarization: the family level; the business/organization level; and the national level. The profiled strategies are just suggestions that might help address the challenges and in fact reduce the level of division/polarization all too common within our culture.

Section V

CHRISTIAN LIVING AND PROPHETIC IMPLICATIONS OF DIVISION

Jesus himself did not try to convert the two thieves on the cross; he waited until one of them turned to him.[576]
—DIETRICH BONHOEFFER, *Letters and Papers from Prison*

Bible-believing Christians should approach the phenomenon of division differently from the secular world. We must appreciate that Satan uses division to accomplish his goal of world dominance. Perhaps Dietrich Bonhoeffer (1906–1945), a German Lutheran pastor and anti-Nazi dissident who was hung by the Nazi regime in 1945, understood the struggle best. In his book, *Letters and Papers from Prison*, Bonhoeffer asks: "Who stands fast?" This is a question that helps believers understand who we are and our role in this world.

"The great masquerade of evil has played havoc with all ethical concepts," Bonhoeffer writes. "For evil to appear disguised as light, charity, historical necessity, or social justice is quite bewildering to anyone brought up on our traditional ethical concepts, while for the Christian who bases his life on the Bible it merely confirms the fundamental wickedness of evil."[577]

Then Bonhoeffer answers his question "Who stands fast?" He writes:

Only the man whose final standard is not his reason, his principles, his conscience, his freedom, or his virtue, but who is ready to sacrifice all this when he is called to be obedient and responsible action in faith and in exclusive allegiance to God—the responsible man, who tries to make his whole life an answer to the question and call of God. Where are these responsible people?[578]

This section in two chapters addresses Bonhoeffer's rhetorical questions: "Who stands fast?" and "Where are these responsible people?" He is addressing Bible-obedient Christians, not the lost. He calls on us to take a spiritual approach to the works of Satan, and in particular, the Devil's evil use of division.

In the previous section, I provided strategies for overcoming division across three venues: the family level, the business level, and the national level. These strategies are written from a secular point of view in that they apply generally to all of us who live in this fallen world. However, for Christians, as Bonhoeffer implies, there is much more to division/polarization, as we learned in chapter 3 of this volume, "Satan's Work among the Vulnerable and Powerful."

Chapter 16 provides Bible-based principles for addressing the truths about the spiritual reality we must live with today. Those principles are critical to apply in helping us—and, by association, others—overcome polarization. Sometimes, because they are Bible-based moral principles, they will overlap with the secular strategies outlined in the previous section.

Ultimately, we must understand that division is a tool in the hand of Satan. After all, his soon-coming Antichrist will seek to further divide the world to usher in the prophetic end times. Chapter 17, the final one in this volume, calls out particular Scripture passages that expose this reality—specifically, how Satan and his army of demons intend to use their polarization means in the end times, and how we must prayerfully discern that agenda and recognize its implications.

chapter sixteen

Spiritual War with Division

> I appeal to you, brothers, to watch out for those who cause divisions and create obstacles contrary to the doctrine that you have been taught; avoid them. For such persons do not serve our Lord Christ, but their own appetites, and by smooth talk and flattery they deceive the hearts of the naive.
> —Romans 16:17–18 (ESV)

I don't believe God ever intended for the world to be filled with angry, divisive people. Today, however, many people are angry about almost everything—from politics to religion and much more. We should blame Satan for the polarization. That anger, which is rooted in our sin, dates back to the book of Genesis, when mankind fell and then God scattered us across the earth (Genesis 11, the account of the Tower of Babel).

That brings us to the spiritual consequences of today's polarized world and how Christians ought to respond to this tragic situation. Although all humans have similar daily challenges, such as securing food and locating a safe place to live, we don't all view the world the same way, as explained in chapter 2, "Roots of the Powerful Who Use Division." Therefore, those of us with a spiritually based worldview are fundamentally disconnected from the world by God's design; therefore, we are naturally polarized from the balance of humanity on very significant, mostly moral issues. After all, in John 16:13, Christ promised to send the Holy Spirit to guide us to the truth, the essence of our polarization from this world.

On a broader view and spiritually speaking, our enemy polarizes all of us, using hate speech and the constant bombardment of negative programming from all media that further inflames our polarization. Therefore, our task in this world is to tune out and turn off the messages presented by this hateful environment and turn on our spiritual discernment with the Spirit's help to see not only the manipulation of our thinking by the father of lies (Satan), but also to take up a biblical approach to all of those polarizing messages and circumstances.

We turn on spiritual discernment by constantly leaning on the Holy Spirit and applying His biblical principles to life's challenges in order to counter polarization. Specifically, the Scriptures give us guidelines to respond to polarization, which admittedly are often difficult to execute because they need to govern how we interact with those with whom we often disagree. Further, we must apply these principles within the context of emulating the example of Jesus Christ in approaching reconciliation.

Biblical Principles about Division: Old Testament

Principles found in both the Old and New Testaments are key to overcoming the effects of division. Below, I paraphrase a few applicable Old Testament Scripture passages, followed by the general application for today's Christians, and then identify the principle that might help defeat polarization. This discussion will be followed by a look at New Testament principles.

Find Strength with Likeminded People (Ecclesiastes 4:12)

Ecclesiastes is a Greek word for a person who calls an assembly, and in Ecclesiastes 1:1 the author identified himself by the Hebrew word *Qoheleth,* which means "preacher." There is good reason to believe the author of the book of Ecclesiastes is King Solomon, the son of David, king in Jerusalem at the time, the one who has increased in "wisdom more than all who were over Jerusalem before me," and the one who collected many proverbs (Ecclesiastes 1:1,16, NAS).

Solomon wrote in Ecclesiastes 4:12 (ESV), "And though a man might prevail against one who is alone, two will withstand him—a threefold cord is not quickly broken." This verse expresses the antithesis of division, the importance of not being alone. Previously in the book of Ecclesiastes, Solomon said life is vanity for a man who is alone and toils for nothing. However, Solomon extolled the virtues of having partners.

The principle: Spend more time with fellow believers (Christians) than with the lost, who tend to be divisive.

Speak the Truth (Genesis 3:4; Exodus 20:16)

Watch your tongue, Christian. It's very easy in today's world to lie, or to do what some try to categorize as "fabricate the truth." You should be reliably known for speaking the truth. After all, we are reminded in John 16:13 that God's Spirit guides the believer into all truth. We should rely on the Holy Spirit and dare to consistently be truthful.

We are reminded in Genesis 3:4 that lies lead to destruction, and, as Exodus 20:16 encourages, we should build relationships on foundations of truth and honesty. Further, according to Psalm 120:2–3 we are to avoid liars and deceivers, and always remember: "The Lord detests lying lips, but he delights in people who are trustworthy" (Proverbs 12:22, NIV).

The principle: Be known for speaking the truth, which defeats division.

Have an Undivided Allegiance to God, with Grace and Gratitude (Ephesians 5:20; Colossians 3:17).

The Apostle Paul is known for being thankful. He wrote about giving thanks for all things, no matter the circumstances (1 Thessalonians 5:18) and seeking the opportunity to do everything in the name of Jesus with all gratefulness (Colossians 3:17). James, the half-brother of Jesus, the likely author of the book of James, wrote about being thankful in suffering: "Consider it all joy my brethren, when you encounter various trials" (James 1:2, NAS).

Living this way is evidence of obedience to Christ and, as a result, we truly stand out in this fallen culture.

The principle: To embrace Paul's encouragement by living a grateful life in the face of division. This is all about the attitude you embrace as division surrounds your life.

Have a Heart Undivided between God and Earthly Treasures (Hosea 10:1–2)

God told the Israelites that when they entered the promised land, they were to totally destroy everything (Deuteronomy 2:34; 20:16–18). Why? To prevent the foreigners there from teaching them to follow all the detestable things they did in worshipping their pagan gods, influencing the Israelites to sin against the Lord God. Of course, the Israelites failed in that mission; they were divided from God's plan for them and disgraced God (Judges 2:1–3; 1 Kings 11:5; 14:24; 2 Kings 16:3–4). The purpose of the commandment to "destroy" was to prevent a greater evil and protect the people of God from harm.

Unfortunately, up to that time, the Israelites had a history of abandoning God to worship other "gods." We saw them quickly turn from God while Moses was on Mount Sinai receiving the Ten Commandments. Time and again, even after they entered the Promised Land, as evidenced in the book of the Judges, the Israelites forgot God's mandate not to abandon Him.

The principle: Avoid worshipping other gods, such as financial security, which diverts (divides) our attention from God.

Biblical Principles about Division: New Testament

A number of New Testament principles address division.

In fact, four Greek words in the New Testament are translated "division," according to *Strong's Concordance*, and these words often sketch out principles.

Diamerismos means "breaking up," "discord," or "hostility." It is found in Galatians 5:19–21 to describe one of the works of the flesh, and in Romans 16:17, it is used to urge believers to avoid those who cause divisions.

The word *dischostasia* means "division," "dissension," or "standing apart." It is used in Luke 12:51 (NIV), where we read that Jesus asks: "Do you think I came to bring peace on earth? No, I tell you, but division."

The third word for "division" in the New Testament is *schisma*, which means "to rend, as in a garment," or "dissension." It is used eight times, such as in Matthew 9:16 (NIV): "No one sews a patch of unshrunk cloth on an old garment, for the patch will pull away from the garment, making the tear worse."

The fourth word, *apodiorizo*, is found in Jude 19 (NIV): "These are the people who divide you, who follow mere natural instincts and do not have the Spirit."

With these definitions in mind, consider some principle-based uses of the term "division" in the New Testament.

Don't Be Divided about the Truth of God (John 17:20–23)

Christ, just prior to the Crucifixion, called for His disciples to be united (John 17:20–23). This call for unity applies more universally for all believers to be united with Christ and each other. Thus, the lesson here is to avoid division. After all, in Romans 16:17 (NIV), the Apostle Paul warns:

> I urge you, brothers and sisters to watch out for those who cause divisions and put obstacles in your way that are contrary to the teaching you have learned. Keep away from them.

This teaching continues in Paul's first letter to the Corinthians:

> I appeal to you, brothers and sisters, in the name of our Lord Jesus Christ, that all of you agree with one another in what you say and that there be no divisions among you, but that you be perfectly united in mind and thought. (1 Corinthians 1:10, NIV)

The conclusion is that division is a result of the flesh (sin), and is contrary to the true fruit of the spirit.

Paul identifies division among our many sinful tendencies in his letter to the Galatians as well:

> Now the works of the flesh are evident: sexual immorality, impurity...dissensions, *divisions,* envy...and things like these. I warn you, as I warned you before, that those who do such things will not inherit the kingdom of God." (Galatians 5:19–21, ESV; emphasis added)

How are we to respond to such division when it shows its ugly head in the body of Christ? We are instructed to correct believers who cause such division. In Titus 3:10 (NIV), we read: "Warn a divisive person once, and then warn them a second time. After that, have nothing to do with them." Evidently, the Bible teaches there can be no unity without truth, and the toleration of teaching that does not promote truth is unacceptable and divisive. Therefore, action to remove that sin or false teaching is necessary.

Division is often the result of selfishness, and as Philippians 2:1–4 (ESV) states:

> So if there is any encouragement in Christ, any comfort from love…do nothing from selfish ambition or conceit…let each of you look not only to his own interests, but also to the interests of others.

The principle: To oppose division, embrace unity within the Body.

Oppose Efforts to Divide and Redefine Marriages (Mark 10:6–8)

In this polarizing world, God's Word counts. Jesus is clear when it comes to divorce: Marriage, between one man and one woman, was ordained by God. As Christ said: "What therefore God has joined together, let no man separate" (Mark 6:9, NAS). That verse also applies to efforts to redefine marriage, as is common in our culture. The so-called same-sex (homosexual) union is nowhere condoned in the Scriptures. In fact, the homosexual's defining behavior is condemned by God (Romans 1:26; 1 Timothy 1:10). Also, don't forget: God specifically names the purpose of marriage in Matthew 19:4–6, that it is for a man and woman to "become one flesh" (Matthew 19:5, NIV) and to be "fruitful" (to produce children; see Genesis 1:22).

The principle: What God created for good, Satan seeks to divide and destroy. Stand on the Word of God, especially when He explicitly defines His intention in the Bible for mankind. Each of us will ultimately give an account of our actions.

Avoid Division within the Family, God's Key Building Block of Society (Luke 11:17)

Division within families is found in the Bible and should be avoided. One of the best-known examples is found in 2 Samuel 15:13, when Absalom turns on his father, King David. The biblical narrative tells us Absalom was angry with David and, in retaliation, he turned an entire nation against the king. It's noteworthy that Absalom's name, which means "peace of my father," resulted in nothing of the kind. In this instance, David sought reconciliation.

The principle: Don't allow division within the household of faith, and, if possible, don't allow it within your earthly family, either (1 Corinthians 1:10).

Oppose Compromising because of Temptations (Romans 6:19–23; 2 Corinthians 7:1; and Ephesians 4:24)

The Christian's allegiance is first to God, no other. We see this clearly outlined in Matthew 10:37 (NIV): "Anyone who loves their father or mother more than me is not worthy of me; anyone who loves their son or daughter more than me is not worthy of me." Further, we can't have a relationship with people who remain in sin. However, we are to treat them as unbelievers and either encourage wayward believers to confess their sin and return to fellowship or to win lost people to a new life through the Gospel of Christ.

The principle: We are followers of Christ exclusively and shouldn't compromise to temptations that are divisive. Be bold and winsome for Christ.

Avoid Worldly People Who Are Devoid of the Spirit (Jude 1:19)

As Christians, we must understand that Satan and his demonic army are prowling about tempting the saved and using the lost to cause division. That's a fact of life. Recognize that division steers us away from God's truth. Also, we know that, upon Christ's return, He will divide all people into two groups, those who are His (the sheep) and those who never came to Him (the goats; see Matthew 25:31–46). Therefore, we are to test the spirits to see whether they are from God, as it says in 1 John 3:24 (NIV):

> The one who keeps God's commands lives in him, and he in them. And this is how we know that he lives in us: We know it by the Spirit he gave us.

The principle is: We are to be Christlike in this world but are not to make our home with those who aren't in Christ.

Avoid Divisive People (Romans 16:17; Titus 3:10)

Why avoid divisive people? Romans 16:18 (ESV) explains the reason: because "such persons do not serve our Lord Christ, but their own appetites, and by smooth talk and flattery they deceive the hearts of the naïve."

What should we conclude about divisive people who teach something other than "the sound instruction of our Lord Jesus Christ" (1 Timothy 6:3, NIV)? We read in 1 Timothy 6:4–5 (NIV) that such divisive people are "conceited and understand nothing. They have an unhealthy interest in controversies and quarrels about words that result in envy, strife, malicious talk, evil suspicions and constant friction between people of corrupt mind, who have been robbed of the truth and who think that godliness is a means to financial gain."

Divisive people cause others to stumble and sin in their walk with

God (Romans. 16:17), and they do not follow God's teaching. Specifically, as we see in Galatians 1:8 (NKJV), the divisive people who preach "any other gospel to you than what we have preached to you, let [them] be accursed." Those people do not serve Jesus, and, more generally: "By their fruit you will recognize them" (Romans 16:18, NIV). Are they imitators of Jesus, or do their works betray them as hypocrites?

The principle: Correct fellow believers who are divisive and call out the lost who are pushing division through their works of dissension, selfish ambition, discord, and more.

One Intentional Division: Live Openly for Christ in this Alien World

It is true that Jesus teaches about division, the outcome when God's people apply God's plan in their lives. According to Luke 6: 22–23, when we stand for Jesus, others will hate us and seek to divide us from society. However, we know from Luke 12:51–53 that Jesus did not come to bring peace, but division. His Word will divide families and set us at variance with one another. We see the same situation in Acts 14:1–4. At that time, the people in Iconium were divided by the preaching of the Gospel: some believed and others were disobedient.

The Christian is to be the "light of the world" by shining for Christ to honor our Father in heaven (Matthew 5:14, KJV). Specifically, the Christian's relationship with the world is to work like light, which exposes evil and produces what is truth. Jesus illustrates the concept in John 8:12, KJV. He declares, "I am the light of the world. He who follows Me shall not walk in darkness, but have the light of life." Therefore, Christians are to reflect the light of Christ in their living, which refers to moral deeds. We are to "put on the armor of light" as stated in Romans 13:12–14 (NKJV), by making "no provision for the flesh." The light of the Christian can change a work environment (Ephesians 5:13) and the believer maintains good conduct among non-Christians, so "when they speak against you as evildoers, they may, by your good works which they observe, glorify God in the day of visitation (1 Peter 2:12, ESV).

The principle: Don't hide your faith. You are a light to the world.

The Cross of Christ Overcomes Enmity

These biblical principles are a good starting point to apply when dealing with division. However, there is more, which has much to do with how we live for Christ in this world.

My research on the topic drew me to an article by Ronald Rolheiser, a Roman Catholic priest and the president of the Oblate School of Theology in San Antonio, Texas. Father Rolheiser penned an insightful article, "Overcoming the Divisions That Divide Us," which states that the real answer to the "enmity" that divides us today is an "understanding of how the cross and death of Jesus brings about reconciliation." That's quite insightful and helpful for contemporary Christians living in this divisive world.[579]

Father Rolheiser admits that we tend to oversimplify our divisions: left-right and liberals-conservatives, as well as pro-life and pro-choice. He agrees that "virtually every social and moral issue is a warzone: the status of women, climate change, gender roles, sexuality, marriage and family as institutions, the role of government, how the LGBTIQ [Lesbian, Gay, Bisexual, Transgender, Intersex, and Queer or Questioning] community is to be understood, among other issues."[580]

He also acknowledges that "civility has disappeared from public discourse even within our churches." Then he advances what I discussed in the last section of this volume, our proclivity to discuss contentious issues only among members of our own ideological circle, which perpetuates the same, polarizing biases.[581]

Next, Father Rolheiser calls out the scriptural term of "enmity," which is really another word for "hatred" and fuels much of today's polarization. He proposes the answer to "enmity" that polarizes us today. Specifically, he states the solution lies in an understanding of how the cross, death, and Resurrection of Jesus brings about reconciliation. He cites the Apostle Paul's words to the Ephesians to demonstrate how Jesus broke down the barrier of hostility (enmity) that existed between communities by creating one person where formerly there had been two—"and that He might reconcile them both in one body to God through the cross, by it having put to death the hostility" (Ephesians 2:16, NAS).[582]

What Christ did is "something that asks for our imitation, not simply our admiration. What happened in the cross and death of Jesus is an example for us to imitate," wrote Rolheiser. Further, thanks to the cross, Jesus transformed "bitterness and division rather than to retransmit them and give them back in kind." Father Rolheiser also wrote: Jesus "took in hatred, held it inside himself, transformed it, and gave back love." In other words, Jesus took "in enmity, bitter division, held it, transformed it, and through that revealed to us the deep secret for forming community, namely, we need to take away the hatred that divides us by absorbing and holding it within ourselves and thereby transforming it."[583]

We are like "a water purifier which holds within itself the toxins and the poisons and gives back only pure water," explained Father Rolheiser using a metaphor. Yes, that's a tall order, but, as he argues: "That stalemate [of division] will remain until one by one, we [followers of Jesus Christ] each transform rather than enflame and retransmit the hatred that divides us."[584]

Conclusion

You and I are called by God to be part of the solution, not part of the problem of division. The challenge is that we live in a very polarized world, and our Christianity makes us a target because the world hates Christ and, by association, it hates His followers as well. Therefore, we must not only embrace biblical principles in our calling to be winsome, but we are to be Christlike, and, as Father Rolheiser suggests, we need to be "water purifiers" for Christ.

chapter seventeen

Division in End-Times Prophecy

We see the storm clouds gathering and events taking place that
herald the second coming of Jesus Christ.[585]
—BILLY GRAHAM (1918—2018), American Christian evangelist

Division is a tool used by both God and Satan to bring about the
prophetic end times. In this chapter, I trace the use of division/
polarization through the prophetic Scriptures to demonstrate its role in
leading to the end times. In some instances, division is subtle, but in
others, it is quite clear and purposeful. What's certain is that division is
a tool that God and Satan will use, according to the Bible, as our world
transitions into a future that leads people to one of two destinations:
Heaven with Jesus or, for those who reject Him, separation from God in
an everlasting Hell.

Coming Great Deception: Division

Jesus warns in Matthew 24:5–8 (NIV) that a time is coming when "many will come in [Jesus'] name, claiming, 'I am the Messiah,' and will deceive many." Unfortunately, some will believe that divisive claim; others who know the true Christ will utterly reject those false Christs. Those make-believers claiming to be "the Christ" will come just as warfare increases and famines and natural disasters occur. The true Christ warns about those times and tells us not to be deceived (divided from Him), because these events are only the beginning of birth pains; the end is still yet to come.

The Apostle Paul writes in his first letter to Timothy that the true end times will be marked by political division (upheaval). Specifically, we read in 1 Timothy 4:1 (NIV) that Satan deceives (divides) people to attempt to compel them to abandon their "faith and follow deceiving spirits and things taught by demons." Further, Paul warns about "terrible times" in the last days. Those "terrible times" will be characterized by "people [being] lovers of themselves, lovers of money, boastful… unholy…unforgiving…treacherous…lovers of pleasure rather than lovers of God." These evil, divisive people will actively oppose God and seek to deceive us and divide us from the True God (2 Timothy 3:1–9, NIV).

The end times will also be marked by more division over the nation of Israel as well. While some will always support Israel, others will be hostile (polarized against) Israel, worse than the current divide experienced in the Palestinian and Arab world today. What's also clear is that having Israel as a nation in its own land as it is today is a significant end-times prophecy, as seen in Daniel 10:14; 11:41; and Revelation 11:8. After all, God promised Abraham that his seed would possess Canaan (the present-day land of Israel) as "an everlasting possession" (Genesis 17:8), and the prophet Ezekiel echoed that foretelling of the physical and spiritual resuscitation of Israel (Ezekiel 37).

Divisions from Rapture to Second Coming of Christ

Dr. John Walvoord (1910–2002), former president of Dallas Theological Seminary, was a prominent evangelical scholar in his generation. He is especially known for his interpretation of biblical prophecy. His article, "Major Events Preceding the Second Coming of Christ," provides a template for me to call out the frequent use of "division" by God and Satan's coming Antichrist in the biblical end times.[586]

Rapture of the Church

The ultimate example of division imposed by God is the Rapture of the Church, whereby Christ comes for believers, both living and dead. First Thessalonians 4:16–17 (NIV) states:

> For the Lord himself will come down from heaven, with a loud command, with the voice of the archangel and with the trumpet call of God, and the dead in Christ will rise first. After that, we who are still alive and are left will be caught up together [raptured] with them in the clouds to meet the Lord in the air. And so, we will be with the Lord forever."

The Rapture, according to Dr. Walvoord, takes place prior to the fulfillment of the last seven years described in Daniel 9:27, the period known as the Tribulation.

The Rapture is simply the removal by God (the dividing out) of all born-again believers from the earth. Specifically, we should be encouraged by these words, because we escape the imminent and hellish Tribulation, described in part in the following paragraphs.

Dr. Walvoord's article outlines the highlights associated with the Tribulation: a time of oppression and persecution—of massive division leading up to the end of the world we know today.

For context, the term "tribulation" is defined in Deuteronomy 4:30 as "trouble" or "affliction," and in Romans 2:9 as "anguish." In terms of the prophetic end times, we turn to Revelation chapters 6, 8, 9, and 16, which describe those times as a living hell for those left behind. It is this seven-year period Dr. Walvoord writes about in his article, and I use it to call out some specific examples of division, which also provide a description of the coming "anguish."

Examples of Division in the Prophetic End Times

Dr. Walvoord describes six prophetic end-times events that illustrate division. The first requires some background to appreciate: the Battle of Gog and Magog.

Gog and Magog are mentioned in four Bible books: Genesis, 1 Chronicles, Ezekiel, and Revelation. Magog was the grandson of Noah (Genesis 10:2), who settled to the north of Israel, likely in Europe and northern Asia (Ezekiel 38:2). The people (descendants) of Magog are described as skilled warriors in Ezekiel 38:15.

Gog, according to Ezekiel's prophecy, will be the leader of a great army that attacks Israel (Ezekiel 38:11). He is described as "of the land of Magog, the chief prince of Meshek and Tubal" (Ezekiel 38:2, NIV).

There are differences of opinion about the timing of the battle of Gog and Magog. Some prophecy experts believe this battle occurs before the Tribulation and others believe it happens during the first half of that seven-year period. Dr. Walvoord's view is that the battle of Gog and Magog occurs in the first half of the Tribulation.

For purposes of illustrating "division" in this biblical prophecy, I believe both Ezekiel's prophecy and John's refer to Gog and Magog as symbols of Satan and His armies—a battle between good and evil, God and Satan.

Battle of Gog and Magog

Dr. Walvoord writes that, unprovoked, there will be a divisive sneak attack by a great nation to the north of Israel, perhaps Russia (Magog), under the command of Gog (Ezekiel 36:15; 38:6, 15). That nation is joined by a coalition of other nations that attack tiny Israel, even though at the time Israel is at peace. Evidently, this attack happens in the first three and a half years of the Tribulation leading up to the Second Coming of Christ. The attack and ensuing war turn out to be disastrous for the aggressors, however (Ezekiel 39:3–6, 11–20).

Once the aggressor (likely Russia and her partners) that attacked Israel is devastated, the ruler who oversees at that time ten nations declares himself the world dictator—the "Antichrist," because he is "against Christ"—and he faces no opposition. This is a divisive, polarizing move. After all, many people at that future time will ask the questions raised in Revelation 13:4: "Who is like the beast [the Antichrist]? Who can make war against him?" Evidently, no one can deny the world's throne to this strong man, this dictator, the Antichrist. That soon-coming world leader isn't identified as to nationality, however.

Antichrist Breaks with Israel

Halfway through the Tribulation (at the three-and-a-half-year mark; see Daniel 9:27), the Antichrist breaks the peace covenant with Israel to make war (divide) against it, and that becomes a time of intense opposition for Israel. Then the Antichrist commits "the abomination of desolation," another act of division, by setting up an image of himself to be worshipped in the Jerusalem Temple (Daniel 9:27; 2 Thessalonians 2:3–10) and claiming to be God—evidence of his worst act of division (Revelation 13:8).

Death for Those Who Refuse to Worship Antichrist

The Antichrist persecutes (divides, calls out) those who refuse his author-ity. We see his reign of terror described in Revelation 6–18, as disasters and persecution fall on those who refuse to recognize him as god. Then, in Revelation 6, we read about the "seven seals"—cold war, open war, famine, death, and physical disturbances—on a scroll that names great catastrophes, such as the fifth seal, which is in the form of a death pen-alty for those who refuse to bow to the world leader as deity.

God Protects a Remnant of Israel

Meanwhile, God protects, divides/separates out 144,000 Israel-ites—12,000 from each Israeli tribe—in the final three and a half years of the Great Tribulation, as described in Revelation 7. Yes, those Israel-ites endure the Great Tribulation and gather on Mount Zion at the end of the period (Revelation 14:1).

The Battle of Armageddon

At the end of the seven-year Tribulation, the Antichrist attacks Jerusa-lem, and the battle ends at Armageddon. Then Jesus returns to earth with the armies of Heaven (Mark 14:62), destroys the Antichrist and his legions of demons, and casts them into the Lake of Fire (divides them from the world; see Revelation 19:11–21). Christ binds Satan in the Abyss for a thousand years and rules His earthly kingdom (Revelation 20:1–6). After that sentence, Satan is once again defeated and cast into the Lake of Fire for eternity (the final division; see Revelation 20:7–10).

Judgment for Unbelievers

At that point, Christ judges all unbelievers (Revelation 20:10–15) at the Great White Throne Judgment. He then divides them, separating the righteous ("sheep") from the wicked ("goats"; see Matthew 25:31–46) by casting the "goats" into the Lake of Fire with Satan and his demonic army.

Conclusion

Division is a recurring theme from the earliest time of humanity in the Garden of Eden until the prophetic end times. Arguably, at the prophetic end times, division is the primary tool that delineates the righteous from the unrighteous, which leads to a final, God-directed solution for every person who has ever breathed air on this earth.

Afterword

Hope is like an anchor. Our hope in Christ stabilizes us in the
storms of life, but unlike an anchor, it does not hold us back.[587]
—CHARLES SWINDOLL (1934), American evangelical Christian pastor,
author, radio preacher

America is increasingly divided, because it long ago abandoned faith
in God and turned to politicians for answers. Unfortunately, most
of our political class serve for all the wrong reasons. A growing number
of them are polarizing in their ideology and rhetoric, and some are no
doubt influenced by the father of lies.

This isn't what our founders intended.

No, it's no longer just our differences in politics, ideology, location
(city versus rural areas), race, ethnicity, and more that divide us. We've
lost our homogeneity, our identity as "just" Americans and as a mostly
Christian people—the glue that long preserved this country's identity.
Today, we argue among ourselves everywhere. Bathrooms have become
battlefields, our workplaces are becoming unsafe, social media outlets
are filled with hatred, our public transport venues are crime scenes, and

our cities are no-go zones. Sex, faith, ethnicity, heritage—our former melting pot of ideas and identities—are boiling over with divisions fueled by our incendiary mainstream and social media. We more often than not scurry to our social ghettos, both physical and virtual, to avoid these divisions and deny our past homogenization, something we long ago lost, to embrace the mantle of self-identities along narrow lines of race, ideology, social class, and ethnicity.

Why is the America that many of us once loved being transformed into a dangerous and unrecognizable place? That's simple. We've allowed division/polarization to prevail across all strata and issues of American society. However, we didn't start this way two and a half centuries ago.

America's founders based our constitutional republic on an idea, *E pluribus unum*, which, as stated earlier, is Latin for the phrase "out of many, one." This expression appears on the Great Seal of the United States thanks to an act of the US Congress in 1782, and it is our de facto motto. Out of necessity at our founding, we bound together our original thirteen colonies around ideas of liberty, freedom, respect, and faith in God. Yes, we more often than not put aside our differences to embrace the idea of a common national identity, even though we continued to treasure our personal independence and right of conscience. Today, however, the ideological left's evil calls for diversity, equity, and inclusion are inconsistent with our founding principles because they divide us, not homogenize our differences. As a result, we are quickly losing the precious gift God, through our founders, gave this nation.

In five sections, *Divided* has explored the phenomenon of "division," especially its spiritual background. Section 1, "Roots of Division," looked at the instrument of division as it applies across society and called out the actors pushing this destructive tool. Its instrumentation is aided by the corrupting worldview of the most powerful people in society, who more often than not serve Satan's evil purposes and, by association, use division as a wedge to accomplish their own often nefarious intentions. This section concluded with a glimpse behind the veil of the unseen world to expose Satan's role in recruiting human proxies—mostly today's powerful, divisive people—to advance His evil objectives.

This book traced division's usefulness to the dawn of mankind, the Garden of Eden. Section II surveyed division and polarization throughout history to demonstrate that it's an ancient tool of the powerful and the handiwork of the father of lies, Satan. We reviewed division internationally over two World Wars, and we profiled some contemporary evil leaders and icons of our polarizing world. Domestically, *Divided* has highlighted our sad, polarized history by considering the American Civil War, the Vietnam War era, and the emergence of two very different divisive social phenomena—the racist KKK and the women's suffrage movement. The section concluded with a review of the instrumentation of division in biblical history from Creation to the Cross of Jesus Christ.

The heart of *Divided* was section III, "Deeply Divided Twenty-first Century America," which took a deep dive into the overwhelming evidence and tragic consequences of division across contemporary America. Here we considered examples of the polarization of American institutions: family, politics, religion, education, the workplace, culture, and government. Division/polarization is a cultural cancer the ideological left intends to use to destroy the America many of us love and replace it with something that serves the powerful—and ultimately assists the intentions of Satan. Evidence of division across each of these institutions is on full display every day in our schools that push critical race theory or a perverse, sexual agenda; in our media that attacks our God and our Christian faith at every turn; and, of course, in our government, which long ago lost sight of its original purpose outlined in our Constitution and now seeks to replace itself as our god.

Section IV, "Strategies for Overcoming Division," provided secular answers to these divisive attacks on the very foundations of our civilization. In chapter 14, I presented three case studies that provide lessons to help mitigate polarization. Chapter 15 provided a wider view of the problem of division to recommend how "we the people" can address the cancer of division to reset our entire nation in the face of rancid polarization.

Section V, "Christian Living and Prophetic Implications of Division," was a personal message to fellow Christians. We have a special role, a God-given mission, in today's very divisive world. Our calling is clear, and our course is outlined in the Scriptures, especially by the very words of our Lord Jesus Christ. Chapter 16 provided the Christian with Bible-based principles to use in this life to help overcome destructive polarization. These moral principles aren't necessarily easy to embrace, but neither is it easy to live in this divisive world. However, with the help of the Holy Spirit, they are our only true hope. *Divided* concluded with a chapter (17) reviewing the role division plays in the prophetic end-times Scriptures, for both good and evil.

When it comes to division, Christians need to take the long view. Since our beginnings in the Garden of Eden, mankind has wrestled and too often lost the fight against evil-inspired polarization. However, there is hope, because we Christians know the end of the story. Yes, division will continue, fueled by Satan and his army of demons using powerful human proxies to keep us off-balance. Only when we recognize the reality of the spiritual battlefield—life on this earth—and embrace God's formula of living by biblical principles guided by His Holy Spirit—do we then come to enjoy the life God intended: a hope-filled life. However, and ultimately, this sinful existence does end for believers in Jesus Christ when we will be ushered into a far better place either at the end of our physical existence on this planet or through the promised Rapture of the Church just prior to the Tribulation.

USE THE QR-CODE BELOW
TO ACCESS MANY SPECIAL
DEALS AND PROMOTIONS ON
BOOKS AND FILMS FEATURING
DISCOVERY, PROPHECY, AND
THE SUPERNATURAL!

Notes

1. Abraham Lincoln, Brainyquote, accessed January 27, 2023, https://www.brainyquote.com/quotes/abraham_lincoln_378182?src=t_divided.

2. James Madison, "The Federalist Number 10," November 22, 1787, https://founders.archives.gov/documents/Madison/01-10-02-0178.

3. Ibid.

4. George Tsakiridis, "Vine and Fig Tree," George Washington's Mount Vernon, accessed February 11, 2023, https://www.mountvernon.org/library/digitalhistory/digital-encyclopedia/article/vine-and-fig-tree/#:~:text=%22Under%20their%20vine%20and%20fig%20tree%22%20is%20a,trees%2C%20and%20no%20one%20shall%20make%20them%20afraid%E2%80%A6.%22.

5. Daniel L. Dreisbach, "The 'Vine and Fig Tree' in George Washington's Letters: Reflections on a Biblical Motif in the Literature of the American Founding Era," *Anglican and Episcopal History* 76, no.3 (September 2007): 299–326, 301.

6. Michael and Jana Novak, *Washington's God: Religion, Liberty, and the Father of Our Country* (New York: Basic Books, 2006), 239 as cited in Tsakiridis, Op. cit.

7. Benjamin Franklin, Brainyquote, accessed January 27, 2023, https://www.brainyquote.com/quotes/benjamin_franklin_109063?src=t_divided.

8. Amanda Penn, "To Know Your Enemy, You Must Become Your Enemy (Sun Tzu Explained)," Shortform, November 17, 2019, https://www.short-form.com/blog/to-know-your-enemy-you-must-become-your-enemy/.

9. "Eloi," Wikipedia, accessed January 27, 2023, https://en.wikipedia.org/wiki/Eloi#:~:text=In%20H.%20G.%20Wells%27%20The%20Time%20Machine%20%5B,providing%20food%2C%20clothing%2C%20and%20inventory%20for%20the%20Eloi.

10. "Biden Slams 'MAGA Republicans,' Compares the Philosophy to 'Semi-fascism,' CBS News, August 26, 2022, https://www.cbsnews.com/news/biden-maga-republicans-semi-fascism/.

11. Jessica Chasmar, "Biden's 'Pandemic of the Unvaccinated' Narrative Nalls apart as Omicron Cases Skyrocket," Fox News, January 24, 2022, https://www.foxnews.com/politics/biden-pandemic-unvaccinated-falls-apart.

12. Condoleezza Rice, azquotes.com, accessed February 11, 2023, https://www.azquotes.com/quotes/topics/social-division.html.

13. John Adams, overallmotivation.com, accessed January 27, 2023, https://www.overallmotivation.com/quotes/division-quotes/.

14. "Biden's Divisive Speech Helped Neither the Nation Nor Him," *New York Post*, September 10, 2021, https://nypost.com/2021/09/10/joe-bidens-divisive-speech-helped-neither-the-nation-nor-him/.

15. Emily Crane, et al., "Biden Claims Afghanistan Withdrawal 'Extraordinary Success' in Address to Nation," *New York Post*, August 31, 2021, https://nypost.com/2021/08/31/biden-to-address-end-of-afghan-war/.

16. Merriam-Webster Dictionary, accessed January 27, 2023, https://www.merriam-webster.com/thesaurus/division.

17   "APA Divisions," American Psychological Association, accessed January 27, 2023, https://www.apa.org/about/division/.

18. Andrew Thomas, Brainyquote, accessed January 27, 2023, https://www.brainyquote.com/quotes/andrew_thomas_476840.

19. "Weltanschauung," Merriam-Webster Dictionary, accessed January 27, 2023, Weltanschauung Definition & Meaning-Merriam-Webster.

20. Robert L. Maginnis, *Collision Course: The Fight to Reclaim Our Moral Compass Before It's Too Late* (Crane, MO: Defender Publishing, 2020), p. 114, https://www.amazon.com/Collision-Course-Reclaim-Compass-Before-ebook/dp/B089ZWNX2T.

21. Jeffrey M. Jones, "How Religious Are Americans?" Gallup, December 23, 2021, https://news.gallup.com/poll/358364/religious-americans.aspx.

22. Sarah Mae Saliong, "Only 6% of Americans Believe Biblical Worldview, Barna Survey Reveals," Christianity Daily, May 27, 2021, https://www.christianitydaily.com/articles/11996/20210527/only-6-percent-of-americans-

believe-biblical-worldview-barna-survey-reveals-family-research-council.htm.

23. Tre Goins-Phillips, "Stunning Poll Reveals 'Shocking' Percentage of American Pastors Holding to Biblical Worldview," Faithwire, May 18, 2022, https://www.faithwire.com/2022/05/18/stunning-poll-reveals-shocking-percentage-of-american-pastors-holding-to-biblical-worldview/.

24. Maginnis, Op. cit., p. 115.

25. Ibid.

26. Sean Salai, "U.S. Adults Increasingly Accept Marxist Views, Poll Shows," *Washington Times*, October 6, 2021, https://www.washingtontimes.com/news/2021/oct/6/us-adults-increasingly-accept-marxist-views-poll/.

27. "Marxist Worldview," All About Worldview, accessed January 25, 2021, https://www.allaboutworldview.org/marxist-worldview.htm#:~:text=The%20Marxist%20worldview%20is%20grounded%20in%20Karl%20Marx,of%20the%20Marxist%20Worldview%20across%20ten%20major%20categories.

28. William Boykin interview, April 26, 2017.

29. Hick Brockmann, Wiebke Drews, and John Torpey, "A Class for Itself? On the Worldviews of the New Tech Elite," PLOS ONE, Public Library of Science, PLoS One, 16(1): e0244071, January 20, 2021.

30. Ibid.

31. Ibid.

32. Alexander Fleishmann, "Does Power Corrupt? How Powerful People React in Moral Dilemmas," SPSP, April 17, 2019, https://spsp.org/news-center/character-context-blog/does-power-corrupt-how-powerful-people-react-moral-dilemmas.

33. Ibid.

34. Ibid.

35. Patrick M. Wright, "Woke Corporations and Worldview: Making Moral Proclamations from Shaky Moral Foundations," Academy of Management Perspectives, amp-2021-0187.r2, October 3, 2022, https://journals.aom.org/doi/abs/10.5465/amp.2021.0187.

36. Ibid.

37. Ibid.

38. As cited in Wright, Ramaswamy, V. (2021). *Woke, Inc., Inside Corporate America's Social Justice Scam.* (New York, NY: Center Street), pp. 29–30.

39. Hadas Gold, "Survey: 7 Percent of Reporters Identify as Republican," Politico, May 6 2014, https://www.politico.com/blogs/media/2014/05/ survey-7-percent-of-reporters-identify-as-republican-188053.

40. Jack Shafer and Tucker Doherty, "The Media Bubble Is Worse Than You Think," Politico, May/June 2017, https://www.politico.com/magazine/ story/2017/04/25/media-bubble-real-journalism-jobs-east-coast-215048.

41. James Ostrowski, "Why Progressives Make Bad Journalists," LewRockwell. com, December 30, 2015, https://www.lewrockwell.com/2015/12/ james-ostrowski/never-trust-progressive-journalist/.

42. Ibid.

43. "Deep State," thoughtco.com, accessed January 27, 2023, https://www. thoughtco.com/deep-state-definition-4142030.

44. Thomas Knapp, "What Is the Deep State?" Fee Stories, July 2, 2017, https://fee.org/articles/what-is-the-deep-state/.

45. Ibid.

46. Ralph R. Smith, "Political Donations and Federal Employees in 2020 Elections," Fedsmith.com, February 12, 2021, https://www.fedsmith. com/2021/02/12/political-donations-and-federal-employees/.

47. "World Economic Forum," Wikipedia, accessed January 29, 2023, https://en.wikipedia.org/wiki/World_Economic_Forum.

48. J. B. Shurk, "The True Evil of the World Economic Forum," *American Thinker*, May 26, 2022, https://www.americanthinker.com/articles/2022/05/ the_true_evil_of_the_world_economic_forum.html

49. Boris Ngounou, "Davos Forum: When Private Jets Reinforce the Climate Crisis," AFRIK, January 16, 2023, https://www.afrik21.africa/en/davos-forum-when-private-jets-reinforce-the-climate-crisis/#:~:text=A%20new%20 analysis%20commissioned%20by%20Greenpeace%20International%20 shows,emissions%20four%20times%20higher%20than%20the%20 average%20week.

50. Katarina Bradford and Glenn Beck, "15 Shocking Quotes from the World Economic Forum Davos Summit That Should...," News Radio

94.3, January 26, 2023, https://943wsc.iheart.com/featured/glenn-beck/content/2023-01-26-glenn-beck-blog-15-shocking-quotes-from-the-world-economic-forum-davos-summit-that-should-deeply-trouble-you/.

51. Ibid.

52. Gabriel Hays, "Al Gore Goes on 'Unhinged' Rant about 'Rain Bombs,' Boiled Oceans, Other Climate Threats at Davos," Fox News, January 18, 2023, https://www.foxnews.com/media/al-gore-goes-unhinged-rant-about-rain-bombs-boiled-oceans-other-climate-threats-davos.

53. Mark J. Perry, "Al Gore's New $9 Million Ocean-View Villa in CA," AEI, May 5, 2010, https://www.aei.org/carpe-diem/al-gores-new-9-million-ocean-view-villa-in-ca/.

54. "Metaverse," Wikipedia, January 31, 2023, https://search.yahoo.com/search?fr=mcafee&type=E211US0G0&p=metaverse+meaning

55. Bradford and Beck, Op. cit.

56. Ibid.

57. Ibid.

58. Ibid.

59. Ibid.

60. There is Scripture to suggest that IAW Zechariah 3 and Hebrews 9 that Satan no longer enjoys access to Heaven as was in the case of being there before God to accuse Job. Further, this demonstrates that Satan is also not omnipresent, because he has been "thrown down" (Revelation 12).

61. "Six Things Satan Wants for Your Life," New Spring Church, accessed January 27, 2023, https://newspring.cc/articles/6-things-satan-wants-for-your-life.

62. "Paul Harvey's 'If I Were the Devil' Transcript from 1965," Word & Work, accessed January 27, 2023, http://www.wordandwork.org/2018/02/paul-harveys-if-i-were-the-devil-transcript-from-1965/.

63. Mark Buchanan, "Get Behind Me, Satan!" *Leadership Journal*, vol. 33, no. 2, Spring 2012, p. 106. Gale Academic OneFile, link.gale.com/apps/doc/A289723924/AONE?u=wash92852&sid=bookmark-AONE&xid=e05919ab. Accessed December 12, 2022.

64. Ibid.

65. Micaiah Bilger, "Satanic Temple Opens New Abortion Clinic to Kill Babies in Ritualistic Abortions," Life News, February 1, 2023, https://www.lifenews.com/2023/02/01/satanic-temple-opens-new-abortion-clinic-to-kill-babies-in-ritualistic-abortions/.

66. Ibid.

67. Ibid.

68. Ibid.

69. Ibid.

70. Katarina Bradford and Glenn Beck, "Satanic Temple Sues GOP-led States to Protect Their 'Satanic Abortion…,'" iHeart, January 5, 2023, https://www.iheart.com/content/2023-01-05-glenn-beck-blog-satanic-temple-sues-gop-led-states-to-protect-their-satanic-abortion-ritualand-the-msm-loves-it/.

71. Ibid.

72. Caleb Parke, "Satanic Temple Designated as Church, Given Tax-exempt Status by IRS: 'Satanism Is Here to Stay,'" Fox News, April 25, 2019, https://www.foxnews.com/us/satanic-temple-irs-has-designated-it-a-tax-exempt-church.

73. Bradford and Beck, Op. cit., and Bilger, Op. cit.

74. Nikita Nikhil, "Who Sponsored the Grammys 2023? Pfizer Backlash Erupts on Twitter in Wake of Satanic Controversy," SK Pop News, February 7, 2023, https://www.sportskeeda.com/pop-culture/news-who-sponsored-grammys-2023-pfizer-backlash-erupts-twitter-wake-satanic-controversy.

75. Kristine Parks, "CBS Tweet about Being 'Ready to Worship' Satanic Sam Smith Raises Eyebrows: 'Compromised by Evil,'" Fox News, February 6, 2023, https://www.foxnews.com/media/cbs-tweet-ready-worship-satanic-sam-smith-raises-eyebrows-compromised-evil.

76. Ibid.

77. Ibid.

78. Ben Cost, "Balenciaga BDSM Scandal Ignites 'Hidden' Child Satan Worship Conspiracy Video," New York Post, November 30, 2022, https://nypost.com/2022/11/30/balenciaga-bdsm-drama-sparks-child-devil-worship-conspiracy-theory/ and Barsha Roy, "What Does Balenciaga Mean in

Latin? Aleister Crowley Satanic Theory Explored Amid Child Campaign
Controversy," SK Pop, November 30, 2022, https://www.sportskeeda.com/
pop-culture/what-balenciaga-mean-latin-aleister-crowley-satanic-theory-
explored-amid-child-campaign-controversy.

79. Cost, Op. cit.

80. Ibid.

81. Ibid.

82. Priscilla DeGregory, "Balenciaga Files $25M Suit over Con-
troversial Ad Amid 'BDSM Teddy Bear' Backlash," *New York
Post*, November 25, 2022, https://nypost.com/2022/11/25/
balenciaga-files-25m-suit-against-bdsm-teddy-bear-ad-producers/.

83. Cost, Op. cit.

84. "What Does the Bible Say about Getting a Sex Change?"gotquestions.
org, accessed February 11, 2023, https://www.gotquestions.org/sex-change.
html.

85. Ibid.

86. Timothy H. J. Nerozzi, "Biden Administration Endorses Transgender
Youth Sex-change Operations, 'Top Surgery,' Hormone Therapy," Fox News,
March 31, 2022, https://www.foxnews.com/politics/biden-administration-
transgender-agenda-youth-sex-change-hormone-therapy.

87. Ibid.

88. Ibid.

89. Ibid.

90. Ryan T. Anderson, "Sex Reassignment Doesn't Work. Here Is the Evidence," Heritage Foundation, March 9, 2018, https://www.heritage.org/
gender/commentary/sex-reassignment-doesnt-work-here-the-evidence.

91. Ibid.

92. Ibid.

93. Michelle Maiese, Tova Norlen, and Heidi Burgess, "*Polarization: Beyond
Intractability,*" Eds. Guy Burgess and Heidi Burgess. Conflict Information
Consortium, University of Colorado, Boulder. Posted: October 2003, http://
www.beyondintractability.org/essay/polarization. Note: The authors are:
Michelle Maiese, a professor of philosophy at Emmanuel College; Tova C.

Norlén, a professor at the George C. Marshall Center; and Heidi Burgess, the codirector of the University of Colorado Conflict Information Consortium.

94. As cited by Maiese in Dean Pruitt and Paul Olczak, "Beyond Hope: Approaches to Resolving Seemingly Intractable Conflict," 59–92, in *Conflict, Cooperation, and Justice: Essays Inspired by the Work of Morton Deutsch,* eds. Barbara Bunker and Jeffrey Rubin, et al. (San Francisco: Jossey-Bass Publishers, 1995), 81.

95. Ibid.

96. Ibid.

97. Ronald Reagan, quotesayings.net, accessed January 28, 2023, https://quotessayings.net/topics/polarization/.

98. David Murrin, "Polarisation: The Road to War," Global Forecaster, July 30, 2019, accessed December 15, 2022, https://www.davidmurrin.co.uk/article/polarisation-the-road-to-war#:~:text=Submitted%20by%20David%20Murrin%20on%20Tue%2C%2030%2F07%2F2019%20-,charges%20or%20a%20magnet%27s%20north%20and%20south%20poles.

99. Ibid.

100. Ibid.

101. Ibid.

102. "The Main Causes of World War I," World Atlas, accessed December 15, 2022, https://www.worldatlas.com/articles/the-main-causes-of-world-war-i.html.

103. Martin Kelly, "5 Key Causes of World War I," March 26, 2020, https://www.thoughtco.com/causes-that-led-to-world-war-i-105515.

104. "Hitler's Beer Hall Putsch," thoughtco.com, accessed January 28, 2023, https://www.thoughtco.com/hitlers-beer-hall-putsch-1778295.

105. Ibid.

106. Michael Stratford, "What Civilization Invented the 'Divide & Conquer' Strategy?" Classroom, June 25, 2018, https://classroom.synonym.com/civilization-invented-divide-conquer-strategy-12746.html.

107. Nicole Hill, "How Did the Nicene Creed Lead to the Break Between Roman Catholic & Greek Orthodox?" Classroom, September 29, 2017,

https://classroom.synonym.com/how-did-the-nicene-creed-lead-to-the-break-between-roman-catholic-greek-orthodox-12087703.html.

108. "Thirty Years War," History.com, accessed January 28, 2023, https://www.history.com/topics/reformation/thirty-years-war.

109. Ibid.

110. "The Protestant Reformation," National Geographic, accessed January 28, 2023, https://education.nationalgeographic.org/resource/protestant-reformation.

111. Andrew O'Donohue and Thomas Carothers, "How to Understand the Global Spread of Political Polarization," Carnegie Endowment for International Peace, October 1, 2019, https://carnegieendowment.org/2019/10/01/how-to-understand-global-spread-of-political-polarization-pub-79893.

112. Ibid.

113. Ibid.

114. Ibid.

115. Ibid.

116. "Countries of the World," worldometer.info, accessed January 28, 2023, https://www.worldometers.info/geography/how-many-countries-are-there-in-the-world/.

117. Judith Bergman, "China's Belt and Road Being Built with Forced Labor," Gatestone Institute, June 2, 2021, https://www.gatestoneinstitute.org/17403/china-belt-road-forced-labor.

118. Alexjandro Avila, "China-basher Enes Kanter Freedom Gets Traded, Then Waived by the Houston Rockets. Coincidence?" Fox News, February 14, 2022, https://www.foxnews.com/sports/china-basher-enes-kanterfreedom-gets-traded-then-waived-by-the-houston-rockets-coincide.

119. Brianna Provenzano, "Is Vladimir Putin a Dictator? Here's What experts Have to Say," MIC.com, October 6, 2016, https://www.mic.com/articles/156026/is-vladimir-putin-a-dictator-here-s-what-experts-have-to-say.

120. Kelsey Vlamis, "Why Is Russia Attacking Ukraine? Here Are 5 Reasons Putin and Others Have Given for the Invasion," Businessinsider.com, February 24, 2022, https://www.businessinsider.com/why-russia-is-attacking-ukraine-putin-justification-for-invasion-2022-2.

121. Olaf Scholz, "The Global Zeitenwende: How to Avoid a New Cold War in a Multipolar Era," Foreign Affairs, January/February 2023, https://www.foreignaffairs.com/germany/olaf-scholz-global-zeiten-wende-how-avoid-new-cold-war?utm_medium=promo_email&utm_source=pre_release&utm_campaign=pre_release_120522&utm_content=20221205&utm_term=all-special-send.

122. "New Revelations Expose Saudi Crown Prince Mohamed bin Salman's Plot to Murder King Abdullah and Former Government Official," DAWN, October 24, 2021, https://dawnmena.org/new-revelations-expose-saudi-crown-prince-mohamed-bin-salmans-plot-to-murder-king-abdullah-and-former-goverment-official/.

123. Jack Lao, "'Bin Salman' The Notorious Dictator," Islam Times, July 13, 2019, https://www.islamtimes.org/en/article/804792/bin-salman-the-notorious-dictator.

124. Frances Martel, "MBS Gives Xi Jinping Lavish Welcome to Saudi Arabia—a Stark Contrast to Failed Biden Fist-Bump Summit," Breitbart, December 8, 2022, https://www.breitbart.com/asia/2022/12/08/mbs-gives-xi-jinping-lavish-welcome-saudi-arabia-a-stark-contrast-failed-biden-fist-bump-summit/.

125. Ibid.

126. "Here's How to Explain Soros' $1 Billion Losing Bet against Trump," The Street, January 17, 2017, https://www.thestreet.com/story/13954459/1/here-s-how-to-explain-soros-1- billion-losing-bet-against-trump.html.

127. George Gimein, "George Soros Is Mad as Hell He Made Billions Anticipating Blowups. Now He Thinks George Bush Is Creating One," Fortune, October 27, 2003, http://archive.fortune.com/magazines/fortune/fortune_archive/2003/10/27/351671/index.htm.

128. Sam Dorman, "Soros Group Investing as Much as $100M in Biden Spending Push," Fox News, April 5, 2021, https://www.foxnews.com/politics/soros-biden-spending-plan-open-society-foundations.

129. Joe Schoffstall, "George Soros-backed District Attorney Candidates Sweep Elections," Fox News, November 10, 2022, https://www.msn.com/en-us/news/opinion/

george-soros-backed-district-attorney-candidates-sweep-elections/
ar-AA13YxUV.

130. "List of George Soros Owned District Attorneys," Clever Jour-
neys Creed, April 25, 2022, https://cleverjourneys.com/2022/04/25/
list-of-george-soros-owned-district-attorneys/.

131. Bart Jansen, "Trump Indictment: Amid Seedy but Simple Allegations,
Critics Decry Case as Politically Motivated," *USA Today*, April 1, 2023,
https://news.yahoo.com/trump-indictment-amid-seedy-simple-090019729.
html?fr=sycsrp_catchall.

132. Chris Enloe, "Alan Dershowitz Explains Why Judge May
Quickly Toss Out Trump Indictment: 'Foolish, Foolish Decision,'" *The Blaze*, March 31, 2023, https://www.theblaze.com/news/
dershowitz-trump-case-tossed-statute-of-limitations.

133. Isabel Vincent, "How George Soros Funded Progressive 'Legal Arsonist' DAs behind US Crime Surge," *New York
Post*, December 16, 2021, https://nypost.com/2021/12/16/
how-george-soros-funded-progressive-das-behind-us-crime-surge/.

134. Tara Isabella, "Pope Francis's Divisive Papacy,
Explained in 5 Moments," Vox.com, March 13, 2018,
https://www.vox.com/identities/2018/3/13/17107702/
pope-francis-divisive-papacy-explained-five-years-catholic-church.

135. Ibid.

136. John Adams. (n.d.). AZQuotes.com. Retrieved December 19, 2022,
from AZQuoates.com Web site: https://www.azquotes.com/quote/1309364.

137. C. James Taylor, "John Adams: Campaigns and Elections," Miller Cen
ter, University of Virginia, accessed January 31, 2023, https://millercenter.
org/president/adams/campaigns-and-elections.

138. Barbara Marznzani, "What Happened to Aaron Burr After He Killed
Alexander Hamilton in a Duel?" History, July 11, 2022, https://www.history.
com/news/burr-hamilton-duel-political-legacy-died.

139. "Sumner-Brooks Affair," USHistory.com, accessed January 31, 2023,
https://www.u-s-history.com/pages/h225.html.

140. Ibid.

141. Ibid.

142. "A Brief History of Polarization," Wilson Quarterly, Autumn 2004, Vol 28, Issue 4.

143. Ibid.

144. Carl von Clausewitz, *On War,* trans. Col. J. J. Graham. New and Revised edition with Introduction and Notes by Col. F. N. Maude, in Three Volumes (London: Kegan Paul, Trench, Trubner & Co., 1918).

145. "Civil War Casualties," American Battlefield Trust, January 26, 2023, https://www.battlefields.org/learn/articles/civil-war-casualties.

146. The Act Prohibiting Importation of Slaves of 1807 (enacted March 2, 1807) became US law that "provided that no new slaves were permitted to be imported into the United States." "Act Prohibiting Importation of Slaves," Wikipedia, accessed February 3, 2023, https://en.wikipedia.org/wiki/Act_Prohibiting_Importation_of_Slaves#:~:text=The%20Act%20Prohibiting%20Importation%20of%20Slaves%20of%201807,earliest%20date%20permitted%20by%20the%20United%20States%20Constitution.

147. "The Antebellum Period: What Happened in America before the Civil War," Historynet, accessed January 31, 2023, https://www.historynet.com/the-antebellum-period-what-happened-in-america-before-the-civil-war/.

148. Ibid.

149. Ibid.

150. Ibid.

151. Ibid.

152. "U.S. Territorial Growth, 1860," Anchor, accessed January 31, 2023, https://www.ncpedia.org/media/map/us-territorial-growth#:~:text=This%20map%20shows%20which%20areas%20of%20the%20United,admission%20of%20Kansas%20and%20Nebraska%20as%20U.S.%20territories.

153. Ibid.

154. Ibid.

155. Ibid.

156. Ibid.

157. James McPherson, "A Brief Overview of the American Civil War,"

American Battlefield Trust, August 24, 2021, https://www.battlefields.org/learn/articles/brief-overview-american-civil-war.

158. Ibid.

159. Vietnam War Casualties, Wikipedia, accessed January 31, 2023, https://en.wikipedia.org/wiki/Vietnam_War_casualties.

160. Ibid.

161. Stuart Lutz, "Vietnam War Protests," history.com, February 22, 2010, https://www.history.com/topics/vietnam-war/vietnam-war-protests.

162. "How the Vietnam War Polarized American Society Essay," IvyPanda, October 7, 2021, https://ivypanda.com/essays/how-the-vietnam-war-polarized-american-society/.

163. Tim Page, "Vietnam War," History.com, accessed January 31, 2023, https://www.history.com/topics/vietnam-war/vietnam-war-history.

164. "Opposition To the Vietnam War—Polarization," liquisearch.com, accessed January 31, 2023, https://www.liquisearch.com/opposition_to_the_vietnam_war/polarization.

165. Henry Louis Gates, Jr., *Stony the Road: Reconstruction, White Supremacy, and the Rise of Jim Crow* (New York, NY: Penguin Press, 2019).

166. Beth Rowland, "Home Grown Terrorists," America's Civil War, Historynet, July 2015, pp. 49-53. http://www.historynet.com/home-grown-terrorists.htm.

167. Ibid.

168. Ibid.

169. David Wark Griffith, *The Birth of a Nation, directed by David Wark Griffith* (1915, United States: Epoch Producing Company, 1915), Film.

170. John Holden Bickford and Jeremiah Clabough, "A Guided Inquiry into a Dubious, Pervasive, All-American Organization: The Ku Klux Klan," *Teaching History: A Journal of Methods*, vol. 45, no. 1, Spring 2020, pp. 1+. Gale Academic OneFile, link.gale.com/apps/doc/A637012909/AONE?u=wash92852&sid=ebsco&xid=635974c2. Accessed December 18, 2022.

171. Virginia Sapiro, "The Power and Fragility of Social Movement Coalitions: The Woman Suffrage Movement to 1870," *Boston University Law Review*, Vol. 100:1557.

172. Sandra Day O'Connor, History of the Women's Suffrage Movement, 49 VAND. L. REV. 657 (1996).

173. As cited by O'Connor from Olivia Coolidge, *Women's Rights: The Suffrage Movement in American, 1848–1920* (Dutton, 1966), and Eleanor Flexner, *Century of Struggle the Woman's Rights Movement in the United States* (Harvard U., 1975).

174. Ibid.

175. As cited by O'Connor from Alfred Tennyson, Locksley Hall 29 (Fields, Osgood, 1869).

176. Sandra Day O'Connor, *History of the Women's Suffrage Movement*, 49 VAND. L. REV. 657 (1996).

177. Ibid.

178. Ibid.

179. As cited by O'Connor from Olivia Coolidge, Women's Rights: The Suffrage Movement in America, 1848–1920 (Dutton, 1966), and Eleanor Flexner, *Century of Struggle the Woman's Rights Movement in the United States* (Harvard U., 1975).

180. Cited by O'Connor, p. 661.

181. Ibid, p. 662.

182. Ibid.

183. Ibid.

184. Ibid., p. 665.

185. Ibid., p. 665, from Coolidge, Women's Rights at 122 (cited in note 1).

186. Brennan Weiss, "RANKED: The 15 Most Polarizing US Presidents, According to Political Scientists," *Insider*, March 6, 2018, https://www.businessinsider.com/most-polarizing-us-presidents-ranked-by-political-scientists-2018-3#1-donald-trump-15.

187. Philip Bump, "Trump Is the Most Polarizing President on Record—and almost Nobody's Opinion of Him Is Changing," *Washington Post*, January 16, 2019, https://www.washingtonpost.com/politics/2019/01/16/trump-is-most-polarizing-president-record-almost-nobodys-opinion-him-is-changing/.

188. Gregory Eady, et al, "Comparing Trump to the Greatest—and the Most Polarizing—Presidents in US History," Brookings, March 20, 2018, https://

www.brookings.edu/blog/fixgov/2018/03/20/comparing-trump-to-the-great-est-and-the-most-polarizing-presidents-in-u-s-history/.

189. Adriana Cohen, "Big Tech Continues to Collude with Democrats," RealClear Politics, August 24, 2022, https://www.realclearpolitics.com/articles/2022/08/24/big_tech_continues_to_collude_with_democrats_148095.html#!

190. Ibid.

191. Peter Gentry, "The Sons of God: Genesis 6," Real Science Radio, accessed February 2, 2023, https://kgov.com/gentry-3#:~:text=%2A%20Dr.%20Gentry%20on%20%22the%20Sons%20of%20God%22,then%20bore%20%22giants%22%2C%20as%20described%20in%20Genesis%206.

192. "Old Testament Priests & Priesthood," Barnes' Bible Charts, accessed February 4, 2023, chrome-extension://efaidnbmnnnibpcajpcglclefindmkaj/http://www.biblecharts.org/oldtestament/oldtestamentpriestsandpriesthood.pdf.

193. Maya Angelou, azquotes.com, accessed January 31, 2023, https://www.azquotes.com/quotes/topics/polarization.html.

194. Janet Adamy, "Inflation, Political Division Put U.S. in a Pessimistic Mood, Poll Finds," *Wall Street Journal*, New York, NY, June 7, 2022, A4, https://www.wsj.com/articles/inflation-political-division-put-u-s-in-a-pessimistic-mood-poll-finds-11654507800.

195. Ibid.

196. Ibid.

197. Ibid.

198. Gordon Heltzel and Kristin Laurin, "Polarization in America," Current Opinion in Behavioral Sciences, 2020, 34:179–184, https://www.ncbi.nlm.nih.gov/pmc/articles/PMC7201237/.

199. Ibid.

200. Ibid.

201. John Adams, groups.io, accessed January 31, 2023, https://groups.io/g/thepegboard/message/771.

202. James Wilson, Goodreads.com, accessed January 31, 2023, https://www.goodreads.com/author/quotes/18918.James_

Wilson#:~:text=%E2%80%9CThe%20culture%20without%20chil-dren%20is%20forever%20immature%2C%20self-obsessed,around%20 to%20show%20them%20otherwise.%E2%80%9D%20%E2%80%95%20 James%20Wilson.

203. "Marital Status of the United States Population in 2021, by Sex," statista.com, accessed January 31, 2023, https://www.statista.com/ statistics/242030/marital-status-of-the-us-population-by-sex/.

204. "The American Family under Siege," Investor's Business Daily, September 19, 2014.

205. "More Children Live with Just Their Fathers Than a Decade Ago," US Census, November 16, 2017, https://www.census.gov/news-room/press-releases/2017/living-arrangements.html#:~:text=Of%20 children%20who%20live%20with%20one%20parent%2C%20 the,percent%29%2C%20and%20ages%2012%20to%2017%20 %2835%20percent%29.

206. John Groove, "What Percentage of Millennials Get Married?" Maine Divorce Law Blog, October 11, 2022, https://mainedivorcelawblog.com/ what-percentage-of-millenials-get-married/.

207. Lynn D. Wardle, "The Alteration and Disintegration of the American Family: Implications for Children and Society," Lynn D. 6 INT'l J. Jurisprudence FAM. 135 (2015).

208. Helen Andrews, "Who Will Defend the American Family?" *New York Times*, New York, April 28, 2019, https://www.nytimes.com/2019/04/27/ opinion/sunday/conservative-women.html.

209. Naomi Schaefer Riley, "Interfaith Unions: A Mixed Blessing," *New York Times*, April 5, 2013, https://www.nytimes.com/2013/04/06/opinion/ interfaith-marriages-a-mixed-blessing.html.

210. Ibid. Note: Mr. Riley's research included a 2010 poll by YouGov, which conducted a national survey of 2,450 Americans, "adjusted to produce an oversampling of couples in interfaith marriages."

211. Wardle, Op. cit.

212. Arthur Zuckeman, "61 Single Parent Statistics: 2020/2021 Overview, Demographics & Facts," CompareCamp, May 26, 2020, https://

comparecamp.com/single-parent-statistics/ and "Number of white, non-Hispanic families with a single mother in the United States from 1990 to 2021," Statista, accessed February 9, 2023, https://www.statista.com/statistics/205048/number-of-white-families-with-a-female-householder-in-the-us/#:~:text=In%202019%2C%20there%20were%20about%206.69%20million%20white%2C,with%20a%20single%20mother%20living%20in%20the%20U.S.

213. Ibid.

214. Mary Eberstadt, "The Fury of the Fatherless," First Things, December 2020, The Fury of the Fatherless by Mary Eberstadt | Articles | First Things.

215. "The American Family Under Siege," Op. cit.

216. Thomas Sowell, "'Favors' to Blacks," The American Spectator, September 27, 2016, https://spectator.org/favors-to-blacks/.

217. Ben Shapiro, *Primetime Propaganda: The True Hollywood Story of How the Left Took Over Your TV* (New York: Broadside Books, 2012), 55–85.

218. Dana Kennedy, "Mount Holyoke Grad Deprogrammed from Women-only Woke Culture," *New York Post*, November 26, 2022, https://nypost.com/2022/11/26/mount-holyoke-grad-deprogrammed-from-women-only-woke-culture/.

219. Ibid.

220. Dan M. Berger, "DeSantis Admin Revoking Liquor License From Orlando Venue for Allowing Children at 'Drag Queen Christmas,'" *Epoch Times*, February 3, 2023, https://www.theepochtimes.com/mkt_app/desantis-admin-revoking-liquor-license-from-orlando-venue-for-allowing-children-at-drag-queen-christmas_5033328.html?utm_source=Morningbrief&src_src=Morningbrief&utm_campaign=mb-2023-02-05&src_cmp=mb-2023-02-05&utm_medium=email&est=PLWcBaeW9qxCqA26yxob3MvkCpRhhDSNbIqJbaN%2Fi9YfzyLQQgU3BeSVYxAYkZb%2F.

221. Ibid.

222. Ibid.

223. Ibid.

224. Hillary Clinton, quotemaster.org, January 31, 2023, https://www.
quotemaster.org/divisive+politics#&gid=1&pid=2.

225. "A Divided America Agrees that Democrats' Failures are Hurting the
Country," States News Service, November 14, 2022, Gale Academic One-
File, link.gale.com/apps/doc/A726659548/AONE?u=wash92852&sid=e
bsco&xid=97eed109. Accessed 19 Nov. 2022. Gale Document Number:
GALE|A72665954.

226. Ypetach Lekes and Sean J. Westwood, "We Study Political Polarization:
The Midterm Election Results Make Us Hopeful," The Hill, November 19,
2022, https://thehill.com/opinion/campaign/3742552-we-study-political-
polarization-the-midterm-election-results-make-us-hopeful/.

227. Ibid.

228. "As Partisan Hostility Grows, Signs of Frustration with
the Two-Party System," Pew Research Center, August 9,
2022, https://www.pewresearch.org/politics/2022/08/09/
as-partisan-hostility-grows-signs-of-frustration-with-the-two-party-system/.

229. PRRI Staff, "Fractured Nation: Widening Partisan Polarization and Key
Issues in 2020 Presidential Elections," October 20, 2019, accessed November
24, 2019, https://www.prri.org/research/fractured-nation-widening-partisan-
polarization-and-key-issues-in2020-presidential-elections/. As cited in https://
digitalcommons.northgeorgia.edu/issr/vol96/iss2/4.

230. Pew Research Center 2017, "The Partisan Divide on Political Values
Grows Even Wider," Available at https://www.people-press.org/2017/10/05/
the-partisan-divide-on-political-values-grows-even-wider/ (Accessed October
2019) [Google Scholar].

231. "Political Polarization in the United States: The Influences of Exceptionalism and Religion," International Social Science Review, Pi Gamma Mu
Inc., https://digitalcommons.northgeorgia.edu/issr/vol96/iss2/4.

232. "Part I. The Need for Greater Party Responsibility," American Political
Science Review, Vol. 44, No. 3, Part 2 Supplement (September 1950), pp.
15–36, Part I. The Need for Greater Party Responsibility on JSTOR.

233. Mike Cummings, "Polarization in US Politics Starts with Weak

Political Parties," Yale University, November 17, 2020, https://news.yale.edu/2020/11/17/polarization-us-politics-starts-weak-political-parties.

234. Ibid.

235. Ibid.

236. Ibid.

237. Ibid.

238. Eric Loepp, "How Does Contemporary Polarization Compare Historically? Is Today's Situation Truly unique?" Divided We Fall, May 25, 2022, https://dividedwefall.org/political-polarization-in-america-past-and-present/.

239. David Blankenhorn, "The Top 14 Causes of Political Polarization," American Interest, May 16, 2018, https://www.the-american-interest.com/2018/05/16/the-top-14-causes-of-political-polarization/.

240. Ibid.

241. Ibid.

242. Drew Desilver, "How the Most Ideologically Polarized Americans Live Different Lives," Pew Research Center, June 13, 2014, https://www.pewresearch.org/fact-tank/2014/06/13/big-houses-art-museums-and-in-laws-how-the-most-ideologically-polarized-americans-live-different-lives/.

243. Ibid.

244. Blankenhorn, Op. cit.

245. "Political Polarization in the United States: The Influences of Exceptionalism and Religion," International Social Science Review, Pi Gamma Mu Inc., https://digitalcommons.northgeorgia.edu/issr/vol96/iss2/4.

246. Ibid.

247. Ibid.

248. Ibid.

249. Ibid.

250. Ibid.

251. Evan Andrews, "8 Reasons Why Rome Fell," History.com, February 10, 2023, https://www.history.com/news/8-reasons-why-rome-fell.

252. Avicenna, Goodreads.com, accessed February 1, 2023, https://www.goodreads.com/quotes/22778-the-world-is-divided-into-men-who-have-wit-and.

253. Mark Weldon Whitten, "Manufactured Myth: America Isn't a 'Christian Nation' as the Religious Right Claims and the Constitutional Convention Proves It," *Church & State*, Vol. 62, Issue 2, February 1, 2009 https://link.gale.com/apps/doc/A194193378/AONE?u=wash92852&sid=AONE&xid= f284fb20.

254. Lyman Stone, "Promise and Peril: The History of American Religiosity and Its Recent Decline," AEI Paper & Studies, The American Enterprise Institute, April 30, 2020, https://www.aei.org/research-products/report/promise-and-peril-the-history-of-american-religiosity-and-its-recent-decline/.

255. "1815–1850: Religion: Overview," encyclopedia.com, accessed February 13, 2023, https://www.encyclopedia.com/history/news-wires-white-papers-and-books/1815-1850-religion-overview.

256. Tobin Grant, "Why 1940s America Wasn't as Religious as You Think—The Rise and Fall of American Religion," Religious News Service, December 11, 2014, https://religionnews.com/2014/12/11/1940s-america-wasnt-religious-think-rise-fall-american-religion/#:~:text=Coming%20out%20of%20World%20War%20II%2C%20America%20was,drain%20on%20resources%20and%20volunteers%20during%20the%20war.

257. Stone, Op. cit., p.1.

258. Ibid.

259. Ibid, pp. 21–22.

260. Ibid, p. 1.

261. Ibid. Pew Research Center, "Religious Landscape Study," 2014. https://www.pewresearch.org/religion/dataset/pew-research-center-2014-u-s-religious-landscape-study/.

262. Ibid. "Religion," Gallup, 2022, https://news.gallup.com/poll/1690/religion.aspx.

263. "Europe: The Future of World Religions: Population Growth Projections, 2010-2050," Pew Research Center, April 2, 2015, https://www.pewresearch.org/religion/2015/04/02/europe/.

264. "Immigration Demographics: A Look at the Native and Foreign-born Populations," USAFACTS, January 20, 2020, https://usafacts.org/articles/immigration-demographics-look-native-and-foreign-born-populations/.

265. Ibid.

266. Stone, Op cit, p. 42.

267. As cited in Ibid. Steve Bruce and Tony Glendinning, "When Was Secularization? Dating the Decline of the British Churches and Locating Its Cause," British Journal of Sociology 61, no. 1 (March 2010): 107–26, https://doi.org/10.1111/j.1468-4446.2009.01304.x.

268. Ibid.

269. David E. Campbell, *Daedalus*, Summer 2020, Vol. 149, No. 3, Religion & Democracy (Summer 2020), pp. 87–104 Published by: The MIT Press on behalf of American Academy of Arts & Sciences Stable URL: https://www.jstor.org/stable/10.2307/48590942.

270. "Christians by Political Party," Pew Research Center, May 30, 2014, https://www.pewresearch.org/religion/religious-landscape-study/compare/christians/by/party-affiliation/.

271. Campbell, Op. cit.

272. Ibid.

273. Carl Desportes et al., "Culture of American Families Executive Report," Institute for Advanced Studies in Culture, University of Virginia, 2012. (Note: The data for the project was collected in two stages: a web-based survey of a national representative sample of 3,000 parents of school-aged children and follow-up, in-person interviews with 101 of the survey respondents.)

274. Ibid.

275. Ibid.

276. Ibid.

277. Ibid.

278. Ibid.

279. C. S. Lewis, wisefamousquotes.com, accessed February, 1, 2023, https://www.wisefamousquotes.com/quotes-about-education-and-parents/.

280. Lydia Saad, "Confidence in Public Schools Turns More Partisan," Gallup, July 14, 2022.

281. Heather L. Schwartz, "What Is Really Polarizing Schools Right Now?" RAND Corporation, March 14, 2022, https://www.rand.org/blog/2022/03/

what-is-really-polarizing-schools-right-now.html#:~:text=Political%20
polarization%20that%20rises%20to%20the%20level%20of,children%20
safe%E2%80%94schools%20are%20at%20risk%20of%20
becoming%20ungovernable.

282. Brian Kennedy, Alec Tyson and Cary Funk, "Americans'
Trust in Scientists, Other Groups Declines," Pew Research, February 15, 2022, https://www.pewresearch.org/science/2022/02/15/
americans-trust-in-scientists-other-groups-declines/.

283. Melissa Kay Diliberti and Heather L. Schwartz, "District Leaders' Concerns About Mental Health and Political Polarization in Schools," RAND
Corporation, 2022, https://www.rand.org/pubs/research_reports/RRA956-8.
html.

284. Ibid.

285. Ibid.

286. Taylor Orth, "Republicans and Democrats Disagree over Problems Facing Local Public Schools," YouGov America, August 23, 2022.

287. J. D. Tuccille, "Americans Increasingly See Political Polarization
Overtaking Public Education," Reason, August 22, 2022, https://reason.
com/2022/08/22/americans-increasingly-see-political-polarization-overtak-
ing-public-education/.

288. Ibid.

289. Peter Grier, "Public Education, Democracy, and the Future
of America," Christian Science Monitor; Boston, Mass. June 8,
2022, https://www.csmonitor.com/USA/Education/2022/0608/
Public-education-democracy-and-the-future-of-America.

290. Ibid.

291. Ibid.

292. Ibid.

293. Marjorie Cortez, "American Family Survey: Are Public Schools the
Battlefield for the Nation's Culture Wars?" October 4, 2022, https://www.
deseret.com/2022/10/4/23363910/public-schools-battlefield-nation-culture-
wars-book-bans-lgbtq-trans-american-family-survey.

294. Ibid.

295. Ibid.

296. Ibid.

297. Ibid.

298. Ibid.

299. "The History Wars; Patriotism and Polarization," *Economist*, July 10, 2021, 26(US). *Gale Academic OneFile*, link.gale.com/apps/doc/A667816501/AONE?u=wash92852&sid=ebsco&xid=fb355875.

300. Jennifer Rubin, "Cynical MAGA Censors Are Damaging Public Education," *Washington Post*, November 30, 2022.

301. "The History Wars; Patriotism and Polarization," Op. cit.

302. Miloon Kothari, "Roosvelt's 'Four Freedoms' Weren't Just an American Idea," Resilience, January 12, 2021, https://www.resilience.org/stories/2021-01-12/roosevelts-four-freedoms-werent-just-an-american-idea/.

303. "The History Wars; Patriotism and Polarization," Op. cit.

304. Sommer Brugal, "'It was shocking': Miami AP African American Studies Students React to DeSantis Rejecting Course," *Miami Herald*, January 31, 2023, https://www.miamiherald.com/news/local/education/article271821682.html#storylink=cpy.

305. Natalie Robehmed, "Why The Rock's Social Media Muscle Made Him Hollywood's Highest-Paid Actor," *Forbes*, July 13, 2018, https://www.forbes.com/sites/forbesdigitalcovers/2018/07/12/why-the-rocks-social-media-muscle-made-him-hollywoods-highest-paid-actor/?sh=39373f05136b.

306. Note: Gloria Jean Watkins wrote poetry under the name "bell hooks," a tribute to her great-grandmother, "Bell Blair Hooks." Ms. Watkins used the lowercase form of the name to distinguish her from her great-grandmother, "and to suggest that what mattered was the substance of the work, not the author's name." As cited in Hua Hsu, "The Revolutionary Writing of bell hooks," *New Yorker*, December 15, 2021, https://www.newyorker.com/culture/postscript/the-revolutionary-writing-of-bell-hooks.

307. Brianna Andrews and Travis Gibson, "Gov. DeSantis Says Florida Rejected AP African-American Class Due to Mentions of 'Queer Theory,' and 'Intersectionality'," News4Jax.com, January 23, 2023, Gov. DeSantis

says Florida rejected AP African-American class due to mentions of 'queer theory,' and 'intersectionality' (news4jax.com).

308. Nayyera Haq, "The AP's African American History Course Still Has a Lot to Teach Students," MSNBC, February 1, 2023, https://www.msnbc.com/opinion/msnbc-opinion/ron-desantis-wins-fight-ap-african-american-history-course-rcna68636.

309. Cortez, Op cit.

310. Emma Camp, "New Data Show COVID School Closures Contributed to Largest Learning Loss in Decades," reason.com, September 6, 2022, https://reason.com/2022/09/06/new-data-show-covid-school-closures-contributed-to-largest-learning-loss-in-decades/.

311. Kimberly Amadeo, "U.S. Education Rankings Are Falling Behind the Rest of the World," *The Balance*, April 13, 2022, https://www.thebalancemoney.com/the-u-s-is-losing-its-competitive-advantage-3306225.

312. Chris Papst, "23 Baltimore Schools Have Zero Students Proficient in Math, Per State Test Results," Fox Baltimore, February 6, 2023, https://foxbaltimore.com/news/project-baltimore/state-test-results-23-baltimore-schools-have-zero-students-proficient-in-math-jovani-patterson-maryland-comprehensive-assessment-program-maryland-governor-wes-moore#.

313. Ibid.

314. Ibid.

315. Ibid.

316. Ibid.

317. Audrey Conklin, "Garland denies DOJ labeling parents as domestic terrorists following school board memo," Fox News, October 21, 2021, https://www.foxnews.com/politics/garland-doj-parents-domestic-terrorists-school-board-memo.

318. Ibid.

319. Jennifer Rubin, "The Cynical MAGA Censors Are Damaging Public Education," *Washington Post*, November 30, 2022, https://www.washingtonpost.com/opinions/2022/11/30/maga-culture-wars-schools-education/.

320. Ibid.

321. Ibid.

322. Charles Creitz, "Leftist Mob Riots after Charlie Kirk Shows up at Campus, Tries to Shut Down Free
Speech Event," Fox News, https://www.foxnews.com/media/
leftist-mob-riots-charlie-kirk-shows-campus-tries-shut-free-speech-event.
323. Ibid.
324. Matthew Yglesias, "Education Polarization Is Only Growing,"
Slow Boring, September 27, 2021, https://www.slowboring.com/p/
education-polarization.
325. Ibid.
326. Ibid.
327. Ibid.
328. Robert L. Maginnis, *Give Me Liberty, Not Marxism*, (Crane, MO:
Defender Publishing, 2021).
329. Mike Shotwell, "The Infiltration of Marxism into Higher Education
(Part 2 of 2)," *Epoch Times*, December 3, 2018, https://www.
330. Paul Gottfried, "The Frankfurt School and Cultural Marxism,"
American Thinker, January 12, 2018, https://www.americanthinker. com/
articles/2018/01/the_frankfurt_school_and_cultural_marxism.html.
331. Ibid.
332. Kim Parker, "The Growing Partisan Divide in Views of
Higher Education," Pew Research Center, August 19, 2019,
https://www.pewresearch.org/social-trends/2019/08/19/
the-growing-partisan-divide-in-views-of-higher-education-2/.
333. Michael Hiltzik, "Column: The GOP Is Now Complaining about
Environmentally Responsible Investing," *Los Angeles Times*, July 1, 2022.
334. "Who Cares Wins 2005 Conference Report: Investing for Long-Term
Value," International Finance Corporation, accessed February 1, 2023, Who
CaresWins_2005ConferenceReport.pdf (ifc.org).
335. Ibid.
336. Lindsay Singleton and Tessa Recendes, "Opinion: The Bipartisan Argument for ESG," DeseretNews, February 4, 2022, https://www.deseret.com/
opinion/2022/2/3/22910986/opinion-the-bipartisan-argument-for-esg-
climate-change-environment-sustainability-polarization.

337. Ibid.

338. "ESG, Scientism & The Coming Tectonic Backlash," Trends EMagazine, April 30, 2022, https://trends-magazine.com/esg-scientism-the-coming-tectonic-backlash/.

339. Ibid.

340. Ibid.

341. Ibid.

342. Jurian Hendrikse, "The False Promise of ESG," Harvard Law School Forum on Corporate Governance, March 16, 2022, https://corpgov.law.harvard.edu/2022/03/16/the-false-promise-of-esg/.

343. Ibid.

344. "ESG, Scientism & the Coming Tectonic Backlash," Op. cit.

345. Hiltzik, Op. Cit.

346. "ESG, Scientism & the Coming Tectonic Backlash," Op. cit.

347. Rosemary Gibson, "Opinion: China Has Cornered the Market on Antibiotics, so the U.S. Must Rebuild Its Manufacturing Capacity," MarketWatch, April 28, 2021, https://www.marketwatch.com/story/china-has-cornered-the-market-on-antibiotics-so-the-u-s-must-rebuild-its-manufacturing-capacity-11619640612#:~:text=Right%20now%2C%20the%20U.S.%20has%20virtually%20no%20capacity,ear%20infections%2C%20and%20life-threatening%20conditions%20such%20as%20sepsis.

348. "In Their Own Words: Behind Americans' Views of 'Socialism' and 'Capitalism,'" Pew Research Center, October 7, 2019, https://www.pewresearch.org/politics/2019/10/07/in-their-own-words-behind-americans-views-of-socialism-and-capitalism/#:~:text=Some%20who%20view%20socialism%20negatively%20portray%20it%20as,for%20a%20system%20that%20blends%20socialism%20and%20capitalism.

349. Emma Gibney, "Progressive Politics Drive the 'S' in ESG," alabamapolicy.org, October 21, 2022, https://alabamapolicy.org/2022/10/21/progressive-politics-drive-the-s-in-esg/.

350. Adam Andrezjewski, "Remembering "Solyndra"—How Many $570M Green Energy Failures Are Hidden Inside Biden's Infrastructure Proposal?"

Forbes, April 12, 2021, https://www.forbes.com/sites/adamandrzejew-
ski/2021/04/12/remembering-solyndra--how-many-570m-green-energy-
failures-are-hidden-inside-bidens-instructure-proposal/?sh=4dec997a2672.

351. Ibid.

352. Ibid.

353. Ibid.

354. Ibid.

355. Ibid.

356. "The Truth about ESG (Environmental Social Governance),"
aMarketology, October 10, 2022, https://www.amarketology.com/
the-truth-about-esg-environmental-social-governance.

357. Bonner Cohen, "Biden Labor Department Pushes ESG Investing and
Will Sshort-Change Investors," CFACT, November 30, 2022, https://www.
cfact.org/2022/11/30/biden-labor-department-pushes-esg-investing-and-will-
short-change-investors/.

358. Ibid.

359. Savannah H. Pointer, Nathan Worcester, and Kevin Stock-
lin, "Biden Issues 1st Veto, Blocks Anti-ESG Investment Measure,"
Epoch Times, March 20, 2023, https://www.theepochtimes.com/
biden-issues-first-veto-blocks-anti-esg-investment-measure_5135934.
html?utm_source=Morningbrief&src_src=Morningbrief&utm_
campaign=mb-2023-03-21&src_cmp=mb-2023-03-21&utm_mediu-
m=email&est=4aRkVEF%2FFSexhbtaW7sANQ388p1jPZM6URcvet1Qp
6gFDy8PU1CuEJnPFyxKPEwM.

360. Ibid.

361. Ibid.

362. Sanjai Bhagat, "An Inconvenient Truth About ESG Investing,"
Harvard Business Review, March 31, 2022, https://hbr.org/2022/03/
an-inconvenient-truth-about-esg-investing.

363. Ibid.

364. Ryan Flugum and Matthew Southern, "Stakeholder Value: A
Convenient Excuse for Underperforming Managers?" SSRN, November
13, 2020, Stakeholder Value: A Convenient Excuse for Underperforming

Managers? by Ryan Flugum, Matthew E. Southern SSRN as cited in Sanjai Bhagat, "An Inconvenient Truth About ESG Investing," *Harvard Business Review*, March 31, 2022, https://hbr.org/2022/03/an-inconvenient-truth-about-esg-investing.

365. Michael Hiltzik, "The GOP Is Now Complaining about Environmentally Responsible Investing," *Los Angeles Times*, July 1, 2022, Hiltzik: For Republicans, ESG Is the New Critical Race Theory—*Los Angeles Times* (latimes.com).

366. Ibid.

367. Ibid.

368. Ibid.

369. Ibid.

370. Ryan Van Velzer, "Kentucky GOP Leaders Say S&P Credit Score Calculation Is 'Political Subjugation,'" WKU Public Radio, July 6, 2022, https://www.wvxu.org/politics/2022-07-06/kentucky-gop-leaders-say-s-p-credit-score-calculation-is-political-subjugation.

371. Ibid.

372. Ibid.

373. Pete Schroeder, "West Virginia Bars Five Financial Firms for Deemed Fossil Fuel 'Boycotts'," *International Business Times*, July 28, 2022, West Virginia Bars Five Financial Firms for Deemed Fossil Fuel 'Boycotts' (ibtimes.com).

374. "Author Michael Shellenberger: The Left's Green Agenda Is an 'Environmental Nightmare,'" Fox News, October 4, 2022, https://www.foxnews.com/media/author-michael-shellenberger-left-green-agenda-environmental-nightmare.

375. Thomas Sowell, brainyquote, accessed January 29, 2023, https://www.brainyquote.com/quotes/thomas_sowell_440790?src=t_media.

376. Art Swift, "Americans' Trust in Mass Media Sinks to New Low," Gallup, September 14, 2016, https://news.gallup.com/poll/195542/americans-trust-mass-media-sinks-new-low.aspx.

377. Ibid.

378. Ibid.

379. Flavia Roscini, "How the American Media Landscape Is Polarizing the Country," Frederick Padee School of Global Studies, Boston University, accessed January 29, 2023, https://sites.bu.edu/pardeeatlas/back2school/how-the-american-media-landscape-is-polarizing-the-country/#:~:text=%20An%20essential%20driver%20of%20this%20polarization%20is,to%20American%20democracy.%20Figure%201.%20Pew%20Research%20Center.

380. Margaret Sullivan, "'Birthing Centers for Polarizing Thetoric': The Outsize Influence of Fox, CNN and MSNBC," *Washington Post*, May 26, 2019, https://www.washingtonpost.com/lifestyle/style/birthing-centers-for-polarizing-rhetoric-the-outsize-influence-of-fox-cnn-and-msnbc/2019/05/23/2bcc429a-7cbe-11e9-8ede-f4abf521ef17_story.html.

381. Tom Jones, "No, Fox News and MSNBC Are Not the Same Thing," *Poynter*, February 1, 2021, https://www.poynter.org/newsletters/2021/no-fox-news-and-msnbc-are-not-the-same-thing/.

382. Dave Chaffey, "Global social media statistics research summary 2023," Smart Insights, January 30, 2023, Global social media statistics research summary 2022 [June 2022] (smartinsights.com) and Poynter Institute, Wikipedia, accessed February 2, 2023, https://en.wikipedia.org/wiki/Poynter_Institute.

384. Ibid.

385. "Vyacheslav Molotov," Russiapedia, accessed January 26, 2021, http://russiapedia.rt.com/prominent-russians/history-and-mythology/vyacheslav-molotov/?gclid=CPqq5-a1xKcCFSVa7AodgAfrCg.

386. Hu Qiaomu 胡喬木, "Baozhi shi jiaokeshu" 報紙是教科書 ("Newspapers Are Textbooks"), in *Hu Qiaomu wenku* 胡喬木文集 (*The Collected Works of Hu Qiaomu*), (Beijing: People's Daily Publishing House, 1994), 3:303. (In Chinese) as cited in Editorial. Team, "The Specter of Communism, Chapter 13: The Media," *Epoch Times*, June 9, 2018, https://www.theepochtimes.com/chapter-thirteen-hijacking-the-media_2684140.html.

387. Editorial Team, "The Specter of Communism, Chapter 13: The

Media," *Epoch Times*, June 9, 2018, https://www.theepochtimes.com/chapter-thirteen-hijacking-the-media_2684140.html.

388. Maginnis, Give Me Liberty, pp. 201–202.

389. David B. Jenkins, "America's Marxist Media," PJ Media, April 3, 2011, https://pjmedia.com/blog/david-b-jenkins/2011/04/03/americas-marxist-media-n11648.

390. Johnathan Gray, "Spreading the Red Stain: The Communist Infiltration of Hollywood," *Epoch Times*, September 21, 2017, https://www.theepochtimes.com/spreading-the-red-stain-the-communist-infiltration-of-hollywood_2299892.html.

391. "Whittaker Chambers," Wikipedia, accessed January 26, 2021, https://en.wikipedia.org/wiki/Whittaker_Chambers.

392. Maginnis, *Give Me Liberty*, p. 201.

393. David B. Jenkins, "America's Marxist Media," PJ Media, April 3, 2011, https://pjmedia.com/blog/david-b-jenkins/2011/04/03/americas-marxist-media-n11648.

394. Ibid.

395. "Trusted News Initiative," KeyWiki, accessed January 29, 2023, https://www.keywiki.org/Trusted_News_Initiative#:~:text=Trusted%20News%20Initiative%20is%20a%20left-wing%20scheme%20among,President%20Donald%20Trump%20and%20Joe%20Biden%20in%20America.

396. Ibid.

397. Ibid.

398. Naman Ramachandran, "Early Warning System Set up to Combat Fake News During U.S. Presidential Election," *Variety*, July 13, 2020, https://variety.com/2020/biz/news/fake-news-us-presidential-election-1234704593/.

399. "Fake News, Fact-checking, and Bias: Media Consolidation in the U.S.," Tacoma Community College, accessed January 29, 2023, https://tacomacc.libguides.com/c.php?g=599051&p=4586162.

400. "Trusted News Initiative (TNI) to Combat Spread of Harmful Vaccine Disinformation and Announces Major Research Project," BBC, December 10, 2020, Media Centre (bbc.com)

401. Robert Malone, "Who Is Behind the Trusted News Initiative?"

Substack, August 19, 2022, https://www.theburningplatform.
com/2022/08/19/who-is-behind-the-trusted-news-initiati ve/.

402. Robert L. Maginnis, *Kings of the East*, (Crane, MO: Defender
Publishing, 2023).

403. David Barstow, "Behind Analysts, the Pentagon's Hidden Hand," *New
York Times*, April 20, 2008, (nytimes.com)

404. Ibid.

405. Ibid.

406. Ibid.

407. "Twitter - microblogging service," Britannica, accessed February 1,
2023, https://www.britannica.com/topic/Twitter.

408. Ibid.

409. Ibid.

410. Ibid.

411. Victor Nava et al., "Hunter Biden Laptop Bombshell:
Twitter Invented Reason to Censor *Post's* Reporting," *New
York Post*, December 2, 2022, https://nypost.com/2022/12/02/
elon-musk-releases-twitters-files-on-censorship-of-post/.

412. Ibid.

413. Ibid.

414. Ibid.

415. Ibid.

416. Ibid.

417. Ibid.

418. John D. Davidson, "The Twitter Files Reveal an Existential Threat,"
Imprimis, Vol. 52, No. 1, Hillsdale College, January 2023, https://imprimis.
hillsdale.edu/the-twitter-files-reveal-an-existential-threat/.

419. Ibid.

420. Ibid.

421. Ibid.

422. Ibid.

423. M. Dowling, "You Need to Know About the Trusted News Initiative,"

Independent Sentinel, August 22, 2022, https://www.independentsentinel.
com/you-need-to-know-about-the-trusted-news-initiative/.

424. Elizabeth Woodworth, "COVID-19 and the Shadowy 'Trusted News
Initiative,'" Global Research, January 22, 2022, https://www.globalresearch.
ca/COVID-19-shadowy-trusted-news-initiative/5752930.

425. Ibid.

426. Rick Edmonds, June 24, 2021, "US Ranks Last among 46 Countries in
Trust in Media, Reuters Institute Report Finds," June 24, 2021, https://www.
poynter.org/ethics-trust/2021/us-ranks-last-among-46-countries-in-trust-in-
media-reuters-institute-report-finds/.

427. "Trusted News Initiative Announces Plans to Tackle Harmful
Coronavirus Disinformation," March 27, 2020, https://cbc.radio-canada.ca/
en/media-centre/trusted-news-initiative-plan-disinformation-coronavirus.

428. Jo Waters, "Trusted News Initiative Steps Up Global Fight Against
Disinformation and Targets US Presidential Election," EBU News, July 13,
2020, https://www.ebu.ch/news/2020/07/trusted-newsinitiative-steps-up-
global-fight-against-disinformation-and-targets-uspresidential-election.

429. "Trusted News Initiative (TNI) to Combat Spread of Harmful
Vaccine Disinformation and Announces Major Research Project,"
BBC, December 10, 2020, https://www.bbc.com/mediacentre/2020/
trusted-news-initiative-vaccine-disinformation.

430. "Therapeutic Management of Non-hospitalized Adults
with COVID-19, Last Updated July 8, 2021" National
Institutes of Health, accessed February 13, 2023, https://www.
COVID19treatmentguidelines.nih.gov/management/clinical-management/
nonhospitalized-adults–therapeutic-management/.

431. "State Rules and Recommendations Regarding Chloroquine,
Hydroxychloroquine and Other Drugs Related to COVID-19," National
Academy for State Health Policy,
posted March 2020, https://www.nashp.org/wp-content/uploads/2020/03/
StateCOVID-drug-chart-3-27-2020.pdf.

432. Elizabeth Woodworth, "COVID-19 and the Shadowy 'Trusted

News Initiative,'" globalresearch.com, January 22, 2022, https://www.globalresearch.ca/covid-19-shadowy-trusted-news-initiative/5752930.

433. Jessica Chasmar, "National Security Experts Slam Media, Scientists for Prematurely Shutting Down COVID-19 Origins Discussion," Fox News, January 11, 2023, https://www.foxnews.com/politics/national-security-experts-slam-media-scientists-prematurely-shutting-down-COVID-19-origins-discussion.

434. Ibid.

435. Bruce Golding, "Chinese Lab Leak Likely behind COVID Outbreak: US Energy Department," *New York Post*, February 26, 2023, https://nypost.com/2023/02/26/chinese-lab-leak-likely-behind-covid-19-outbreak/.

436. Zachary Stieber, "COVID-19 Could Stem from Risky Experiments at Chinese Lab: Fauci," *Epoch Times*, March 13, 2023, https://www.theepochtimes.com/covid-19-could-stem-from-risky-experiments-at-chinese-lab-fauci_5118654.html?utm_source=Morningbrief&src_src=Morningbrief&utm_campaign=mb-2023-03-14&src_cmp=mb-2023-03-14&utm_medium=email&est=mClhj7HxhMvN%2B1xkT%2F3IbW5tYcX2e5lVz8B5DZmEVFAyT%2Fkk%2Fft8bF3olvloX%2BTa.

437. Michelle Rabin, "The Irony of the Trusted News Initiative," Musing of a Retired Shrink (blog), December 23, 2021, https://michellerabinphd.substack.com/p/the-irony-of-the-trusted-news-initiative.

438. Ibid.

439. United States. CDC. VAERS, https://wonder.cdc.gov/vaers.html, via Karen Selick, July 25, 2021, https://www.bitchute.com/video/3bmfKOGpkuGD/.

440. Lien Davies, "Open Letter from Dr Tess Lawrie to Chief Exec MHRA Dr Raine—URGENT Report—COVID-19 Vaccines Unsafe for Use in Humans," June 10, 2021, https://freedomalliance.co.uk/2021/06/10/open-letter-from-dr-tess-lawrie-to-chief-exec-mhra-dr-raine-urgent-report-COVID-19-vaccines-unsafe-for-use-in-humans/.

441. Jon Sanders, "Why Is There Such Reluctance to Discuss Natural Immunity?" American Institute for Economic

Research, June 4, 2021, https://www.aier.org/article/
why-is-there-such-reluctance-to-discuss-natural-immunity/.

442. Ibid.

443. Ibid.

444. Free West Media, "German Chief Pathologist Sounds Alarm on Fatal
Vaccine Injuries," August 3, 2021, https://freewestmedia.com/2021/08/03/
german-chief-pathologist-sounds-alarm-on-fatal-vaccine-injuries/.

445. Berkeley Lovelace Jr., "CDC: 78% of People Hospitalized for COVID
Were Overweight or Obese," *Journal of Nursing*, March 1, 2021, https://
www.asrn.org/journal-nursing/2517-cdc-78-of-people-hospitalized-for-
COVID-were-overweight-or-obese.html.

446. Dieter De Smet, et al., "Serum 25(OH)D Level on Hospital Admission
Associated With COVID-19 Stage and Mortality," *Am J Clin Pathol.*,
February 11, 2021, ;155(3):381–388. doi: 10.1093/ajcp/aqaa252, https://
pubmed.ncbi.nlm.nih.gov/33236114/.

447. Piers Robinson, "COVID Is a Global Propaganda Operation," *Asia
Pacific Today*, August 4, 2021, https://rumble.com/vkppo0-COVID-is-a-
global-propaganda-operation.html).

448. Alexander Hamilton, Brainyquote, accessed
January 29, 2023, https://www.brainyquote.com/quotes/
alexander_hamilton_383897?src=t_federal_government.

449. Adam Edelman, "Clinching Victory, President-elect Biden Declares
'Time to Heal in America,'" NBC News, November 7, 2020, https://www.
nbcnews.com/politics/2020-election/clinching-victory-president-elect-biden-
declares-time-heal-america-n1247013.

450. "Divided Government in the United States," Wikipedia.
org, accessed January 29, 2023, https://en.wikipedia.org/wiki/
Divided_government_in_the_United_States.

451. Jeffrey M. Jones, "U.S. Political Party Preferences Shifted Greatly
During 2021," Gallup, January 17, 2022, https://news.gallup.com/
poll/388781/political-party-preferences-shifted-greatly-during-2021.aspx.

452. "The Rise of the Independents," Office of the University Provost,

Arizona State University, October 13, 2022, https://provost.asu.edu/
rise-independents.
453. Ibid.
454. Ibid.
455. "George Washington Warned against Political Infighting in His Farewell
Address," History, accessed January 29, 2023, https://www.history.com/
news/george-washington-farewell-address-warnings.
456. Ibid.
457. Abigail Adams, Goodreads.com, accessed January 29, 2023, The Letters
of John and Abigail Adams Quotes by Abigail Adams (goodreads.com).
458. Abraham Lincoln Online, Annual Message to Congress—Concluding
Remarks, December 1, 1862, http://www.abrahamlincolnonline.org/lincoln/
speeches/congress.htm.
459. "Partisan Antipathy: More Intense, More Personal," Pew Research
Center, October 10, 2019, Partisan Antipathy: More Intense, More Personal
| Pew Research Center.
460. Philip Bump, "Two-thirds of Americans Think That the Democratic
Party Is Out of Touch with the Country," Washington Post, April 23, 2017..
461. R. J. Reinhart, "Majority in U.S. Still Say a Third Party Is Needed,"
Gallup, October 28, 2016.
462. David Blankenhorn, "Why Polarization Matters," American Interest,
December 22, 2015, https://www.the-american-interest.com/2015/12/22/
why-polarization-matters/.
463. Ibid.
464. Ibid.
465. Elliott Davis Jr., "Political Polarization Around U.S. Immigration
Policy Heightens, Survey Finds," US News, August 8, 2022, https://
www.usnews.com/news/national-news/articles/2022-08-08/
political-polarization-around-u-s-immigration-policy-heightens-survey-finds.
466. Ibid.
467. "Fentanyl Deaths Climbing, DEA Washington Continues the Fight;
Drug Enforcement Administration," Drug Enforcement Administration,

February 16, 2022, https://www.dea.gov/stories/2022/2022-02/2022-02-16/
fentanyl-deaths-climbing-dea-washington-continues-fight.
468. Ibid.
469. Ibid.
470. Audrey Conklin, "Garland Denies DOJ Labeling Parents
as Domestic Terrorists Following School Board Memo," Fox
News, October 21, 2021, https://www.foxnews.com/politics/
garland-doj-parents-domestic-terrorists-school-board-memo.
471. Sarah Weaver, "Father Raided by FBI Found Not Guilty of
Federal Charges Alleging He Assaulted Abortion Worker," *Daily
Caller*, January 30, 2023, https://dailycaller.com/2023/01/30/
mark-houck-fbi-doj-merrick-garland-pro-life-verdict-not-guilty-charges/.
472. Ibid.
473. Kyle Seraphin, "The FBI Doubles Down on Christians
and White Supremacy in 2023," uncoverdc.com, February
8, 2023, https://www.uncoverdc.com/2023/02/08/
the-fbi-doubles-down-on-christians-and-white-supremacy-in-2023/.
474. Ibid.
475. Ibid.
476. Note: Groypers, according to Wikipedia, also called the Groyper Army,
is identified as white nationalist provocateurs and Internet trolls who attempt
to introduce far-right politics to American conservatism. Wikipedia alleges
Groypers participated in the 2021 US Capitol protest and are described
as "white nationalist, homophobic, nativist, fascists, sexist, antisemitic,
and an attempt to rebrand the declining alt-right movement." Cited from
"Groypers," Wikipedia, accessed March 25, 2023, https://en.wikipedia.org/
wiki/Groypers.
477. Seraphin, Op cit..
478. Ibid.
479. Ibid.
480. John Solomon, "FBI Suffers Fresh Bias Episode, Retracts Intel Memo
Portraying Catholics as Extremist Threats," justthenews.com, February 9,

2023, https://justthenews.com/accountability/fbi-suffers-fresh-bias-episode-retracts-intel-memo-portraying-catholics-extremist.

481. "Biden's Fight for Racial Discrimination," *Washington Examiner*, July 7, 2021, https://www.washingtonexaminer.com/opinion/editorials/bidens-fight-for-racial-discrimination.

482. *The Wisdom of China and India*, edited by Lin Yutang, (Random House, Inc., 1942), p. 839, https://archive.org/details/in.ernet.dli.2015.187364/page/n1/mode/2up.

483. Robert Dallek, "Franklin D. Roosevelt: A Political Life, 9780525427902: Amazon.com: Books.

484. "Presidential Job Approval Center," Gallup, accessed January 29, 2023, (gallup.com).

485. Katabella Roberts, "'Stray Papers': Biden Downplays Contents of Classified Documents," NTD, February 9, 2023, https://www.ntd.com/stray-papers-biden-downplays-contents-of-classified-documents_900213.html.

486. Christi Craddick, "Biden's EPA Oversteps Authority to Target Oil and Gas Industry," *National Review*, August 26, 2022, https://www.nationalreview.com/2022/08/bidens-epa-oversteps-authority-to-target-oil-and-gas-industry/.

487. Tara Copp, "Keep COVID-19 Military Vaccine Mandate, Defense Secretary Says," Defense News, December 4, 2022, https://www.defensenews.com/news/pentagon-congress/2022/12/04/keep-COVID-19-military-vaccine-mandate-defense-secretary-says/.

488. 2022 Reagan National Defense Survey," Ronald Reagan Presidential Foundation and Institute, accessed January 29, 2023, https://www.reaganfoundation.org/reagan-institute/centers/peace-through-strength/reagan-institute-national-defense-survey/.

489. Ibid.

490. Aaron Kliegman, "Biden Expected to Call for Unity at State of the Union after Repeated Attacks against Republicans," Fox News, February 7, 2023, https://www.foxnews.com/politics/biden-expected-call-unity-state-union-repeated-attacks-republicans?yptr=yahoo.

491. "Transcript: Biden's Second State of the Union Address," Associated Press, February 7, 2023, https://www.sfgate.com/news/article/transcript-biden-s-second-state-of-the-union-17770533.php.

492. Jessica Chasmar, "Biden's State of the Union Address: Top 5 Moments," Fox News, February 8, 2023, https://www.foxnews.com/politics/bidens-state-union-address-top-5-moments.

493. Ibid.

494. Grace Panetta, "Biden Calls Georgia's New Voting Law 'Jim Crow in the 21st Century' and 'a Blatant Attack on the Constitution,'" Insider, March 26, 2021, https://www.businessinsider.com/biden-georgia-voting-law-attack-constitution-jim-crow-2021-3.

495. Kliegman, Op. cit.

496. Ibid.

497. Ibid.

498. Ibid.

499. Ibid.

500. Ibid.

501. Barack Obama, "65 Division Quotes on Success in Life," overallmotivation.com, accessed February 11, 2023, https://www.overallmotivation.com/quotes/division-quotes/.

502. Leonardo da Vinci, Goodreads, accessed January 29, 2023, https://www.goodreads.com/quotes/tag/division.

503. Lynn Uzzell, "Madison's Five Lessons for Overcoming Polarization," the 1776 series, RealClear Public Affairs, accessed January 29, 2023, https://www.realclearpublicaffairs.com/articles/2021/03/18/madisons_five_lessons_for_overcoming_polarization_660476.html#!.

504. Ibid.

505. Ibid.

506. Ibid.

507. Ibid.

508. Ibid.

509. Ibid.

510. Ibid.

511. Ibid.

512. Ibid.

513. Ibid.

514. Ibid.

515. See Letter from James Madison to Thomas Jefferson (July 30, 1793), in
15 The Papers of James Madison 48 (Thomas A. Mason et al. eds., 1985).
An endnote in Powell, H. Jefferson. "The Founders and the President's
Authority over Foreign Affairs," *William and Mary Law Review*, vol. 40, no.
5, May 1999, p. 1471.

516. Uzzell, Op cit.

517. Vivian Bradfor, "Lessons on Political Polarization from Lincoln's 'House
Divided' Speech, 160 Years Later," Roundup, https://historynewsnetwork.
org/article/169300.

518. Ibid.

519. Ibid.

520. Ibid.

521. Ibid.

522. Ibid.

523. Ibid.

524. Abraham Lincoln, "A House Divided," Voices of Democracy, June
16, 1858, Lincoln, "A House Divided," Speech Text - Voices of Democracy
(umd.edu).

525. Matthijis Tieleman, "Dutch Lessons for Political Polarization in the
United States," *Journal of Applied History*, December 2, 2021, https://brill.
com/view/journals/joah/3/1 2/article p121_7.xml?language=en.

526. Ibid.

527. Ibid.

528. Ibid.

529. Ibid.

530. Ibid.

531. Ibid.

532. Ibid.

533. Ibid.

534. Ibid.

535. Ibid.

536. Ibid.

537. Ibid.

538. Ibid.

539. Ibid.

540. Ibid.

541. "Swahili Proverb," quotemaster.org, accessed January 29, 2023, https://www.quotemaster.org/Divisions#&gid=1&pid=15.

542. Nick Cady, "4 Strategies for Families Divided by Politics," nickcady.org, November 11, 2016, https://nickcady.org/2016/11/11/3-strategies-for-families-divided-by-politics/.

543. Ibid.

544. Ibid.

545. John Maxwell, "Leading in Polarized Times," November 13, 2018, https://www.johnmaxwell.com/blog/leading-in-polarized-times/.

546. Ibid.

547. Ibid.

548. Ibid.

549. Ibid.

550. Ibid.

551. Ibid.

552. Ibid.

553. Martin Reeves et al., "How Business Leaders Can Reduce Polarization," *Harvard Business Review*, October 8, 2021, https://hbr.org/2021/10/how-business-leaders-can-reduce-polarization.

554. Ibid.

555. Ibid.

556. Ibid.

557. Ibid.

558. Ibid.

559. Ibid.

560. Ibid.

561. Lee de-Wit, et al., "What Are the Solutions to Political Polarization?" Greater Good Magazine, July 2, 2019, https://greatergood.berkeley.edu/article/item/what_are_the_solutions_to_political_polarization.

562. Ibid.

563. Carlee Beth Hawkins and Brian A. Nosek, "Motivated Independence? Implicit Party Identity Predicts Political Judgments among Self-proclaimed Independents," Pers Soc Psychol Bull, 38(11):1437–52, November 2012, and Psychological Barriers to Bipartisan Public Support for Climate Policy—Leaf Van Boven, Phillip J. Ehret, David K. Sherman, 2018 (sagepub.com).

564. Annemarie S. Walter and David P. Redlawsk, "Voters' Partisan Responses to Politicians' Immoral Behavior," *Political Psychology*, March 27, 2019, Voters' Partisan Responses to Politicians' Immoral Behavior - Walter - 2019 - Political Psychology - Wiley Online Library.

565. Hawkins, Op. cit.

566. Ibid.

567. Ibid.

568. de-Wit, Op. cit.

569. Ibid.

570. Ibid.

571. Ibid.

572. Ibid.

573. Ibid.

574. Jeffrey A. Karp and Susan A. Banducci, "Political Efficacy and Participation in Twenty-Seven Democracies: How Electoral Systems Shape Political Behaviour," *British Journal of Political Science*, Cambridge University Press, February 8, 2008, JSTOR.

575. de-Wit, Op. cit.

576. Dietrich Bonhoeffer, *Letters and Papers from Prison*, Evangelism Quotes, Goodreads, accessed January 28, 2023, https://www.goodreads.com/quotes/tag/evangelism.

577. Dietrich Bonhoeffer, *Letters and Papers from Prison*, (Simon & Schuster), https://www.amazon.com/dp/B004PYDAXG?ref_=x_gr_w_preview_kcr-20&tag=x_gr_w_preview_kcr-20&linkCode=kpdt.

578. Ibid.

579. Ron Rolheiser, "Overcoming the Divisions That Divide Us," January 22, 2018, https://ronrolheiser.com/overcoming-the-divisions-that-divide-us/#.Y8WlgHbMLq4.

580. Ibid.

581. Ibid.

582. Ibid.

583. Ibid.

584. Ibid.

585. Billy Graham, Billy Graham Library, accessed January 28, 2023, https://billygrahamlibrary.org/blog-10-quotes-from-billy-graham-on-end-times/.

586. John Walvoord, "Major Events Preceding the Second Coming of Christ," bible.org, accessed January 28, 2023, https://bible.org/seriespage/14-major-events-preceding-second-coming-christ.

587. Charles Swindoll, azquotes.com, accessed January 28, 2023, https://www.azquotes.com/quotes/topics/hope-in-christ.html.